S0-ARH-544

FLORIDA STATE
UNIVERSITY LIBRARIES

JUN 17 1997

TALLAHASSEE, FLORIDA

The Imperatives of Power

American University Studies

Series XXI
Regional Studies

Vol. 15

PETER LANG
New York • Washington, D.C./Baltimore
Bern • Frankfurt am Main • Berlin • Vienna • Paris

Pedro A. Noguera

The Imperatives of Power

Political Change and the Social Basis of Regime Support in Grenada from 1951–1991

PETER LANG
New York • Washington, D.C./Baltimore
Bern • Frankfurt am Main • Berlin • Vienna • Paris

Library of Congress Cataloging-in-Publication Data

Noguera, Pedro.
The imperatives of power: political change and the social basis of regime
support in Grenada from 1951–1991/ by Pedro A. Noguera.
p. cm. — (American university studies. Series XXI, Regional studies; vol. 15)
Includes bibliographical references (p.   ) and index.
1. Grenada—Politics and government. 2. Power (Social sciences)—Grenada—
History—20th century. 3. Political leadership—Grenada—History—20th
century. 4. Political stability—Grenada—History—20th century. 5. Political
culture—Grenada—History—20th century. 6. Social change—Grenada—
History—20th century. I. Title. II. Series.
F2056.8.N64   320.9729845'09'045—dc20   95-26225
ISBN 0-8204-3095-1
ISSN 0895-0482

Die Deutsche Bibliothek-CIP-Einheitsaufnahme

Noguera, Pedro A.:
The imperatives of power: political change and the social
basis of regime support in Grenada from 1951–1991/ by Pedro A. Noguera.
–New York; Washington, D.C./Baltimore; Bern; Frankfurt am Main;
Berlin; Vienna; Paris: Lang.
(American university studies. Ser. 21, Regional studies; Vol. 15)
ISBN 0-8204-3095-1
NE: American university studies/ 21

The paper in this book meets the guidelines for permanence and durability
of the Committee on Production Guidelines for Book Longevity
of the Council of Library Resources.

© 1997 Peter Lang Publishing, Inc., New York

All rights reserved.
Reprint or reproduction, even partially, in all forms such as microfilm,
xerography, microfiche, microcard, and offset strictly prohibited.

Printed in the United States of America.

Contents

Acknowledgements

Completion of this book would not have been possible without the support of several individuals. In Grenada, Donald Alexis (a.k.a. Gambi) and John Bernard (a.k.a. Jaleh) provided invaluable support as research assistants, guides and friends. The staff at the Grenada National Library under the direction of Ms. Joan Sylvester were extremely helpful in providing me with access to documents, books, newspapers and other materials contained in the National Archives. There were also numerous individuals throughout the island who willingly spent a great deal of time talking with me about their views on the issues covered in this book.

In Berkeley and other parts of the United States I received guidance and critical feedback from several notable scholars. In particular, Dr. Percy Hintzen provided me with the benefit of his vast knowledge of Caribbean societies. His willingness to review numerous drafts of this work, enabled me to produce a book which reflects my strengths and creative abilities as a scholar. Franz Schurmann, Paget Henry and Carlene Edie, also provided constructive criticisms which helped me to revise and improve earlier drafts of this work.

Finally, I want to acknowledge the patience and support of my wife Patricia, without whom completion of this book would have been impossible. She not only endured the hardships created by the time I spent in Grenada, but also provided me with the distraction-free time I needed to carry out the writing once I returned. My eldest son Joaquin served as my most important research assistant while I was doing field research in Grenada in 1987 and 1988, even though he was only four years old at the time. His constant presence provided me with much needed companionship and made it much easier for Grenadians who were tired and suspicious of yet another American researcher to consent to being interviewed by me. And last but not least, my three other children, Amaya, Antonio and Naima, who though not present at the time this work was done, have enriched my life and given me the motivation to pursue this and other important goals.

Funding for this study was provided by the U.S. Department of Education Fulbright Hays Doctoral Dissertation Fellowship.

Chapter 1

Introduction

Placing Grenada in Context

Grenada is a small island located in the eastern Caribbean, the southern most island in the Windward archipelago. Until 1983, it was not a place that was well known to many outside of the Caribbean. Like the other small island nations of the Caribbean, Grenada was an obscure and politically unimportant country, known outside of the area by only a small number of north American and European tourists. With a land area of 133 square miles and a population of less than 100,000 people, it is smaller than many American cities. It has no precious minerals or valuable natural resources, nor has it historically been regarded as strategically significant to commerce or security in the Caribbean region.

Prior to the notoriety it gained after the U.S. invasion in 1983, Grenada experienced dramatic fluctuations in its political leadership which created a climate and context that deviated substantially from the norms of the Commonwealth Caribbean. During the span of forty years (1951-1991), control of the Grenadian government shifted back and forth between three leaders, each possessing significantly different styles of leadership and ideological orientations. Eric Gairy, a right wing populist, rose to power through his leadership in the labor movement of the 1950s, and went on to occupy a position of leadership in national politics until he was overthrown by the left wing New Jewel Movement (NJM) in 1979. NJM leader Maurice Bishop, a young radical lawyer, served as Prime Minister of the People's Revolutionary Government (PRG) which

ruled the island for four and one half years until it collapsed
as a result of internal conflict and was overthrown by the U.S.
military in the invasion of the 1983. Finally, Herbert Blaize, a
conservative, pro-business politician, was elected in 1984. He
had previously served in national office twice before, during
the 1950s and 1960s and held power until his death in 1989.

Whether measured by the results achieved through national
elections or by an ability to mobilize large numbers of people,
all three regimes could legitimately claim to have had popular
support at some time. Despite having had this support, all three
regimes eventually lost power and much of the support that
they had previously enjoyed.

Using Grenada as a case study, this book seeks to explain
two related phenomena: the factors influencing regime survival and the social and political basis of regime support. This
study will explain how it was possible that the island of Grenada
could have produced and supported, even temporarily, these
three strikingly different leaders and their regimes. In carrying out this investigation, I will attempt to identify and interpret the social basis of support for political leadership in
Grenada by exploring the reasons why popular support can be
obtained at certain times and lost at other times. Such an investigation necessarily involves an analysis of the political culture of Grenadian society, a probing of the values and priorities of the populace, and an ascertainment of how these
manifest themselves in collective political behavior. It also requires an awareness of how structural conditions, namely, relations between social classes and the island's political
economy, influence political culture, since these forces have
historically played a major role in shaping the attitudes and
behavior of the populace.

This study also attempts to explain the rise and fall of the
three regimes. The issue of regime survival, and the factors
that influence political instability and political change, have
been central to the study of social change and development,
particularly in Third World nations (Moore, 1965; Lerner 1958;
Apter, 1965; Huntington, 1968; Skocpol 1979; Hintzen, 1989).
This study attempts to build upon that vast body of work
through an in-depth historical investigation of political change
in Grenada. Grenada provides a case in which a comparison

of distinct political leadership styles is possible. Gairy, Bishop and Blaize utilized different approaches to rise to positions of national leadership in Grenada. Once power was attained, the three regimes devised and implemented different strategies to maintain power. A variety of factors influenced how these strategies were conceptualized and implemented by the three regimes. The ideological leanings of the parties and individuals in power, the personalities and leadership styles of the three leaders, and the relationships developed by the three regimes to various class forces within the society all had bearing upon their actions and policies. However, despite their differences, common ground for comparison can be found in the need for each regime to devise strategies for addressing the most fundamental issue confronting Grenada and other small developing nations: the economic and political vulnerability created by Grenada's structural dependence within the world economy. This ever present state of vulnerability creates a set of "structural imperatives" which define the parameters under which leaders and regimes must act. How each regime attempted to respond to and confront this condition of vulnerability becomes yet another basis of comparison.

Throughout the forty year period (1951-1991) upon which this study is focused, there was an ongoing interaction between the three leaders and the parties they represented. An important feature of this interaction was that the ascension of one leader was contingent upon the decline of the one in power. Within such a scenario, the question of popular support and the relationship of domestic and international class forces to the regime in power has been central. While there are other nations and leaders that have been able to retain power even without popular support, the weakness of the state in Grenada has tended to make the absence of substantial support result in the strengthening of the opposition and, consequently, increased the vulnerability of the regime in power. The central focus of this work examines the vicissitudes of national leadership in Grenada by treating the interaction between leaders and parties, and the varied reactions of the populace to these players.

However, because of its small size and population, any study of Grenada must begin by locating the island within an appropriate geo-political context. Obviously, since past and present happenings in Grenada affect only a small number of people, it may not be immediately obvious to outsiders that Grenada's recent history could be relevant or potentially useful as a case study from which to understand larger and more complex units of analysis. Yet, in this respect, the island's size makes it particularly appropriate for this kind of analysis. Whereas larger and more developed societies often possess characteristics related to their geography, their ethnic and religious diversity, and the complexity of their economic and social systems, which make comparative analysis difficult, as a micro-society, Grenada offers a relatively "pure" case in which it is possible to study political processes and social behavior without the influences of an array of intervening variables.

As shall be shown in the pages ahead, this work is also intended to add to the existing body of literature on the state in the Anglophone Caribbean. Drawing on the concepts and theoretical propositions utilized in other studies on the political sociology of the Caribbean, (Singham, 1968; Lewis, 1968; Munroe, 1972; Beckford, 1972; Thomas, 1974; Stone, 1980; Stone and Henry 1983; Reviere, 1985; Stephens and Stephens, 1986; Hintzen,1989), this work aims at shedding new light on the process of political change. Despite its small size and relative obscurity, this is not the first time that Grenada has been chosen as a case for illuminating such issues. Archie Singham's study on Grenada, focused on the conflict between Eric Gairy and the British colonial government in *The Hero and the Crowd*, made an important contribution to the study of conflicts between charismatic and bureaucratic modes of authority within colonial polities. Along the same lines, it is my intention to utilize the Grenadian case to further deepen understanding of the process of political change in the Caribbean and other non-industrialized nations.

The Significance of the U.S. Invasion

Undoubtedly, had it not been for the events of October 1983, the tiny island of Grenada would have remained obscure and largely insignificant to outsiders. The events of that month brought Grenada to the center of international political discourse and, for a brief period thereafter, generated an interest in Grenada that extended well beyond the Caribbean. In the days and weeks following the U.S. military intervention, foreign journalists descended on the island to report on the brief battle and its implications for what was then an ongoing east-west competition for global power and influence. At the United Nations General Assembly, the Organization of American States, and in other international fora, diplomats and ambassadors debated the ethics of the invasion and voted on resolutions of condemnation and support for the military assault. Several writers set out quickly to write books about what had happened on the island, hoping to be the first to shed light and provide information to those who wanted to know more about the tiny island and the background that led up to the events of October 1983.[1]

Then suddenly, and perhaps understandably, interest in Grenada quickly subsided. Within weeks of the invasion, Grenada moved from the front pages of major newspapers, to short articles buried deep within, to eventually nothing but an occasional update. Though political and financial affairs on the island would remain tense and unstable for the next several years, Grenada had returned once again to its previous obscurity, surpassed by the happenings within larger, more complex societies. For politicians who had been closely identified with the invasion, it retained a degree of symbolic importance. This was particularly true for U.S. president Ronald Reagan and the Republican party, who used the military victory in the presidential campaign of 1984 as a way of reminding American voters of the president's resolve to fight communism throughout the world.[2] However, even by then, Grenada had become a distant memory to most American voters, a place which most outsiders had trouble locating on a map or even pronouncing correctly. Writing in the April 1989 edition of the *New Republic*, Gary Krist summed up the decline of American interest in Grenada in this way: "What started out as a marriage made in heaven has begun to look more like a one-night stand." (April 12, 1989)

Still, despite its seeming insignificance, the invasion proved to be one of the most important measures the Reagan administration had undertaken in the area of foreign policy during its eight year tenure. Setting a pattern for future military operations, the invasion served as proof that the United States could effectively utilize force to achieve its objectives in foreign policy without incurring a barrage of domestic criticism, particularly from the national media (Pearce 1981; LaFeber 1983). To other nations, the invasion demonstrated that the U.S. had overcome its trepidation over foreign involvements that lingered in the wake of the war in Vietnam. The military assault on Grenada helped to convince skeptical U.S. policy makers that strategic military actions could be staged without inciting a larger military confrontation with the Soviet Union or its allies, or arousing substantial domestic opposition. The invasion of Grenada was the first time since 1965 that the United States used direct military force to intervene in the affairs of a sovereign Caribbean state. It was also the first and only occasion in which such an intervention had occurred in the entire history of the Anglophone Caribbean.[3]

It is not surprising then, that for the English speaking Caribbean generally, and the people of Grenada in particular, the U.S. led invasion of October of 1983 produced repercussions that would be felt for years to come. In Grenada, there would be no speedy return to normalcy and business as usual after the troops departed. The invasion raised expectations in Grenada and throughout the region that the U.S. would use the intervention as an occasion for launching a new and improved relationship with its largely ignored neighbors in the Caribbean. Having finally become significant as a geopolitical entity within the super power conflict, the region now hoped to be wooed with aid and investment as had happened in Central America, Southeast Asia and other areas of the world considered strategically important by the U.S. (Barnet 1983; Chomsky 1991).

The aftershocks of the Grenada invasion were most profound in the recently independent territories formerly known as the British West Indies. In its aftermath, the U.S. assumed an even greater role in the political and economic affairs of the region than it had previously, completely surpassing the British as the dominant power there. The increased U.S. presence provided its political allies in the region with a major boost to their influence and prestige. Nations that had supported and minimally participated in the invasion were rewarded through the trade provisions of the Caribbean Basin Initiative (C.B.I.).[4] Aside from the Central American countries which continued to receive the bulk of foreign aid as a part of the Reagan administration's counterinsurgency strategy in the region (El Salvador received 21% of the funds initially allocated), Jamaica, Barbados and to a lesser extent Dominica, accrued the lion's share of bonuses, at least partially as a result of extending their political support for the invasion. The ruling parties in these countries and a few others went on to establish a formal political alliance with each other and the United States, known as the Caribbean Democratic Union (CDU).[5] Conversely, the leadership of nations that opposed the invasion, such as Trinidad and Tobago, Belize, the Bahamas and Guyana were penalized through their omission in C.B.I. There were political reprimands for these regimes as well. In the months that followed, governments that had opposed the Grenada invasion were faced with significant challenges internally to their leadership, and in many cases, the opposition openly boasted of having the support of the U.S. As evidence of the increase in U.S. influence, two years after the invasion only one of the four regimes that opposed the invasion managed to retain power. Moreover, in the wake of the invasion, the U.S. proceeded with efforts to increase militarization throughout the region, under the guise of improving security for island-states that previously had only minimal defense forces.[6]

While the invasion had a major impact upon the region, its effects upon Grenada were most profound and monumental. The battle itself between U.S. armed forces and the Cuban and Grenadian combatants, which lasted no more than four days, was by far the most violent incident in the island's history. The 12,000 U.S. servicemen that were deployed in the operation, supported by aircraft carriers, jets and modern military hardware, quickly overcame the resistance and completely overwhelmed the island's inhabitants. The loss of human lives and property far exceeded that which had occurred at any previous time in Grenada's history. In its aftermath, many of the island's inhabitants were left traumatized, stripped of their sovereignty, and more dependent than ever on foreign assistance to recover.

This, however, is not a study on the U.S. invasion of Grenada, though the incident is central to this analysis. Several authors have written about the invasion and the collapse of the People's Revolutionary government, most having done so for the purpose of condemning or supporting the U.S. invasion.[7] I have selected Grenada as the focus of this study because it serves as a useful case for analyzing the process of political change in a small developing nation. It is my contention that there are lessons to be derived from the Grenadian experience that may have bearing on our understanding of political processes that are common to large and small nations, as well to various levels of government. The fact that Grenada was invaded by the United States not too long ago adds to the contemporary significance of the case and provides a useful starting point for this study of political change.

Re-Entering the Field

I had been initially attracted to Grenada after hearing about the socialist oriented revolution that had occurred there on March 13, 1979. Grenada was the first and only nation in the Anglophone Caribbean to have experienced an armed socialist oriented revolution. It also gained the distinction as the only member of that group to have been subjected to a military invasion by the United States. I had read about the social welfare programs initiated by the new government and of its intention to develop and to implement a new form of participatory democracy. I had also heard about the revolution's plan to build socialism through agricultural development, emphasizing the export of cocoa, nutmeg and bananas, and the expansion of tourism. I was particularly interested in learning more about the adult literacy campaign that was launched in 1980 because of the opportunity it created for observing firsthand a mass voluntary educational mobilization at a moment of dramatic political change.

These attempts at reforming the political economy of the island intrigued me. Having visited other Caribbean islands before, and because I felt a personal affinity to the islands due to my heritage (my mother was born in Jamaica and my father grew up in Trinidad), I wanted to witness and observe these changes first hand. The West Indians I had known struck me as a somewhat conservative and extremely pragmatic group of people. The idea of constructing an anti-imperialist form of socialism in such a society seemed to be a radical departure from the customs and beliefs I had known. I was interested in seeing how the Grenadian people were reacting to the changes introduced by the new socialist government; could Marxism and calypso mix? Moreover, after hearing about the efforts of the revolutionary government to provide the citizens of Grenada with the opportunity to participate in the process of producing these changes, I wanted to see how this was being done, and what effects, if any, this had upon political behavior and attitudes.

I first visited Grenada in the summer of 1982. From July through February of 1983, I worked as a consultant to the Center for Popular Education (CPE), the state agency responsible for administering the adult literacy campaign. While providing technical assistance to the campaign, I also conducted research on adult education and political socialization. At the time, I was primarily interested in studying the role of the literacy campaign in the transformation of political culture in Grenada. Working with the literacy campaign allowed me to directly observe and participate in a collective undertaking which departed significantly from past political practices and social norms.

During those six months in Grenada, part of my time was spent at the headquarters of the CPE in the capital of St. George's, preparing reports and supplemental materials for teachers and local administrators. However, most of my work was carried out in the countryside, visiting with volunteer staff who were responsible for the literacy work in the rural villages. My assignment was to meet with literacy workers to discuss how the work was proceeding, and to prepare reports for the national office on the status of the work. The leadership of the People's Revolutionary Government declared 1983 the year of Academic and Political Education, and the adult literacy campaign directed by the CPE was envisioned as the major initiative to be undertaken during this period.[9]

As I began speaking with students and teachers involved with the campaign, I was immediately impressed by the degree of support expressed for the "Revo" (revolution), the PRG, and most of all its leader, Maurice Bishop. I was told by both students and teachers alike of the great progress that was occurring in the country as a result of the revolution. Several commented on the new sense of national pride and new openness to participation and volunteerism which had been generated by the revolution and which led large numbers of Grenadians to become involved in a variety of mass organizations. Most often, praise for the revolution was expressed in personal terms, with emphasis given to the particular ways in which an individual or family had benefited from new opportunities created as a result of the revolution.

There were also many people who spoke freely of their reservations about the revolution and of their opposition to certain policies undertaken by the government. I heard scathing criticisms directed at government officials who were considered lazy, corrupt or discourteous toward the people. Numerous individuals raised questions about the presence of Cubans on the island, and several expressed fear and concern over the antagonisms which had developed between Grenada and the United States. There were also some who worried that atheism would become official government policy and that religious freedoms would come under attack.

However, the vast majority of people I met and encountered seemed to accept and support the PRG and its policies. I left Grenada in December of 1982 feeling that the majority of Grenadians supported the "revolution", its policies and especially its social welfare programs. I sensed that for the vast majority of Grenadians, political support was not necessarily based upon embracement of the socialist ideas which motivated the leaders. Rather, it appeared that support was based on a more general feeling of satisfaction and approval over the direction being taken by the government. While there were criticisms and fears expressed about some of the actions taken by the government, there also seemed to be widespread support for most of its initiatives, and in many cases, a willingness to become actively involved in the programs initiated by the PRG. I observed mobilizations of the People's Militia, comprised of armed teenagers, senior citizens, housewives, farmers, fishermen, and others who spoke militantly of their will-

ingness to defend the revolution with their lives if it was attacked. I attended zonal council meetings held in the rural
villages, where government officials explained national policies, both foreign and domestic, to gatherings of local folk,
who responded with questions and statements of opinion, and
who raised concerns relevant to their needs as a community.[11]
I spoke freely with market women who complained about the
prices of imported foodstuffs, to taxi cab drivers who assailed
the government for driving away American tourists, and to
businessman who felt unfairly treated by a government which
stated openly its plans to regulate and restrict the private
sector. Nonetheless, there seemed to be widespread acceptance
and approval of the revolution, the government and the
leader.

Nine months after returning to the United States, I was
stunned by news of a split in the central committee of the New
Jewel Movement in September of 1983. This was followed by
reports that Maurice Bishop had been placed under house arrest, and that shortly thereafter, on the 19th of October, had
been executed by members of the People's Revolutionary Army.
It was reported that a new government had been formed led
by officers from the People's Revolutionary Army (PRA), and
that a dawn to dusk and shoot on site curfew had gone into
effect.

Then on the morning of October 25th I was awakened at
4:00 a.m. by a call from a relative in Trinidad who told me that
the U.S. military had led a multi-national force in an invasion
of Grenada. Over twelve thousand U.S. troops, many of whom
were reportedly on their way to Lebanon following the deaths
of over two hundred marines at a U.S. military base, participated in the invasion of Grenada. The battle itself lasted only
four days. The invasion was described as a mission undertaken
to rescue American medical students who were on the island.
In the days and weeks after the attack, other reasons were cited
by the Reagan administration as justification for the action.
Primary among these was the suggestion that the Grenadian
people wanted the Revolutionary Military Council (RMC),
which had formed briefly after the assassination of Bishop, to
be overthrown. The American media broadcast scenes of
Grenadians welcoming U.S. troops. and opinion polls were

cited which suggested overwhelming support among Grenadians for the U.S. led assault.[12]

I reacted to these pictures of Grenadians carrying signs reading "God Bless America" and "We Love You Reagan" suspiciously. Such images clashed immediately with my memories of revolutionary Grenada, a society which seemed to have been relatively united in its support of the anti-imperialist stance taken by the government. Still, I found it difficult to dismiss the possibility of Grenadian support for the invasion, particularly after hearing from friends in Grenada who confirmed the reports carried by the U.S. media. Over the months and years that followed, I remained perplexed and curious about what had happened in Grenada. I awaited an opportunity to return to the island to find the answer myself.

The opportunity did not present itself until nearly five years later, when I was finally able to return to Grenada. Shortly after my arrival, I came to realize that there was indeed considerable support for the U.S. invasion. I decided to try to explain why. Had the events of October 1983 produced such a drastic change in political attitudes? Was it possible that I had been misled or fooled during my previous visit, when I had seen large numbers of ordinary citizens pledge their willingness to defend the island in the event of an attack by the United States? Or was the apparent shift in political sympathies due to some sort of collective disillusionment with the goals and aspirations of the revolution? Was it possible that support for the revolution was completely linked to support for Bishop, and that with his execution, the anti-imperialist militancy that I had seen had dissipated? The skeptic in me wanted to know whether or not public opinion polls accurately gauged and solicited the sentiments and understandings of the populace about the changes that had occurred.

There was also a personal and pragmatic reason for embarking on this project. First, despite my prior contact and familiarity with Grenada prior to the invasion, I was completely dumbfounded by the events which occurred in October of 1983 and the apparent popular response to these. My knowledge of the island and its history were of little value to me in understanding or explaining what had happened. I wanted to know whether or not there had been a fundamental change in attitudes toward the PRG and its goals, and if so, why.

Secondly, I felt some pressure to understand the nature of the changes that had occurred in Grenada because since the U.S. invasion, Grenada had become a highly politicized issue in U.S. politics and the Caribbean region. For the Reagan Administration and its supporters, the U.S. invasion represented one of its greatest achievements in foreign policy during its eight year tenure. It became the concrete example of the Reagan Doctrine at work, a signal to American allies and enemies that the U.S. possessed the resolve to use force if necessary to combat what it perceived as the spread of communism in the Western Hemisphere. I was by no means neutral in my feelings about the invasion. After returning to the U.S. from Grenada in 1983, I had spoken publicly on several occasions about the great strides that were being made on the island under the direction of the PRG. After the invasion, I spoke out publicly in opposition to the U.S. led assault on Grenada, and was part of the small group of critics who assailed the Reagan Administration for its aggression against the tiny Caribbean nation.

Still, I could not explain what had actually happened in Grenada. Moreover, I wondered if a majority of Grenadians actually did support the invasion, did it make sense for me to oppose it? The reports of Grenadian support for the invasion could not be dismissed even though I had no way of interpreting what they actually meant. I returned to Grenada in 1987 to find the answers to these questions and with the hope of understanding what the political changes that had occurred in Grenada meant to the Grenadian people.

Research Methods

Based upon my prior familiarity with Grenada, I decided that it was necessary to place the collapse of the PRG and the U.S. invasion within the context of Grenada's recent political history. Though the events of October 1983 were by far the most profound political changes to have occurred in the island's history, an understanding of the history leading up to this upheaval seemed essential to interpreting popular reactions to the changes that had occurred. Moreover, given that Grenadian politics had already been characterized by substantial deviations from the norms of the Commonwealth Caribbean, a historical backdrop seemed essential to the analysis. Dramatic shifts in leadership had occurred in the past involving Eric Gairy, Herbert Blaize and ultimately, Maurice Bishop. Assessing how Grenadians viewed the three regimes that held power over the last forty years seemed to provide the only avenue for explaining how this small society had experienced such radical fluctuations in its national political leadership.

To generate an empirical basis for carrying out this analysis, I decided that a survey and interviews would provide the most effective means to assess Grenadian attitudes toward the three leaders that had held power on the island, and to determine on what basis they developed and held opinions toward them. (Issues related to selection of the sample and the process of conducting the survey are contained in Chapter 7.) Through the survey I hoped to create an opportunity for ordinary Grenadians to express their political values and their attitudes toward politics and politicians in general. I wanted to create an open ended questionnaire that would allow the respondents to express their views freely, while providing me with data which was not overly influenced by my own prejudices. The selection and framing of the questions would naturally reflect my familiarity with the subject and my bias, however. Therefore, I kept the questions simple and open-ended to counter my bias and to allow for free flowing interviews.

During the course of conducting one hundred and twenty interviews (N=120), it became clear that the survey could not suffice as my sole source of data collection. As I began interviewing, I could see that the views of the respondents toward the three regimes and the leaders had changed over time. Individual reactions to present circumstances involving the regime in power tended to color the attitudes they expressed toward past regimes. I realized that the survey would not enable me to gain an accurate assessment of how a leader or regime may have been viewed during an earlier period. There was evidence that all three leaders had been supported at one time, a fact which was not supported by the survey.[13] Hence, I realized that the survey would have to be complimented by other methods of research.

For that reason, I also conducted an extensive review of the available historical data. A review of national newspapers, starting from 1951 to the present, provided me with a means of ascertaining how the three regimes and leaders had been viewed in the past. It also shed light on the strategies employed by the three regimes to maintain power during various periods. Although the *West Indian,* the *Torchlight,* the *Free West Indian,* the *Grenada Voice,* and the *National Informer* might all be considered partisan newspapers, a careful examination of their news coverage, the letters-to-the editor, and the editorials, provided some sense of how a particular regime or leader was viewed at a particular time. Moreover, because each of these papers was sympathetic to a different political party (ie. the *Torchlight* was pro-GNP, the *West Indian* was pro-Gairy, and the *Free West Indian* was pro-NJM), a comparative review of the newspapers enabled me to balance the bias present in the newspapers.

In addition to newspapers, historical documents maintained at the National Archives were also used to obtain additional information on government policies. Government manuscripts and official documents produced by the colonial administration were made available to me by Ms. Joan Sylvester, the National Librarian. The so-called Grenada Papers, government documents of the PRG and minutes of the Central Committee meetings of the NJM, which were confiscated during the U.S. invasion, were also obtained and used in part to carry out analysis of the internal workings of the PRG.

I also sought to obtain information from community leaders and influential individuals who possessed knowledge and insights about the three regimes, which was derived from their privileged access to the three leaders or was based upon the special role they played within Grenadian society. I conducted thirty, in-depth interviews with political leaders from different political parties, labor leaders, clergymen, journalists, businessmen, senior civil servants and community leaders. The views of such individuals served as an effective means of assessing and interpreting the opinions solicited through the survey, and proved particularly valuable as a way of gaining an insiders' view of the three regimes.

Finally, participant observation research methods also served as a very important component to the data collection strategies employed during the research. My impressions of Grenada had been based upon the six months I had spent there in 1982, during the tenure of the PRG. When I was able to return for seven months in 1987, this time while Blaize was in power, I had a unique vantage point from which to analyze events on the island. With the coup against Bishop, the U.S. invasion, the installation of the Interim Government, and the election of 1984 having occurred in between my two visits to the island, I was able to make comparisons of the attitudes and behavior I observed before and after these extremely significant events. My presence on the island, my attendance at social and political functions, my casual interactions with ordinary islanders, and the friendships and acquaintances I developed during my two visits all served to make me familiar with the Grenadian lifestyle and culture. This intensive contact with Grenadian society enabled me to compensate for my status as an outsider and foreigner. Over time, I was able to understand the nuances of Grenadian speech and customs, and my ability to communicate and establish rapport with the people I interviewed improved substantially. The ethnographic data obtained provided me with an intellectual context from which to carry out this study and interpret my observations.

The extensive field work that I carried out in Grenada is also the primary characteristic which distinguishes this work on Grenada from others. Among the volumes that have been written on Grenada since the U.S. invasion, this is the first that is based upon field research conducted in Grenada. As such, it differs substantially from those earlier works which have relied heavily upon government documents and interviews with political actors. It is my hope that by combining ethnographic and historical research to explain the nature of political change in Grenada, I will have more accurately conveyed the complexities of this society and culture, rather than replicating past characterizations which have portrayed the majority of Grenadians as mere extras in the drama of their own history.

Notes

1   The more well known books that were written about Grenada immediately after the U.S. invasion include: *Grenada: Revolution, Invasion and Aftermath* by Hugh O'Shaughnessy (London: Sphere Books, 1984); *American Intervention in Grenada: The Implications of Operation Urgent Fury* by Peter M. Dunn and Bruce W. Watson, editors (Boulder: Westview, 1985); *Grenada: Revolution and Invasion* by Anthony Payne, Paul Sutton and Tony Thorndike (London: Croom Helm, 1984) *Grenada Whose Freedom?* (London: Latin American Bureau, 1984) *The Grenada Papers* edited by Paul Seabury and Walter McDougall (San Francisco: Institute for Contemporary Studies, 1984).

2   During the presidential campaign of 1984, several medical students who had been "rescued" during the assault on the island were used by the Republican party to drum up support for Ronald Reagan in his bid for re-election. See *San Francisco Chronicle* September 21, 1984 "Medical Student Endorses U.S. Military Action."

3   The United States has employed military intervention in the Caribbean on several occasions. Most often, U.S. military intervention has been directed at the Spanish and French speaking islands, in particular Haiti (1915-1934), Dominican Republic (1904, 1916-1924, 1932-1934, 1965), Puerto Rico (1898- 1900, 1934) and Cuba (1989-1902, 1906-1909, 1912, 1917-1923).

    Although the U.S. threatened to intervene militarily in Guyana in 1953 and in Trinidad in 1970, the U.S. did not directly send troops to either country. The presence of U.S. military bases throughout the region serves as an important reminder of U.S. capability to intervene when ever it is deemed necessary. See Barry, Wood, Preusch *The Other Side of Paradise: Foreign Control in the Caribbean* (Albuquerque, New Mexico: The Resource Center, 1984) and Ambursley and Cohen, *Crisis in the Caribbean*, (London: Heineman Educational Books, 1983) Also see Hintzen, P. *The Costs of Regime Survival* (Cambridge, U.K.: Cambridge University Press, 1989) p. 80 and 81.

4   For a discussion of how the CBI was used to support U.S. allies in the region see McAfee, K. (Boston: Southend Press, 1991) p. 33-465. In the years following the U.S. invasion of Grenada, the four governments in Caricom which opposed the action (Belize, Trinidad and Tobago, the Bahamas and Guyana) came under attack. All were excluded by the U.S. from receiving the trade benefits made available to other nations in the region through the Caribbean Basin Initiative.

The PUP government in Belize headed by Price and the PNM government in Trinidad and Tobago headed by George Chambers, were defeated in elections in 1984 by political parties that were openly supportive of U.S. policy in the region. Though there was no change of government in Guyana following the death of Forbes Burnham in 1987, Desmond Hoyte, who was selected to head the government after his death, made it clear that he intended to be more supportive of U.S. policies in the region. Lynden Pinderling, the Prime Minister of the Bahamas, is the only one of the four heads of state that opposed the U.S. invasion, who managed to remain in office after the invasion. However, during his campaign for re-election he was accused by the United States of being involved with drug trafficking and was nearly defeated in the elections of 1987.

5   The CDU was established shortly after the U.S. invasion. Its members included the then ruling parties of Jamaica, Barbados, Dominica, St. Vincent, Montserrat, Belize, St. Kitts-Nevis, St. Lucia and the New National Party in Grenada. For a discussion of the CDU and its links to the Republican party, see Ferguson, J. *Grenada: Revolution in Reverse* (London: Latin American Bureau, 1990) p. 118.

6   For a discussion of the U.S. military build up in the eastern Caribbean that occurred in the wake of the Grenada invasion see "Mare Nostrom: U.S. Security in the English-Speaking Caribbean" in *NACLA*, Vol. XIX No. 4, July/August 1985, p. 27-35.

7   The following authors could be included among those who have written in support of the U.S. invasion: *The Grenada Papers* edited by Paul Seabury and Walter McDougall (San Francisco: Institute for Contemporary Studies, 1984), *Grenada: The Untold Story* by Gregory Sandiford and Richard Valente (Lantham, Md: Madison Books, 1984), The New Jewel Movement: Grenada's Revolution 1979-'83 by (Washington, D.C.: Foreign Service Institute, U.S. Department of State, 1985). The following authors could be included among the opponents of the invasion: *Grenada: Revolution, Invasion and Aftermath* by Hugh O'Shaughnessy (London: Sphere Books, 1984); *Grenada: Revolution and Invasion* by Anthony Payne, Paul Sutton and Tony Thorndike (London: Croom Helm, 1984), *Grenada Whose Freedom?* (London: Latin American Bureau, 1984), *Death of a Revolution* by Cathy Sunshine (Washington, D.C.: EPICA, 1984), *Grenada: Revolution, Counterrevolution* by Trevor Munroe (Kingston, Jamaica: Vanguard, 1984), *Grenada: The Jewel Despoiled* by Gordon K. Lewis (Baltimore: Johns Hopkins University, 1987), *Big Revolution, Small Country: The Rise and Fall of Grenada Revolution* by Jay Mandle (Lanham, Md: North-South, 1985).

8   Grenada is the only English speaking island that has been invaded by a super power. Threats of military intervention were made by the British against the Jagan government in Guyana in 1953 and by the United

States against Trinidad in 1970. For a detailed discussion of both incidents see *The Other Side of Paradise* by Barry, T., Wood, B. and Preusch, D. (New York: Grove Press, 1984) p. 322-328, p. 364-367.

9   PRG leaders explained their emphasis on mass literacy as both an economic and political goal. Education would enhance the productivity of workers and simultaneously help to facilitate the cultural transformation they hoped to bring about through the revolution. For an example of how these goals were articulated, see *Education Is Production Too* (St. George's, Grenada: Ministry of Education, 1981).

11 The zonal council meetings were part of the structure of participatory democracy that was being established by the PRG. The councils were intended to serve as a form of local government and as a vehicle for conveying the sentiment of the residents to the national government. For more information about the zonal councils and how they fit into the PRG's plan for participatory democracy, see *Is Freedom We Making* (St. George's, Grenada: Government Printing Office, 1980).

12 One such poll was cited in the November 3, 1983 issue of the *N.Y. Times* in an article entitled "Grenadians Express Support For U.S. Military Action."

13 Less than ten percent of the respondents to my survey indicated support for Herbert Blaize even though he received more than seventy percent of the popular vote in the election of 1984.

Chapter 2

Developing A Theoretical Framework For An Explanation of Political Change in Grenada

The Imperatives of Power

To explain the process of political change in Grenada, we must begin by placing the case in a regional and international context in order to establish an appropriate frame of reference. This is necessary for two reasons. First, Grenada is an extremely small nation, a mini-state, whose political experiences, regardless of their brief prominence, appear almost inconsequential when viewed in isolation. Secondly, when examined in fine detail, the process of political change in Grenada is too easily interpreted as a tragic drama involving some exceptional and not so exceptional individual leaders whose actions and policies bear primary responsibility for influencing the course of events. While these tendencies may seem compelling, particularly to those who know Grenada well, by decontextualizing the case or over emphasizing the role of individuals, it becomes too easy to lose sight of the larger structural forces which have shaped the context in which political events have occurred and which make it possible to derive important lessons from Grenada's experience.

This study seeks to avoid this error by framing the analysis around two broad theoretical questions that have relevance for a wide range of cases at varying levels of analysis. First, how important is political support to the survival of any government? Or, under what conditions does the degree of support experienced by a regime become significant in determining whether or not that regime will be able to retain political power? In answering these questions within the context of

Grenada's political history, we will explore the ways in which the island's political culture has influenced popular attitudes and expectations toward political leaders, and government more generally. We will also explore in great detail the factors that seem to be most salient in influencing popular support toward government.

This study also seeks to answer questions concerning the factors influencing regime survival and longevity. In explaining the rise and fall of the three regimes, how are we to distinguish and assign weight to factors that exerted internal and external pressures and strains? How important is regime legitimacy, both domestic and international, or the lack thereof, and how does it influence the range of options available to a regime that seeks to retain power under adverse economic and social conditions? In what ways are the survival strategies for regimes that pursue elite support different from those that are directed toward cultivating a more popular base? To what extent does Grenada's vulnerability to external economic and political pressures create problems for the survival of any regime, regardless of its ideological orientation or the personality of the leader? Finally, is political stability in a small impoverished country such as Grenada simply not attainable for an extended period of time because of the vulnerability created by geo-political and macro-economic structures?

This study seeks to explain and interpret the unusual set of political events that occurred during a forty year period in Grenada. The events themselves challenge conventional wisdom and common sense explanations, and therefore require an analysis that is both theoretically compelling and historically situated. My approach to this task relies upon what Hamza Alavi (1982) has referred to as a recognition of the "structural imperatives" that influence patterns of social, economic and political change in developing societies. Such an approach begins by acknowledging and identifying the structural and cultural factors that set the parameters and conditions under which various actors, whether those be individual leaders or broad social categories (i.e. social classes, institutions, organizations, etc.), operate and make decisions. I intend to do so without adopting reductionist or overly deterministic formulation of social action, relying instead upon an approach that is rooted in the history of the island and based upon an analysis of contemporary social and political conditions. Regarding how such an approach can be applied to the study of political change, Alavi writes: "The concept of structural imperative allows us to recognize the possibility of disjunction, within limits and at particular moments, between the making of public policy and the contending interests of the dominant classes, the indigenous bourgeoisie, the metropolitan bourgeoisie and landowning classes, as well as the fact that such deviations not only have limits but can persist over time" (Alavi and Shanin, 1982: 193).

The approach taken in this study of political change in Grenada follows the theoretical framework that has been developed by Evans and Stephens (1989) and utilized by Skocpol (1979) in her study of social revolutions. Though the comparative aspect is limited to the case itself, an analysis of the Gairy, Bishop and Blaize regimes, references are made throughout the text to other relevant cases. The approach taken is substantively historical, one which sets out to interpret the process of political change in Grenada, by rooting it firmly within the island's contemporary political history. However, it is also an approach that aims at establishing Grenada's importance to the study of political change generally, through its emphasis on the following themes that form the parameters of the analytical framework used in this work: 1) how alignments between class forces and their relationship to the state influence the character and orientation of government; 2) the factors influencing the degree of state autonomy at various points in history; and 3) the transnational structures of power that influence Grenada's political economy, both historically and at the present.

This analysis focuses on the issue of regime survival as the key element to understanding the process of political change in Grenada. It does so because since 1951 the question of who controls political power, the particular configuration of class forces and their relations to external actors, has had tremendous bearing upon political activity and the direction of political events. Political actors and organizations have emerged in Grenada to challenge central authority for control over the power to distribute resources and to make decisions that effect the fate of the nation. The contest for political power has historically been manifest as a contest between three leaders: Eric Gairy, Maurice Bishop and Herbert Blaize, and the constituencies they represent, both internal and external to Grenada. These conflicts have defined and shaped the political process in Grenada for the last forty years. An analysis of the efforts utilized by the three leaders and the regimes they led to retain power will be central to this study, as we attempt to identify the ways in which the imperatives of power in Grenada have produced patterns of leadership that were common to the three regimes despite their significant differences.

Of equal importance to this study of political change in Grenada is an explanation of the basis of regime support. Through survey research we will attempt to ascertain on what basis and for what reasons Grenadian citizens have chosen to support or oppose a particular leader. This will involve an assessment of how the expressed political sentiments of individual citizens have affected or become manifest in their political behavior, and under what conditions has support or opposition led to mobilization for or against a regime in power. At a basic and fundamental level, we will seek to understand what Grenadian citizens expect from their leaders and government and what are the factors that influence these expectations. The answers to such questions necessitate an investigation into the island's political culture, as well a review of its history. Such questions also drive the perspectives, sensibilities and priorities of ordinary Grenadians to the forefront of this analysis.

For the purpose of this study on Grenada, political culture is conceived both as a product of history and as a system of collective meaning that mediates social structure and human action. As the collective body of values and norms that have emerged over the course of a nation's history in response to its experience with politics, political culture establishes the social-psychological constraints that affect ". . . the conduct of individuals in their political roles, the content of their political demands, and their responses to political authority" (Almond and Powell, 1978:25). Recognition of the significance of political culture ensures that social actors are not seen as passive role players whose actions and decisions are influenced or determined by forces beyond their control. Instead, the actors are seen as being influenced by established patterns of behavior that are conditioned by social and economic structures, as well as having the capacity to influence the ever changing political culture themselves (Almond and Verber, 1963).

An analysis of political culture is particularly important because it sheds light on the factors influencing legitimacy and on the strategies utilized by regimes to obtain it. In our effort to understand the basis of regime support in Grenada, the extent to which a regime is perceived as legitimate is extremely important because it has tremendous bearing upon the capacity of the state to ". . . extract resources, regulate behavior and distribute goods and services" (Almond and Powell, 1978: 31). As the degree of legitimacy possessed by a regime declines, it may be forced to rely increasingly upon coercion to achieve its objectives. Its ability to use coercive means is in turn influenced by popular perceptions of regime legitimacy.

The Basis of Regime Support

This study seeks to analyze political events in Grenada, both from the perspective of the political leadership of the Gairy, Bishop and Blaize regimes, as well as from the perspective of the citizenry. For me, the task of undertaking this analysis began shortly after the U.S. invasion as I sought to make sense of the political upheaval that had occurred on the island. However, it was not until I returned to Grenada in 1987 that I was gradually able to gain new insights, which both deepened my understanding of what had transpired during my absence from the island and prompted new and different kinds of questions.

Even before my return to Grenada, I had come to realize that my inability to interpret and make sense of the political changes that had taken place in Grenada compelled me to adopt an inductive approach to my research. I had been skeptical of the interpretations of events that I had read and heard from various commentators, almost all of whom seemed more wedded to framing their analysis within a particular ideological framework, rather than pursuing a more objective reading of events. While I by no means saw myself as an objective observer, I was certainly open to devising a research strategy that would produce an explanation of political change on the island that was grounded in the reality of the Grenadian experience. For me, such an approach seemed to provide the only means for arriving at an explanation of political change that would be credible and believable.

Adopting the approach to grounded theory advocated by Glaser and Strauss (1967), I used my prior knowledge of Grenadian politics and my initial observations and interviews to generate meaningful hypotheses. At the same time, I reviewed comparable research and the relevant literature in the field of political sociology of developing societies to assist in my search for plausible explanations. Both processes led me to the following possibilities for explaining political change and the basis of regime support. These are that political support and political change can be based on: 1) the effectiveness of a charismatic leader who generates popular support and maintains power through the strength of personality; 2) the promotion and dissemination of an ideology that is embraced or rejected by large segments of the population; 3) the effective use of patronage to punish or support key constituencies; 4) the use of coercion in a variety of forms against opponents; 5) the use of foreign support from powerful nations in the form of military, economic and/or political assistance. Throughout this study these five hypotheses (charisma, ideology, patronage, coercion and foreign support) are used as themes through which the three regimes are analyzed and compared. We shall now analyze each of these with a view toward examining their relevance to the political scene in Grenada from 1951 to 1991.

1. Projection of a Charismatic Personality

Charismatic leadership is defined by Max Weber as a "certain quality of an individual personality by virtue of which he is set apart from ordinary men and treated as endowed with supernatural, superhuman, or at least specifically exceptional powers or qualities" (Weber,1947: 358). Weber's definition is generally used as an "ideal type," a hypothetical construct that serves as a basis for classifying similar cases that appear in the real world. Weber uses the concept of charisma to characterize the form of political leadership typical to traditional societies in contrast to bureaucratic leadership, which he envisioned as the form of authority modern governments would increasingly adopt.

Many writers have suggested that the emergence of charismatic leadership is a phenomena common to post-colonial societies that are in the process of rapid modernization, or as in the case of Maurice Bishop, during the aftermath of a period of radical political change. The flux created by rapid urbanization, the introduction of foreign values and ideas, and the accompanying changes in production and politics increases the likelihood of political disorder. However, such circumstances also set the stage for the emergence of the charismatic leader. Wriggins writes:

> In most emerging countries the institutions for endowing political leaders with the authority to rule are ill-formed. Traditional ways of acquiring legitimacy no longer remain; the legal and political methods introduced by colonial regimes have been discredited in many places; and the innovations adopted after independence lack roots. By his direct appeal to a multitude of individuals or leaders of autonomous groups, the personality can gain acceptance for his exercise of power (Wriggins: 98).

Charismatic leaders can be particularly useful during periods of rapid change because of what Edward Shils has described as an

> ". . . order-destroying power that arouses the charismatic propensity . . . It does so because it promises in some instance to provide a new and better order of existence. Order-destroying power also arouses the charismatic propensity because of a profound ambivalence in men's relations to the central authority"(Shils, 1965: 203).

Once political power has been secured, Weber suggests that charisma tends to become routinized and may either evolve toward bureaucratic leadership or lead to a deterioration in the power of government as the original appeal associated with charisma begins to wear off and the problem of succession is confronted (Weber, 1947). George Danns suggests that as charisma is routinized, the popular appeal of the leader may become what he terms "mesmeratic" leadership. Unlike charisma which was based upon the ability of a leader to articulate the

genuine concerns, demands and aspirations of his/her supporters, mesmeratic leadership is little more than a shadow of
its predecessor in that it is used to whip up support by drawing on the collective memory of past struggles. It does so without calling up the energies and activism of the past since these
now pose a threat to the regime in power.

In Grenada, both Eric Gairy and Maurice Bishop have been
characterized as charismatic leaders (Lewis 1984;
O'Shaughnessy 1984). In contrast, Herbert Blaize has generally been described as a rather dull, uninspiring leader. In the
pages ahead we will consider the role of charismatic leadership in cultivating and sustaining popular support. We will also
consider whether or not the absence of a charismatic leader
increased the difficulties faced by the various regimes headed
by Blaize.

2. The Promotion and Dissemination
of a Popular Ideology

Several writers have identified ideology as an important factor in the cultivation of support and legitimacy for governments in developing nations. In many cases, governments attempt to utilize an ideology or doctrine as a means of cultivating
and promoting support among the populace. In some cases,
ideology is also used as a means of creating a new sense of
national identity, while simultaneously introducing new values that support the direction chosen by the political leadership. Ideology may also serve a more general purpose and be
utilized primarily as a means of justifying the policies and actions of government. Sigmund describes such an ideology as
"a systematic scheme or coordinate body of ideas about human life and culture" (Sigmund, 1966: 3). The use of the term
ideology employed in this study will be more general so that it
may encompass both more rigid ideological doctrines and more
general political orientations or political philosophies.

In many cases, the ideological orientation of a regime is not
represented by a coherent, neatly packaged doctrine. Nonetheless, evidence of the influence of ideology may be seen
through rhetorical strategies employed to justify state policies
and priorities and to rationalize resource allocations. In the

Anglophone Caribbean, most often ideological appeals have been aimed at mobilizing the lower classes. To secure power after independence, Hintzen argues that Black middle class leaders often used nationalism, and in some cases (Guyana and Trinidad), direct appeals to race to secure lower class support (Hintzen, 1991:16). However, he also points out that such appeals often have no actual bearing on government policy but are used primarily to create the illusion that the regime is promoting the interests of a particular segment of the lower class (Hintzen: 25).

As we compare and contrast the three regimes, we will examine the way in which the ideological character of each regime influenced its policies. We will also consider how the ideological orientation of the regime influenced attitudes toward it, both within and outside of Grenada. Only the PRG headed by Bishop explicitly espoused an ideology. However, to varying degrees, the ideological orientation of all three regimes influenced the nature and content of the policies that were developed and pursued. Whether or not the more explicit ideological orientation of the PRG or the more subtle ideological influences of the Gairy and Blaize regimes played a primary role in influencing popular reactions to the three governments will also be explored in the pages ahead.

3. Patronage and Mass Organizations

In many developing countries, the political system is characterized by a network of alliances between individuals and social groups (clients) and powerful elites (patrons), who exchange political support for some type of service or material benefit. Typically, organizations such as political parties or trade unions serve as the vehicle through which the exchange of services and support takes place. While the nature of the exchanges may vary, (i.e. military protection in exchange for food, social services in exchange for votes, etc.) in many cases, political systems that are based upon patronage have been relatively stable, and the patron-client relationship has been able to endure over long periods of time (Stone, 1977).

The patronage system which exists in many developing nations closely resembles the political machines that were common in many cities in the United States in the late nineteenth century.[1] As was the case in cities such as Chicago, New York and Boston, patronage systems in the Third World have enabled political leaders and their associates to become entrenched in public office, while simultaneously providing them with a means to obtain wealth and other benefits that they might not have had access to otherwise. Based on exchange and reciprocity, patron-client relations tend to work best with poor, socially fragmented communities within competitive political systems. In such a context, the relationship that develops between the patron and client is imbalanced, predicated upon a disparity in wealth, power and authority that favors the patron (Scott, 1975: 178). Patronage systems can also be developed to achieve cooperation among competing interests groups.

In Grenada, all three regimes relied on some form of patronage to cultivate and maintain political support. Despite their vulnerability to corruption, patronage systems have proven to be sustainable for long periods, due largely to the stability they bring to politics, generally, and the regime in power in particular. As we analyze the three regimes, we will consider how the use of patronage influenced attitudes toward them.

4. The Use of Coercion

When all else fails, the state can rely upon its officially sanctioned ability to use force to intimidate its opponents or punish dissidents. The state's monopoly over the legitimate instruments of force, (i.e. the police, military, militia, etc.) provides it with the means to maintain stability and retain power when other means of quelling opposition or enlisting support for the regime have proven ineffective. The use of coercion by the state may take many forms, depending on the nature of the threat, the extent to which it threatens order and stability, and the degree to which political leaders perceive themselves to be secure in their positions of power and authority.

However, excessive use of force or over reliance upon repressive measures may eventually lead to a regime's demise.

Fragile governments may be weakened further if they are forced to rely upon repression as the primary means of contending with opponents. Percy Hintzen argues that only a "strong executive" is capable of using force effectively. A strong executive which is able to "functionally integrate the military, paramilitary units, and the police creates the conditions for more centralized and coordinated control of the state coercive machinery by the political executive" (Hintzen, 1987: 19). Through such control, the state has the ability to "defuse and demobilize the most serious challenges to its own legitimacy or to that of the state" (Hintzen: 21). In societies where the state is "soft", meaning that it must rely on the support of powerful elites for the performance of essential functions by the state, it often can not act unilaterally but must take into consideration the interests of those powerful elites, and at times, consult with them prior to taking action.

Several scholars have noted that the precarious state of economic and social conditions in developing societies often makes it more likely that regimes will rely upon some form of violence as an essential element of their regime survival strategy (Huntington 1968). Wriggins argues that "the level of intimidation in developing nations will have to be higher than in more developed policies where political institutions are well established, procedures accepted, and consensus on major issues more easily evoked" (Wriggins: 176). Making a similar point, Shanin writes that "The special political characteristics, the military regimes' brutality of oppression and instability, are not an aberration, but reflect the specific nature of the state in developing societies...The less secure its control, the more visible the oppressive nature of the state"(Shanin: 319).

Coercive measures were employed by all three regimes in Grenada to deter the activities of opponents. While often providing at least temporary relief from political pressure, invariably the use of coercion comes at the expense of regime support and in some cases undermines regime legitimacy. Hence, while Machiavelli's warning to the Prince that it is better to be feared than loved may be an axiom that has been fully embraced by Grenada's leaders, they have also understood that the cost of becoming feared is high and at times self defeating.

5. The Role of Foreign Support

For a variety of economic, geographic, political and historic reasons, governments in many developing nations often rely quite heavily upon foreign policy as a means to obtain support which may be essential to regime survival. In many cases, domination by a large, technologically advanced nation over the economic and sometimes political affairs of a developing nation is linked to the history of colonialism, and the unequal economic relationships that developed during that period (Chirot, 1977: 181). Because of Grenada's size and economic vulnerability, foreign support has been an important element in the regime survival strategy of the Gairy, Bishop and Blaize regimes. While larger countries such as China, North Korea, Burma and Iran have in the past attempted to develop their economies through strategies based on self-reliance carried out in relative isolation by reducing trade with core nations, Grenada has never been able to seriously entertain that option. Its dependence on food and energy imports, its lack of industry and technology, and its low level of social services with respect to health, education and welfare, have made even the prospect of self sufficiency and self reliance out of the question. Moreover, the country's relatively long history of colonialism (independence was achieved in 1974) has fostered a high degree of political and economic dependence among the population on larger countries such as Great Britain, the United States, and even toward Trinidad and Venezuela.

Although all three regimes in Grenada recognized the need for strategic foreign support, each pursued a different strategy to obtain it. In this respect, the differences in the ideological orientations adopted by the three regimes had a profound effect upon the foreign policy course pursued. In analyzing the factors that led to the fall of all three regimes, we will consider the role and effectiveness of their foreign policies and the actions of foreign powers toward the three regimes.

The five themes identified as potential explanations of regime survival are not intended to serve as an exhaustive listing. They are rather elements of explanations for political support that seemed to resonate among the Grenadians I interviewed. The themes have also" featured prominently in various studies of political change in other developing societies, and therefore provide a means to avoid the specificity and particularity inherent in a case study. The usefulness of these themes is derived from their potential value as a frame of reference for conducting a comparison of the three regimes. It will also allow us to generalize to other cases from the lessons obtained from an intensive study on political change in Grenada.

Notes

1 The political machines established in the United States during the latter part of the nineteenth century were dominated by European immigrants, many of whom had experienced discrimination. Control over municipal government provided these groups with access to patronage and, thereby, provided them with a means to obtain financial security and upward mobility. Through access to civil service jobs and government contracts, these immigrant groups experienced a degree of upward mobility that would not have been possible without patronage. For a discussion of the Irish political machines, see Erie, S. *Rainbow's End* (Los Angeles: University of California Press, 1988).

Chapter 3

Political, Economic and Social Conditions Prior to 1951

The Colonial Legacy and Its Influence on Grenada and the English Speaking Caribbean

As a starting point for analyzing the history of political change in Grenada, it is important to begin with some discussion of how modern politics evolved in Grenada and the area once known as the British West Indies. The economic and political forces at work at the time the structures of the state were created, the class forces which were most responsible for their development, and a recognition of the purposes intended to be served by these structures are all pertinent to an understanding of government and politics in the present day Anglophone Caribbean. Such an historical retreat is necessary for it makes it possible to recognize whether any of the antecedents to the state's development have lingering influences on the present structures. Moreover, given the regional and international dynamics that once influenced the politics and administration of the West Indies, due to the common legacy of British colonialism, such an historical analysis also helps in identifying features of Grenada's political experience that sets it apart from its counterparts in the region.

Most of the developing world, with the exception of Latin America, established independent forms of government within the last forty to fifty years. Often, the forms of government created were modeled after the political institutions of the colonizing nation. Typically, colonial subjects who had been

trained to manage and direct the operations of the state under colonialism continued to occupy positions of leadership
after independence since they possessed the required skills
and knowledge. In many less developed societies, these civil
servants served as a buffer class between the colonial authorities and the indigenous population,[1] making it possible for the
European authorities to exercise control over economic and
political affairs within the colonies in many cases without direct involvement (Fanon,1963; Memmi, 1965; Rodney, 1974).

Some sociologists have referred to the structures of government created by the colonial state as "over developed" (Hintzen,
1978) because the structures created were modeled after the
system of government existent within the colonizing nation and
corresponded to the needs and level of development of the
mother country rather than the colony itself. These structures,
having been created by the colonizing nation, were primarily
intended to facilitate domination over the colony and the exploitation of its resources. When viewed in contrast to Western European societies, where nation-states were created by
an indigenous bourgeoisie "in the wake of their ascendant
power, to provide a framework of law and various institutions
which are essential for the development of capitalist relations
of production" (Shanin,1972:42), the state in post-colonial societies can be seen as having an origin that is not indigenous
but foreign, and as such was not originally intended to serve
the needs and interests of the local population.

As was true for the civil servants, many of the political leaders who came to inherit the reigns of power, whether through
force or peaceful transition, were most often individuals who
had received training in colonial schools and universities and
who had assimilated the values and norms of the colonizing
culture. In the West Indies, these were often the individuals
who led the fight for independence through labor protests and
through the limited official channels for petition and redress.
This cohort of nationalist leaders which emerged out of the
labor struggles of the 1930s and 1940s established its credibility as representatives of the mass interests, through their leadership in trade unions and nascent political parties.[2] Though
many of these leaders occupied positions of relative privilege
within the social hierarchy by virtue of their class, education

and in some cases color, they formed parties that were both nationalist and populist in their political orientation (Bell 1967; Hart 1993). Many of the leaders were intellectuals and professionals who, as Oxaal described, projected "the public image of a party based upon an appeal to intellect and reason . . . and brought into the political arena lofty ideals and even the paraphernalia of academic life" (Oxaal, 1968:3). There were also others such as Alexander Bustamante in Jamaica and Vere Bird in Antigua who adopted a more militant image and style, having emerged onto the political scene as leaders of the labor movement, and veterans of the bitter strikes and conflicts of the 1930s and 40s (Beckford, 1971: 8).

Independence came to the larger nations of the Anglophone Caribbean in the early 1960s at approximately the same time that decolonization was occurring among the former British colonies in Africa. Jamaica, and later Trinidad, became independent in 1961, shortly after the dissolution of the West Indies Federation which had originally been envisioned as the governmental entity under which the entire Caribbean Commonwealth would achieve independence.[3] After independence, the administrative bureaucracies created by the British remained largely intact, as did the civil service personnel they had trained. Aside from the new flag and the darker faces occupying political office, the institution of government, including much of the legal infrastructure, remained largely unchanged (Lewis 1993; Nettleford 1993).

Under colonialism, the state was largely controlled by the economic interests of the metropolitan bourgeoisie and the local plantocracy, whose interlocking relationships based upon trade of agricultural products and raw materials led to a mutual interest in its affairs. Although these interest were by no means uniform and conflicts did develop between estate owners and their British trading partners, the ever present colonial state could always be called upon to intervene and serve as arbiter and mediator to ensure cooperation among elites and the continuous flow of trade. George Beckford described the primary motive of the British in their administration of their colonies in the Caribbean as one of overseeing "production for trade and the extraction of wealth" and thus helps to explain why the colonial state could play a more or less neutral role between competing interests among the economic elites of the Caribbean (Beckford: 19).

Despite the protections afforded by the mother country, the power exerted by the planter class over civil society in the English speaking Caribbean gradually declined during the early part of the twentieth century due to a variety of factors. The decline of labor intensive agriculture, in particular the gradual collapse of sugar cultivation in the region due to competition with more efficient producers in Cuba, the Dominican Republic and Hawaii, and the advent of industrially produced beet sugar in Europe, was a major factor that contributed to a reduction in political influence (Smith 1965; Lewis 1968). Perhaps equally important to the decline of the planter class was the willingness of the British to allow unionization of agricultural labor in the wake of the massive labor upheavals that occurred throughout the region during the 1930's. The willingness of the British colonial government to tolerate the existence of labor unions even after it had tried unsuccessfully to repress the labor movement in its West Indian colonies, allowed these organizations to become the driving forces for independence in the years that followed.

For much of the twentieth century the large estates on many of the small islands in the Eastern Caribbean were owned by absentee landlords, though in some industries, namely sugar, multinational corporations owned and managed production and trade (Lewis 1968:162). The detachment of such major actors from the islands tended to limit their involvement in the political affairs of the local population in matters which directly affected their business operations. This contrasted with settler colonies such as the United States and South Africa, where conflicts between metropolitan business interests and the producers based in the colonies eventually led to violent opposition to British colonial rule (Fredrickson 1980: 150-178). In such colonies, the colonial state proved incapable of responding adequately to both interests, particularly given that it had a stake in many of the commercial enterprises that were undertaken.[4] In the British West Indies, the state was able to avoid such a fate because of the mediating role it played between the competing interests of metropolitan and local capital, and because a large European settler population never established a permanent presence in the region.

In relation to demands for reform emanating from the peasantry and the middle class, the colonial state played a role characterized by paternalism and benign neglect. Although effective maintenance of the empire and all of the territories subject to its rule was generally regarded as a serious affair by the British colonial state, the mini states of the Caribbean were simply too small and poor to warrant the attention they occasionally demanded. Though the colonial state was largely indifferent to the plight of the peasantry and few efforts were made to improve living conditions, raise wages or provide adequate plots of land to independent farmers, the state did intervene when demands for reform blossomed into civil strife and rebellion, as occurred during the Morant Bay Rebellion in Jamaica in 1865 and the peasant uprising in Grenada in 1951. During periods of crisis, the colonial state often intervened with force to squash rebellions and restore order. In some cases, the crushing of a revolt would be followed by the enactment of reforms designed to reduce the possibility of future disturbances. This occured, for example, in the aftermath of the labor uprisings when the Moyne Commission was established by the British Crown in 1938 and charged with the task of investigating the causes of the uprisings which occurred on several of the British West Indian colonies during the preceding years (Brizan, 1984: 67). Aside from these episodes of unrest, the colonial authorities generally left local matters to local government and to the Agricultural Societies, both of which were dominated by the large estate owners.

Poltical Culture and Social Structure in the Post-Colonial Caribbean

Though clearly aligned with the local elites and metropolitan capital, the paternalism of the British colonial state also brought some social benefits to the subordinate classes in the colonies. For example, mass public education at the primary and later secondary level was extended to the West Indian colonies during the mid nineteenth century, nearly one hundred

years before similar public educational systems were created
in most nations of Asia, Africa and Latin America (Miller 1991).
Similarly, in response to demands for representation in local
government, the British gradually extended limited avenues
for petition and political participation in its Caribbean colonies. Over time, the legislative powers of local government were
strengthened and representation in public office eventually
went beyond the local plantocracy to include elements of the
middle class. The gradual empowerment of the Legislative
Councils, the enactment of universal suffrage in the late 1940s
and 1950s, and the transition to Associated Statehood for the
smaller islands in the 1960s allowed for a peaceful transition
from colonialism to independence. It also helped to ensure
that the institutions and political traditions established by the
British would remain largely intact after independence.

Several writers have argued that the reason why there were
relatively few violent clashes between the British and their
colonial subjects (particularly as compared with the French
and Portuguese colonial experience) is due to the paternalism
which characterized British colonialism.[5] In Grenada and the
rest of the West Indies, British paternalism combined with the
unfettered exploitation of the lower class majority created a
political culture that produced enormous contradictions in the
political life of the island and the region. One such paradox is
the relatively high degree of political stability found throughout the region and the persistence of democratic forms of government despite the continued marginalization of the impoverished lower classes from political and economic
opportunities. Carl Stone has described the West Indies as
". . . the only area in the third world where politics based on
free elections, multiple parties, and liberal democratic freedoms are still predominant . . ." (Stone, 1985: 14). The maintenance of the Westminster system of government, left over by
the British, and the general absence of a strong military apparatus among these states, stands in stark contrast to its Central
American neighbors. Whereas those nations, with the exception of Costa Rica, have been frequently led by authoritarian
and military regimes, in the West Indies transfers of state power
between opposing political parties have occurred with considerably less upheaval. Political interference and manipulation,

violence between political parties, as well as gross infringe-ments on political and civil rights have occurred in the En-glish speaking Caribbean. However, such practices have, to some extent, been off set by the legacy of free press, political pluralism and the firmly established rule of law that has char-acterized the region.[6]

However, despite its relative success in retaining democratic practices and institutions, independence has not led to the realization of the idealistic future which was once envisioned for the West Indies.[7] Once the middle class assumed control over government after independence, the political leadership of the independent states of the West Indies were confronted with several challenges for which they were largely unprepared. In the past, the colonial state could rely upon the British for military and economic backing during periods of crisis. How-ever, with the absence of imperial support as the ultimate guar-antor for the retention of power, the post-colonial state has become preoccupied with what Wriggins (1977) calls the "rul-ers imperative—the need to stay in power." Challenges to the political leadership of West Indian governments, whether origi-nating from an opposition committed to democratic norms or emanating from more radical challengers willing to employ "any means necessary" to attain state power, tend to preoc-cupy the leadership, who in most cases are extremely concerned with holding on to power. With the spoils of government and a variety of forms of patronage at stake in any challenge, the struggle for power, which had been relatively low-key during the colonial period, has taken on a new intensity in the post-indepenence period.

Moreover, these nations remain economically vulnerable. As a mini state located within the back yard of the United States, Grenada and most of its Caribbean neighbors (with the pos-sible exception of Trinidad), has no "comparative advantage" or market niche to provide its economy with some measure of protection from the vagaries of the international market. Their dependence on agricultural exports and tourism as the pri-mary sources of foreign exchange makes these islands extremely vulnerable to and dependent upon their major trading part-ners and severely limits the possibilities for economic and so-cial progress. Though independent since 1974, Grenada is a classic "neo-colony", importing most of what its population consumes while exporting non-strategic primary products and large numbers of its well trained and able-bodied citizens to core countries.

As plantation economies, or using Beckford's terminology, colonies of exploitation (Beckford, 1972; Best, 1966; Patterson, 1967; Girvan 1976), the region's economies have been distorted by a colonial legacy that geared all trade of a single product, sugar, to the colonial center. Even as the commodities of exchange have diversified to include other agricultural products, minerals, petroleum and more recently components of a "disaggregated manufacturing industry" (Harris, 1989), the dependent nature of external relations have been maintained. The lack of economic diversity in these countries and their traditional reliance on export oriented growth strategies has allowed the fortunes of Caribbean economies to fluctuate dramatically with the short term cycles of the world economy.

The possibilities for altering the Caribbean's dependent relations to core countries have been severely constrained by the relations that exist between the political elites of the region and foreign capital. The middle class leaders who inherited control of the Caribbean state from the colonial authorities were never a land or capital owning class. Their primary source of wealth was derived from their "cultural capital" (e.g. education and training) and their status as a buffer between the planter class and the lower class majority. However, once in control of the state, the middle class leadership used the bureaucratic apparatus as a vehicle for accumulating wealth and power (Henry and Stone 1983; Hintzen 1987). It accomplished this by using its control of the state to "guarantee a number of property rights and conditions of capital realization and expatriation, all in an effort to make capital 'feel at home'" (Henry and Stone, 1983: 43). Efforts to court foreign capital have consisted of a variety of measures intended to make the country attractive to foreign investors, including measures which have severely undermined the economic interests of workers. In exchange for their compliance, local political elites have been able to accumulate wealth and power through their control of parastatal enterprises, the acquisition of government contracts for themselves or their supporters, and control over the jobs that are created by foreign investment which can be used to expand networks of patronage. The social pact between the ruling middle class political elites and the lower class majority has been strained by such developments, but so far the pact remains more or less intact. Grenada may be the one exception to this norm, for the class alignments in place elsewhere in the region never completely took hold in Grenada. In the following pages we will examine why this did not occur and what the consequences have been for politics on the island.

Social and Economic Conditions

Since the abolition of slavery in 1838, Grenada has been largely a peasant society in which the source of an individual's wealth and status has been derived primarily from his/her relation to the primary means of production, the agricultural economy. The vast majority of people in Grenada earn their income either directly or indirectly from agriculture, and social relations between classes within the society have been influenced largely by one's relationship to the agricultural mode of production. Land distribution has traditionally not been even among the population, with the vast majority of cultivable land belonging to a few large estate owners.[8] However, since the end of slavery, there have also been a significant number of small farmers (88.5% of the total landholders), most of whom own less than five acres of land (Ambursley and Cohen, 1984: 185). These peasant proprietors, together with the landless estate workers and tenant farmers, comprise the rural lower classes in Grenadian society.

The transition from slavery to free labor in 1838 did little to change the hierarchical structure of the society, nor did it significantly alter relations between social classes. As a British colony, political power remained in the hands of the colonial authorities, while control of the economy, both in trade and production, was retained by the white and near white former plantation owners. The colonial political economy created a class structure in which white planters and merchants owned most of the land and dominated the local government. Individuals of brown complexion were predominant in the professions and small business, and the Black majority comprised the peasantry and held the low status occupations. The class structure therefore, produced a caste system in which ". . . correlations between social status, pigmentation, association, and family are extremely high" (Smith: 268).

To a large extent, social relations between classes were influenced by land ownership patterns. The lack of control over land from which one could obtain subsistence fostered the creation of an agroproletariate that continued to provide labor on the estates after the end of slavery. As was true elsewhere in the Caribbean, due to the historic association between agricultural work and exploitation, the end of slavery prompted a gradual exodus of agricultural workers from the estates (Segal 1993). However, this trend did not lead to massive rural-urban migration such as occurred elsewhere in the Caribbean (Watts 1987:481). Instead, former slaves were more likely to claim plots of land for subsistence cultivation and retail on the local market. According to the Grenada Handbook and Directory of 1946 "The effect of freedom upon the African in Grenada seems to have been to fill him with a distaste for regular labor on the sugar estates for fixed wages . . ." which in turn "caused the establishment almost immediately of numerous gardens therein" (Grenada Handbook, 1946: 23).

The loss of labor on the estates, combined with the comparative advantage maintained by Cuba and the larger Caribbean islands in sugar production, brought about the demise of the sugar industry in Grenada, which had been extremely labor intensive, and its replacement by cultivation of cocoa and nutmeg. This shift in agricultural production accommodated the desires of the new peasant proprietors, who spent more time tending their own gardens for subsistence and sale on the local market and who took on work on the estates largely as a means of obtaining cash to purchase those things they could not produce themselves. While this development did little to transform power relations between classes, it did have a tremendous impact upon the quality of life of the peasant majority who became less dependent upon the estate owners. Several authors have argued that landownership patterns in Grenada have produced a degree of independence in the attitudes of the Grenadian peasantry and influenced their atti-

tudes negatively toward highly exploitative work in light manufacturing, tourism and other low paying service sector jobs
generally (Singham 1968:87-92; and Lewis 1987: 64).

Despite changes in the legal status of freed Africans, the
political environment in Grenada remained largely unchanged
from 1838 through 1950. While other British West Indian possessions such as Jamaica, Trinidad, British Guiana, Barbados
and St. Kitts experienced riots and labor unrest during the
1930s, Grenada remained relatively dormant. The mobilization of labor in the Trinidadian oil fields and sugar estates of
Jamaica posed a serious threat to British colonial rule over the
region and prompted the British government in 1938 to establish the West Indian Royal Commission headed by Lord Moyne
to investigate the living and working conditions of the peasantry on the islands (Smith: 269-271). The Commission was
charged with the task of identifying the causes of the uprisings that had taken place and was instructed to recommend
appropriate reform measures which would avert similar occurrences.

While in Grenada, members of the Commission decried what
they regarded as the deplorable conditions of the peasantry,
with respect to housing, health and educational needs. The
Commission noted that "the housing of agricultural laborers
is disgraceful, it is impossible to use any other word to describe it . . ."(Moyne Commission Report 1939:16). It did, however, note that ". . . large portions of the population have the
ability to supplement their cash earnings by home grown food
stuffs . . ."(Moyne Commission Report: 19) and thereby withstand the adverse effects of crop failure or reductions in earnings due to declines in prices for cash crops on the international market. Moreover, while it applauded the stability that
had prevailed on the island for many years, the Commission
recognized that it was ". . . doubtful whether any schemes of
social reform, however wisely conceived and efficiently conducted, would be completely successful unless they were accompanied by the largest measure of constitutional
development..."(Moyne Commission Report: 36). The constitutional development vaguely referred to by the Commission
concerned the growing demand within Grenada for self-government based upon universal suffrage. Though the Commis-

sion was not prepared to concede this demand, it did recommend a broadening of suffrage and changing the form of Crown colony rule (Brizan, 1984: 134).

Opposition to the Crown Colony form of government had been led for many years by W.G. Donovan, and later T.A. Maryshow. The Crown Colony system provided for the election of British subjects residing within the colony, who met the requirements regarding wealth and land ownership, to the Legislative Council. However, it did not permit locals to serve on the Executive Council which controlled the external affairs, defense and finances of the colony. In 1896 Donovan established "The Federalist and Grenada People", a newspaper devoted to expressing local opposition to various colonial policies. On occasion, it even criticized the colonial leadership for their treatment of the peasantry (Singham: 156). Later, Maryshow, an associate of Donovan, and C.B. Renwick started the *West Indian* newspaper which served as their vehicle for airing demands for self-rule. Maryshow went on to be elected to the Legislative Council from the town of St. George's. He later became the leading proponent for the creation of the West Indies Federation, which briefly came into being in 1958, the year of his death (Lewis, 1987: 27).

Aside from the activities of Donovan and Maryshow, resistance to colonial rule and protest over the plight of the peasantry were largely non-existent prior to 1950. Moreover, Maryshow, unlike labor leaders such as Alexander Bustamante or Norman Manley of Jamaica, never developed an organized base among the lower class through the formation of a union or political party with whom he could press his demands for self-rule upon the British. West Indian historian Gordan K. Lewis put forth the following explanation of Maryshow's leadership style: "For all his noble gifts, Maryshow was a West Indian Fabian, a Royalist loyalist, whose staunchly Whig constitutionalism never permitted him to fight the colonial powers except on its own polite terms" (Lewis 1987: 16).

Given the existence of conditions that were potentially favorable to labor activity, one can only attribute the seeming passivity of the Grenadian populace and the relative calm which pervaded the social environment for decades to the lack of leadership and organization among the peasantry. As the Royal

West Indian Commission discovered, conditions were certainly severe enough to have produced the type of unrest that took place on the other islands. Undoubtedly, the constant migration of thousands of Grenadian workers to the oil fields in Trinidad, the cane fields of Cuba, the oil refineries of Aruba and the Panama Canal served as a means of relieving some of the tension which might have built up as a result of the widespread poverty and exploitation on the island.[31] However, the absence of peasant based leadership and organization seems to have been the primary factor which contributed to the continued subordination of the peasant majority without organized resistance.

This point is critical to an understanding of Grenadian politics and the reason for its deviation from the political norms of the English-speaking Caribbean. Whereas on other islands, the Black middle class had emerged to lead the peasantry, in Grenada, the inability or unwillingness of the Black middle class to lead the peasantry in either the labor movement or the nationalist movement for independence left a void in Grenadian politics. The Black intellectuals who have been described by Oxaal (Oxaal:23), Bell (Bell, 1972: 26-64) and Hintzen (1989) in their work on other Caribbean islands failed to assume positions of leadership over the lower classes. Middle class professionals such as Maryshow were politically active, both locally and regionally, but they had no base among the peasant majority, and therefore could not claim to represent them in the political process. As a consequence, the void in leadership created a situation which was ripe for an aspiring political leader with vision and organizing ability. Eric Mathew Gairy, a native of the rural parish of St. Andrews, returned to Grenada in 1949, fresh from his experience organizing in the oil fields of Aruba, to fill that void.[9]

Notes

1   Both Franz Fanon (1967) and Albert Memi (1965) have described how European colonizers in Africa cultivated a class of people from within the colonized population to serve as functionaries for the colonial government and as the intermediaries or "buffers" between the European and indigenous populations. In the English speaking Caribbean, those who constituted the buffer class went on to assume control over the state once independence was attained. See Fanon, F. *Black Skin White Mask* (New York: Grove Press, 1967) and Memi, A. *The Colonizer and the Colonized* (Boston: Beacon Press, 1965).

2   For a discussion of the background of Caribbean leaders, see Brooks, Wendell *Jamaican Leaders: Political Attitudes in a New State* (Berkeley, CA: University of California Press, 1964) and *The Democratic Revolution in the West Indies* (Cambridge: Schenkman Publishers, 1967) and Oxaal, Ivor *Black Intellectuals Come to Power* (Cambridge: Schenkman Publishers, 1968).

3   For a discussion of the history of the Federation and the reasons for its collapse, see Lewis, Gordon K. *The Growth of the Modern West Indies* (London: Modern Reader, 1968) and "Attitudes Toward Political Independence" by Charles C. Moskos in *The Democratic Revolution in the West Indies* edited by Wendell Bell.

4   The relationship between the British Crown and private commercial interests in colonizing the Caribbean is described well by George Beckford in *Persistent Poverty* (New York: Oxford University Press, 1972). *The Modern World System* by Immanuel Wallerstein (Academic Press, 1974) provides a more elaborate historical discussion of the role of private capital in the development of the capitalist world economy.

5   Unlike several other European colonial powers who tenaciously sought to hold onto to their colonial possessions, the British adopted a more paternalistic approach, which resulted in considerably less confrontation in most cases. In *The Poor and the Powerless* (New York: Monthly Review Press, 1988), Clive Thomas describes the British approach in the following manner: The colonial office generally portrayed its colonial mission as one of "trusteeship," a view in which the aim of a good colonial administration was to foster and encourage a progressive and orderly movement toward representative self-government." Such an approach made it possible for the British to grant independence through a relatively peaceful transition process and retain relatively amicable

relations with its former possessions through their membership in the Commonwealth.

6 Those who have followed political developments in Jamaica might contest these assertions. Political conflicts between the People's National Party and the Jamaica Labor Party took a violent turn throughout much of the 1980's. Similarly, the coup attempt by Muslims in Trinidad in 1990 might also seem to contradict the image that has been presented. However, in both Trinidad and Jamaica, political succession has been determined by elections. Moreover, the courts and the press have remained largely independent, so much so that in Trinidad, Abu Bakaar, the leader of the failed coup, was granted an early release from prison by the courts. For further discussion of both of these cases and the vicissitudes of democracy in the Caribbean, see *Democracy in the Caribbean, Myths and Realities* edited by Carlene Edie (Westport, CN: Preager, 1994).

7 Visions of a promising future for the West Indies were expressed by several Caribbean leaders and the British at the time of independence. For further discussion, see *The Growth of the Modern West Indies* by Gordon K. Lewis (New York: Monthly Review, 1968) p. 75.

8 According to Grenadian historian George Brizan, in 1930, out of 15,319 proprietors, 95.8% were peasants owning no more than 2-5 acres of land; 2.6% could be classified as middle-size proprietors (10-100 acres) and 1.6% were large estate owners. Despite the uneven distribution of land, the relatively large number of peasant proprietors contributed to the existence of a small but insignificant subsistent economy. See Brizan, G. *Grenada Island of Conflict* (London, Zed Books, 1984) p. 229.

9 Many Grenadians migrated to Aruba during the 1930s and 1940s to work in the oil fields. Maurice Bishop was born in Aruba while his parents were living there. Most Grenadians, like Bishop's parents, stayed temporarily and returned to Grenada once they had earned enough money or when there was no longer sufficient work available.

Chapter 4

The Populist Roots of Grenadian Politics: The Rise of Eric Gairy

Eric Gairy's early rise to power was made possible to a large extent by his ability to mobilize the peasant majority through the skills he had acquired as a labor organizer and his knowledge of the sensibilities of the Grenadian peasantry. The return of Eric Gairy to Grenada in December of 1949 coincided with the beginning of a change in the political and social order in Grenadian society, influenced largely by constitutional reforms that were instituted in response to the Moyne Commission Report. These reforms included the enactment of universal adult suffrage in 1951 and increased power for the locally elected Legislative Council. Together they constituted the most substantial changes in political conditions on the island in the post-emancipation era. As a result of these changes a new political opening was created for the Grenadian peasantry. However, to take advantage of this opportunity the peasantry would have to be organized. Gairy's arrival on the scene helped to bring that organization about.

Eric Mathew Gairy was born in Grenada in 1922 near the western port city of Grenville to a poor family. At the age of 20 he set off for Trinidad where he was employed at a United States military base. From Trinidad he went to Aruba where he, like hundreds of other Grenadians, found work in the oil refineries (Brizan: 242). While there, he became involved in trade union organizing among the employees of the Esso Company. His activities there led to his eventual removal from the island by local authorities and prompted his return to Grenada (Smith: 254).

Gairy's interest in Grenadian affairs had been sparked prior to his return by contact with T.A. Maryshow in Aruba. Maryshow spoke to many of the migrant Grenadian workers in Aruba about the deplorable conditions back home (Smith: 245). Upon his return to Grenada in 1949, Gairy established the Grenada People's Party in March 1950, and later a trade union, the Grenada Manual and Mental Workers Union (GMMWU). By June of 1951, Gairy claimed to have registered 27,000 members and boasted: "I organized more people in one year than any other man in the West Indies" (Jacobs and Jacobs, 1980: 102).

Conditions were ripe for an organizer with the energy and vision of Eric Gairy, whom M.G. Smith described as "well suited for the role" due to his background and experience (Smith: 283). He quickly became recognized by the peasantry as a spokesman who could be called upon to articulate their grievances and as an advocate who could champion their cause in disputes with employers or the colonial administration. His first victory as a labor leader came early in 1950 when he represented tenant farmers who were threatened with eviction by an absentee British estate owner who had recently purchased the property. Making use of the Tenant Compensation Ordinance, Gairy claimed full cash indemnity for the tenants and won (Brizan: 267).

Soon after his first victory as a labor leader, Gairy launched a more ambitious challenge against the local elite. In August of 1950, the GMMWU demanded a 50% wage increase for workers employed at Grenada Sugar Factory Ltd. Following an unsatisfactory exchange of letters with the management, Gairy called on the five hundred workers employed there to go on strike. Shortly after, workers on eleven other estates joined the strike in sympathy. In September, the matter was brought before the Arbitration Tribunal, who awarded a 25% increase to the workers, as well as holiday pay and double pay for holiday work (Brizan: 261).

While the dispute was before the Tribunal, Gairy demanded a 20% wage increase for all estate workers on the island from the Grenada Agricultural Employers' Society. Fearing that any recognition of Gairy would only serve to further empower him, the Society negotiated instead with the less militant Grenada

Trade Union Council (GTUC). An agreement linking wages to cocoa prices was reached with the more moderate GTUC, which temporarily eased the pressure. The Agricultural Society was relieved, thinking that they had found a way to neutralize Gairy, and that they had found a more moderate group of peasant leaders with whom they could recognize and negotiate labor contracts.

The GTUC was led largely by representatives of the Longshoreman's Union and the St. John's Labor Party. Both of these organizations were led by labor bureaucrats from the middle class who viewed the GTUC as a partner of the Employers' Society. Brizan described "a spirit of amity and cooperation" which seems to have existed between the two bodies (Brizan: 262). Their unwillingness to raise the demands of the agricultural workers forcefully enabled Gairy to challenge their credibility and claim leadership of the trade union movement.

In October, Gairy confronted the Employers' Society again, despite their refusal to recognize him or his union. He demanded a 45.5% increase in wages for all estate workers. He also demanded sick pay, holiday pay, overtime and general improvement in working conditions. The Employers' Society responded by conceding on the issue of vacation pay, but refused to grant the other demands. At about the same time, there was a substantial decline in cocoa prices, which in accord with the agreement reached with the GTUC, led to a fall in wages (Brizan: 263; Lewis 1968: 146).

Gairy took advantage of the situation, and on January 29, 1951 called for a strike at the La Sagesse estate, the same estate where he had obtained compensation for the tenant farmers the previous year. The following day, workers on neighboring estates joined the strike. Gairy was persistent in his demand that the Employers' Society agree to his demands and recognize him and his union. They attempted to ignore Gairy, and reiterated their commitment to the earlier agreement reached with the GTUC (*West Indian* 2/2/51).

At the time of this upheaval, the traditional patron-client relations that existed between peasants and estate owners on the larger estates were beginning to break down. Rising nutmeg and cocoa prices in the 1940's prompted a new cohort of agricultural entrepreneurs to buy abandoned and idle estates cheaply in Grenada. This new group of planters were unaware of the expectations of the estate workers who had grown accustomed to the semi-feudal relations on the estates and the roles and obligations associated with it. Instead of honoring and maintaining their commitments which would have allowed the estate workers to continue to live on the estates, producing food for themselves and their families as part of their compensation for working the land, the new owners sought to formalize the worker-employer relationship by paying set hourly wages. In his first action as a labor leader, Gairy capitalized on the disruption in the relations between owners and workers at the La Sagesse Estate, where peasants were threatened with eviction from their homes by the new proprietors. The labor unrest of 1951 was fueled by this break down in the relations of production in agriculture and the simultaneous proletarianization of the workforce.

On February 18, 1951, Gairy brought his followers together and called for a general strike the following day. This was followed by incidents of violence and arson on estates throughout the countryside. On February 21, Gairy led a massive demonstration into the St. George's capitol, outside of the chambers of the Legislative Council at York House. There, Gairy demanded that he be allowed to meet with the Governor and told his followers not to sleep or work until this demand was met (*West Indian* 2/18/51).

An observer described the scene in front of York House in the following manner: "Shouts went up when Mr. Gairy arrived on the scene, dressed in a mixture of sports and evening wear, bare-headed and carrying his walking stick" (*West Indian*, 2/18/51). In response to altercations between the police and his supporters, Gairy told the crowd that their "fight is not against the police but the employers who will be hunted out should anything happen" (*West Indian*, 2/18/51). The occasion provided the colorful Gairy an opportunity to demonstrate his control over the labor protesters. As the hours passed and the pressure mounted, Gairy was threatened with arrest if he would not disperse the crowd. Gairy responded to the threat by warning his followers that "Things have come to a stage when I may be arrested at any time, but you shall not sleep a night nor do a stroke of work until I am released" (Brizan: 179).

Throughout the day and night Gairy led the crowd in chants of "Don't work, but don't sleep". Adding to the intensity of the situation was the fact that Governor Arundell was not on the island, thus compelling the Acting Governor to decide on his own how to respond. He was faced with the choice of meeting with Gairy and thereby further empowering him and his union through the act of recognition and negotiation or ignoring him and risking further violence. The decision was finally made to detain Gairy and his assistant, Cascigone Blaize (no relation to Herbert Blaize). They were taken aboard the *HMS Devonshire* and sent to the neighboring island of Carriacou. Meanwhile, police were brought in from Trinidad and St. Lucia to contain the violence caused by the island-wide strike (Jacobs, 1980: 77).

While Gairy was held in custody on Carriacou, violence and arson by striking estate workers spread across the island. An official report of the Labor Department described the strike in the following text:

> . . . for one month commencing 19th February 1951, Grenada experi-
> enced a strike of agricultural and road workers which caused an up-
> heaval such as has not been known within living memory. Workers
> who showed a disinclination to go on strike were intimidated and
> beaten by their co-workers, by the unemployed and by unemployables;
> estates were looted in broad daylight, while Management stood by
> unable to interfere; valuable produce, trees, were deliberately dam-
> aged; rioting and bloodshed occurred; the small police force appeared
> totally inadequate to deal with the situation, and it became necessary
> to seek police assistance from St. Lucia and Trinidad. Units of the
> British Navy were hastily summoned, and a small garrison of British
> troops were stationed here for months afterwards (Grenada Labor
> Department Report, November 1951).

As the upheaval progressed, the code word "Sky Red" was used by the strikers to indicate when another burning would take place. The Acting Governor declared a state of emergency and enacted a series of laws to contain the uprising. These measures were unable to deter the revolt, leading one fright-ened estate owner to warn Governor Arundell on March 11, that "unless Government is prepared to rule, we, the planters and the merchants, will have to take the government into our own hands, and we hope that you will give us the license which you have given to these communistic hooligans when we do act".[1] Dennise Henry, another large estate owner, warned the Governor that "Gairyism is not only a trade union, it bears all the hallmarks of communism".[2] Such attempts to portray Gairy as a communist would prove particularly ironic later on, when Gairy himself would attempt to use the same charge to discredit his opponents.

Messages of support for the strike came from trade union leaders throughout the Caribbean, including Uriah Butler, a Grenadian by birth who was a major labor leader in Trinidad, and Alexander Bustamante, a Jamaican labor leader. As the strike and the violence which accompanied it persisted, pressure mounted for the Governor to recognize Gairy and negotiate an end to the uprising with him. E.W. Baltrop, a labor advisor to the Secretary of State in Great Britain, was dispatched to Grenada to assist the Governor in resolving the dispute. On March 5th, Gairy and Blaize were released from Carriacou. Gairy agreed to call for an end to the strike and the Governor agreed to establish a commission to look into the demands of the union.

Upon his return to Grenada, Gairy held meetings with his followers to inform them of the agreement reached with the Governor. On March 8th, Gairy addressed the island over the radio in an appeal for an end to the uprising. His first attempt at quelling the unrest went largely unheeded, leading him to utilize the airwaves a second time the following week to issue yet another call for an end to the protest, but this time in a more forceful and personalized manner:

> Yes folks, this is your leader Uncle Gairy speaking to you . . . I am deeply concerned over the present state of affairs on this our dear little island . . . I feel obligated morally and spiritually to do something to alleviate, to stop, and when I say stop I mean stop, the burning of buildings and fields . . . I say this—everyone has that love for Uncle Gairy. Everyone was disturbed when Blaize and myself were arrested and detained, and as a result lots of bad things happened . . . Gairy and Blaize are out again with you, therefore now is high time you stopped . . . Come on now, those of you listening, let's say no more violence three times together—No more violence! No more violence! No more violence! (*West Indian* 2/27/51).

On March 19th, the general strike came to an end. Negotiations began between the GMMWU and the Grenada Agricultural Employers' Society, with Baltrop serving as mediator. The agreement signed on April 4th was highly favorable to the workers and represented a clear victory for Gairy (Singham: 182). He was now fully acknowledged as the leader of a powerful workers movement and the undisputed spokesman for the peasantry on the island.

The Significance of the 1951 Uprising

The peace and stability that had prevailed in Grenada prior to 1951 came to a dramatic end with the revolt of that year. While labor protests had occurred earlier on the other islands, these mobilizations were either controlled or coopted by Black middle class leaders, who later used the movements to enhance their own bids for power. As a consequence of the middle class control of these labor movements, the demands of the lower class were often narrowed in scope to higher wages and better working conditions, rather than producing changes that would institutionalize working class participation in governance. The exception to this pattern occurred in Guyana where Chedi Jagan, though a member of the middle class, pressed for more radical demands on behalf of the peasantry (Hintzen, 1989). Like Jagan, Gairy was not content with merely pursuing higher wages for his followers. Gairy used the uprising to challenge the social hierarchy in Grenada and "presented himself as the popular champion against the white oligarchy" as he encouraged his peasant followers to "destroy their ingrained deference to their betters" (Jacobs: 83).

Gairy clearly did not identify himself as a communist, but his demands for change did call for an alteration in the power structure in Grenadian society. Many writers on Grenada have suggested that Gairy was far more concerned with obtaining power and wealth for himself than in leveling the differences between social classes in Grenadian society.[3] However, the strategies and tactics employed by Gairy in the uprising of 1951 had the effect of completely shaking up the status-quo in Grenada. For the first time in the island's history, local elites were confronted with demands from an organized peasantry. Likewise, the colonial authorities who had no prior history of being petitioned by the peasantry or their representatives, found themselves forced to negotiate with Gairy. The British authorities had fully expected the establishment of representative local government to result in the election of middle class leaders with whom they felt comfortable, as had occurred elsewhere in the Caribbean. However, the inability of the Grenadian middle class to develop a base among the lower class, combined with the subsequent emergence of Gairy, resulted in an unanticipated political development for the British. The peasantry, that had previously been a docile mass largely marginal to the political affairs of the island, were now mobilized to participate in politics under the leadership of Eric Gairy.

Gairy was instrumental in bringing about a temporary end to the marginalization of the peasantry through the movement of 1951. It is for this reason that some writers on Grenada have described the rebellion of 1951 as a social revolution, a reference not used to describe the protests that occurred elsewhere in the British West Indies. Grenadian historian George Brizan writes:

> The 1951 unrest was a belated attempt by the Grenadian working class to catch up with the developments of similar movements in the rest of the Caribbean. It provided a leap forward in the consciousness of the worker, and one hundred years of docility and subservience seemed to have evaporated over night. A social revolution had occurred that marked the apotheosis of the estate laborers post-emancipation struggle" (Brizan: 256).

Commenting further on the impact of the events of 1951 on the consciousness of Grenadian peasants, Richard and Ian Jacobs write:

> That victory by the agro-proletariate released them from the bondage of superstition that had previously tied them to the belief that only white and off-white people were capable of providing national leadership . . . Every strike, every confrontation that developed at the work place, instilled in the workers a consciousness of themselves as a class and contributed to the development of antagonistic relationships between themselves and their employers (Jacobs: 86).

The significance of the events of 1951 for Grenadian society should not be underestimated. This grassroots social movement prevented political parties such as the Grenada National Party, headed by middle class professionals, from assuming leadership over the peasant movement, as occurred on most of the islands in the British West Indies. It also served as a powerful cultural and political challenge to the hegemony exerted by the local elites and the British over the society, a hegemony that provided the basis for the cultural and psychological domination of the peasant majority.

Gairy's own philosophy of social change has been described by Gordon Lewis as "a curious mixture of God, Marx and the British Empire" (Lewis: 26). His motives for spurring on the rebellion have been called into question by most observers, many of whom have regarded his own intentions as a personal lust for power, wealth and acceptance among the social circles of the elites. Former Governor Arundel described Gairy as "an egoist, ambitious for power and with an inferiority complex apparently because of his dark color, determined to show the world that he can rise above birth and color to political leadership of his people" (Lewis 1984: 32). Regardless of what Gairy's motives might have been, it is impossible to deny that his leadership was decisive in making the uprising of 1951 possible. By leading the peasantry in a confrontation against the local elites and by organizing them into the first credible trade union on the island that genuinely articulated their interests, Gairy played a major role in changing the character of class relations in Grenada. As a result of his efforts, he became the primary beneficiary of the movement, and was elected to the Legislative Council in 1951.

Regardless of how his intentions may have been perceived, the emergence of Eric Gairy as a leader of the peasant majority in 1951 significantly altered relations between classes and castes in Grenadian society. Gairy not only addressed the plight of the agro-proletariate whose domination had gone unchallenged since the days of slavery, he also challenged the color caste system which relegated the Black majority to low status positions throughout the society. By asserting the rights of Black people, he made it possible for others to reject the notion that the poor should passively accept their inferior status in the society. The exploitation of the peasantry continued long after the rebellion of 1951, but their participation in the political process on the island could never again be taken for granted.

The Struggle Over Control of State Resources

Having proven himself an effective labor leader, Gairy quickly went on to establish himself as a political leader on the island. He took advantage of the momentum and power of the labor movement and formed the Grenada United Labor Party (GULP) to launch his campaign for public office. His emergence as a player in the political arena coincided with the enactment of universal adult suffrage in 1951 (Brizan: 223). For the first time in Grenada's history, the majority of citizens would have the opportunity to determine who would serve as the colony's local leaders. The powers of elected representatives were still limited by the constitution of 1951, which constrained their role to legislation over domestic affairs. Ultimate power over the affairs of the colony remained in the hands of the Governor who retained the power to enact and veto legislation. Nonetheless, Gairy's overwhelming victory at the polls compelled the Governor to include him on the Executive Council.

In the aftermath of the uprising of 1951, Gairy viewed political power as the logical progression of his movement, and quickly moved with the GULP to take advantage of the democratic opening. In the October elections of 1951, Gairy and his party won six out of the eight seats on the Legislative Council. In a polling pattern which would repeat itself in the years ahead, the GULP lost in the town of St. George's which was taken by T.A. Maryshow, who ran as an independent, and in the parish of Carriacou.

During his first few years in office, Gairy continued to organize labor through targeted strikes led by the GMMWU. This enabled him to assert himself in the political arena by using his ability to organize workers as an effective form of leverage against his political opponents. In 1952 there were several incidents of independent action by estate workers as well as a strike called by the GMMWU in the parish of St. David's which involved approximately four hundred workers and lasted for three weeks (Singham: 194). Toward the end of 1953, Gairy pressed the Sugar Company and the Employers' Society, who together employed most of the agricultural labor on the island, for wage increases and improved working conditions. Negotiations between the GMMWU and the Employers' Society broke down, resulting in the intervention of an Arbitration Tribunal to resolve the dispute. The Tribunal rejected the union's demands for wage increases, prompting the GMMWU to call a strike of all agricultural workers, with the exception of those employed in the sugar industry on November 6, 1953. The strike was not successful, however, with only one third of the workers actually participating, and by the end of February, it had petered out on its own. To make matters worse for the union, the Agricultural Employers' Society announced a voluntary wage increase on April 28 to demonstrate to the workers that the tactics of the union had not been effective.

The strike of 1953-'54 was the last major labor action called by the GMMWU. From that point onward, trade union activities took a back seat to politics for Gairy and his supporters. Because both the GULP and the GMMWU were run in a highly personalized manner by Gairy, he had difficulty maintaining both operations. His fear of being challenged by leadership from within the ranks of either organization prevented him from delegating leadership responsibilities to his subordinates. Thus, it was impossible for Gairy to maintain the labor activity, while simultaneously managing the affairs of public office. Nonetheless, despite the failure of the strike, the GULP captured six out of eight seats on the Legislative Council in the 1954 elections. Although voter support for Gairy and the GULP declined substantially from what it had been in 1951 (71% of the registered voters voted in 1951 compared to 58% in 1954), Gairy retained his position of leadership on the island (Brizan: 263).

A combination of events coming in the aftermath of the failed strike of 1954 led to a gradual decline in support for Gairy. In that year, thousands of unskilled Grenadians began migrating to Trinidad in search of employment, resulting in the loss of some of Gairy's most ardent followers.[4] In 1955, the island's agricultural economy was devastated by Hurricane Janet, and in its aftermath, Gairy was accused of corruption for misuse of relief funds.

In 1956, Dr. John Watts, a dentist educated in the United States, formed the Grenada National Party (GNP), which became the first party organized in opposition to the GULP. The GNP pledged to "bring back our dear little island to an even keel morally, socio-economically, and politically" (Singham: 196). It was comprised largely of educated middle class professionals, and, in that respect, was very similar to the nationalist parties led by Black intellectuals on the other West Indian islands.

With his political base eroding, his honesty as a public official questioned, and a well financed opponent challenging him in the political arena, Gairy's future as a political leader appeared to be in doubt. To make matters worse, the colonial administration remained suspicious and hostile toward him and cooperated openly with his opponents in their efforts to undermine him (Jacobs: 46). Though they were officially prohibited from becoming involved in electoral politics on the island, they made it clear that Gairy was not the person they wanted to see managing the affairs of the colony.

In the election of 1957, Gairy's GULP won only two seats on the Legislative Council. The GNP also won two seats, one of which was captured by Herbert A. Blaize from the island parish of Carriacou.[5] The remaining four seats were divided evenly between independents and the short lived People's Democratic Movement (PDM). The election of 1957 had a higher turn out than 1954, with 68% of the eligible voters participating, and 44% of those voting for the GULP. Though Gairy easily won his seat from the constituency of St. George's parish, he was suspended from the Legislative Council shortly after the election and prohibited from participating in elections for the next five years. His right to hold office was taken away from him by the colonial authorities as a result of charges that he had disrupted the campaign meeting of a political opponent, L.A. Purcell, by leading a steel band into the gathering (*West Indian* 9/16/57). With defections from the PDM, the GNP became the majority party on the Legislative Council, and in 1960, Herbert Blaize was selected to serve as the Chief Minister.

Patronage, Corruption and Colonial Intervention

Gairy deeply resented what he accurately recognized as a deliberate attempt by colonial authorities to undermine his leadership on the island. He blamed J.M. Lloyd, the Jamaican born colonial administrator, for denying him his franchise and thereby preventing him from holding public office. His charge of victimization became a campaign tactic for gaining sympathy from voters, as he portrayed himself as a humble David confronting the colonial Goliath. The tactic proved effective, and even the West Indian newspaper, which had traditionally criticized and opposed Gairy, printed the following editorial regarding his ban from politics:

> Gairy was found guilty of an electoral offence—that of walking through a political meeting at the head of a steel band. It was the type of incident that would have been laughed off had it happened to any other person but Gairy. Now that he has shown he is a man in full control, we feel every effort should be made as quickly as possible to ensure that he is given back his franchise (*West Indian* 4/9/61).

Despite widespread support for his return to politics, Gairy was prohibited from participating in the elections of 1961. Nonetheless, he was able to lead his party to victory at the polls, gaining 53% of the popular vote and eight out of ten seats on the Legislative Council.[6] Though barred from taking office himself, Gairy was recognized by his supporters on the Council as the defacto leader of government. He discussed government policy at his home with members of his party, and expressed his views on issues coming before the Legislative Council before crowds in the market square. Eventually, the colonial administrators began to see that as an outsider to government, Gairy was even more troublesome and disruptive. Whereas the stature and recognition he received as a public official compelled him to conform to the decorum and norms of the political establishment, as an outsider to government, he engaged in personal attacks against members of the colonial government, in particular, Administrator James A. Lloyd, whom he threatened to dismiss once he returned to office.

In the summer of 1961, Gairy's ban from politics was lifted by the colonial authorities, and in accordance with an arrange-

ment made with GULP member Joshua Thorne prior to the
election, Gairy replaced Thorne on the Legislative Council. In
his first speech to the Council, Gairy boldly asserted that:

> ... praises are not due me, but are due the Divine Maker, the Divine
> Architect, who in his divine scheme of things saw fit to have me come
> back to the scene. I am reminded of this divine and equitable law—a
> law which lends itself to the maxim that 'cream will always float' (Leg-
> islative Council Minutes, December 1961).

Once again, Gairy had demonstrated his ability to overcome
his opponents, and in keeping with is acquired leadership style,
attributed his success to divine intervention.

With GULP controlling the majority of Legislative Council
seats, Gairy was soon elected Chief Minister and Minister of
Finance by his colleagues on the Council. One of his first actions after taking office was to dismiss the Information Officer, who was a member of the civil service, and replace him
with a public relations officer who answered directly to him.
Gairy also took control of the government gazette, the *Citizens
Weekly*, and changed its name to *The Star*, which effectively
became the propaganda organ of his party. These measures
were undertaken by him to counter what he perceived as a
conspiracy against him involving the local elite, colonial administration, and the local press.

It did not take long for Gairy's opponents to respond with a
strategy aimed at removing him from public office once again.
Within a short period of time, charges were levelled against
him by the political opposition, accusing him of improper and
illegal use of public funds. Before long, charges of
"Squandermania" were directed at Gairy by the two major newspapers on the island. Among other allegations, he was accused
of bypassing the Financial Secretary and intimidating the civil
service. He was also charged with using government contracts
to reward friends, wasting public funds on unjustified pur-
chases of land at prices higher than the assessed value, and
using public funds for personal benefit.[7]

On January 22, 1962, a commission of inquiry was established by the Administrator, J.M. Lloyd, to investigate the corruption charges against Gairy. Thirty-seven persons testified
before the Commission to give evidence against Gairy related

to his alleged misuse of government funds. After hearing testimony and examining government records, the Commission concluded that Gairy as Chief Minister and Minister of Finance had been responsible for fiscal mismanagement and wasteful expenditure. Acting as the Queen's representative, Lloyd admonished that "proper control over the expenditure of public funds is essential..the abuses disclosed by the Commission of Inquiry struck at the roots of government."[8] The Commission added that "the Executive has deliberately destroyed the morale of the civil service by an undesirable interference with the administrative duties and by improper threats against the security of his office; the civil service has been induced to commit or condone improprieties or irregularities in the expenditure of public funds."[9] With that, he dismissed the Gairy led government by suspending the constitution and assuming direct control over government.

Gairy tried to dismiss the charges by retorting sarcastically that "this inquiry offers sufficient matter to cause an inquiry into itself." (*Torchlight* 10/18/61). Among his followers, Gairy pointed to the dismissal of his government as further evidence of a conspiracy by the colonial masters and the elite to undermine his leadership. He argued that he had not done anything worse than the previous administrations, a fact that was substantiated by the members of the Commission who discovered improper practices in the expenditure of public finances by the GNP government during their term in office (1957-1961).[10] Furthermore, he charged that those who sought to challenge his use of public finances to furnish his residence were merely opposed to seeing a Black man live so well.

Gairy's strategy proved effective as a means of diffusing the Squandermania issue. Reaction to the findings of the Commission were divided, with most middle and upper class people accepting the legitimacy of the report and supporting the action of the Administrator, and most poor people viewing the Commission and its report as yet another attempt by the colonial authorities and the elite to attack their leader. As a result, Squandermania did not become a central campaign issue during the election of 1962. Instead, the GNP promise to form a unitary state with Trinidad became the main issue. As it turned out, Grenadians responded positively to the proposal, and the

GNP was able to win the next general election with 50.4% of the votes and six out of ten seats on the Legislative Council.[11]

The Blaize government initiated talks with Trinidad on the prospects for a unitary state, but the idea was eventually aborted by Eric Williams, the Trinidadian Prime Minister, who felt Trinidad had little to gain from the merger. Despite this failure, Blaize and the GNP were able to retain political power for the next four years, largely because they had the approval and support of the colonial authorities and the local elites. Establishing a pattern that would characterize the party for years to come, the GNP pursued policies that benefited the interests of the middle class and local elites, the primary constituents and benefactors of the party, while largely ignoring the plight of the poor. It was a pattern that would consistently ensure the victory of GNP opponents in every election following a GNP term in government.

Gairy's confrontation with the civil service and the colonial authorities in 1961 would prove to be only a temporary setback in what had become an ongoing conflict between the two parties. The basic issues involved, control over the civil service and control over government finances, would resurface again as a source of controversy when Gairy returned to office in 1967. What was at stake was how much power locally elected officials would be allowed in managing the affairs of the colony. The ensuing debate was not unlike that which Maryshow had waged years before. The difference now was that Eric Gairy and the party he represented would be the clear beneficiaries of any concessions in power made by the British authorities. For this reason, the GNP and other anti-Gairy elements, who in all likelihood would have fought strenuously for local control over government in years past, now sided with the colonial administration in their conflicts with Gairy.

For Eric Gairy, much more was at stake than the mere principle of local control. In order to maintain the support of his followers and in order to develop a base of support in the business sector, Gairy found it necessary to use government and its resources as a means of distributing rewards and services to his constituents. To accomplish this, Gairy needed to bring the civil service under his control, particularly those departments responsible for issuing contracts, regulating government expenditures and hiring workers for public works projects sponsored by the government. Gairy's efforts to do this were stymied by Chief Administrator Lloyd, whose professional ethos as a colonial bureaucrat clashed with Gairy's unorthodox personalistic style. Singham writes that "the bureaucracy is not a neutral, rational agency. It is merely the only organization with skill in manipulating local interest in the community" (Singham: 203). As such, some of the civil servants sought to utilize forms of bureaucratic sabotage to undermine Gairy, with the Financial Secretary going so far as withholding government documents from him at a time when he was serving as Minister of Finance.

Faced with the obstacles set up by the colonial authorities, Gairy sought to increase government revenue by raising taxes, hoping that it would be easier to exercise control over locally generated funds than those acquired through grants administered by the Federal Treasury. Gairy was surprised by the response to this action,which drew strong protests from the business sector as well as petitions of opposition from his rural constituents. Gairy responded by chastising his followers, saying:

> It is very unfortunate that some of the same people who this government is trying to lift from their low state are joining this mad affair to bring to disgrace the plans and ambitions of government. Why can't our people distinguish between the liberator and those who have dedicated their lives to the return of the whip? (*The Star* 1/13/62)

His remarks, with the explicit reference to slavery and racial oppression, did little to change the sentiments of those who opposed the new taxes. Reaction to the tax increase combined with the GNP's promise for unification with Trinidad resulted in Gairy's defeat at the polls in the 1962 election and signified a significant weakening in his base of support on the island.

During the next five years (1962-1967) while out of public office, Gairy experienced considerable financial hardship and became even more determined to regain political power (Brizan: 268). He was able to use the time out of office to increase the activity of the GMMWU on behalf of agricultural workers, and as a direct result of their agitation, wages over those five years increased by 22% for agricultural workers (Brizan: 269). He also made demands for the GNP government to resign for its failure to fulfill its promise of unitary statehood with Trinidad. The Blaize government ignored Gairy's attacks against them and proceeded with the pro-business policies that had characterized the party's orientation during its first term in office. An indication of this orientation was evidenced through adoption of the Essential Services Ordinance of 1966 which prohibited strikes by workers in the telephone, electric and water companies and in "any industry that might be deemed essential by the Minister" (Jacobs: 95). Such measures added to the unpopularity of the Blaize government and led to the defeat of the GNP during the elections of 1967, with the GULP capturing 54% of the unspoilt votes cast. [12]

Notes

1 *Grenada Disturbances*, Report of the Governor of the Colonial Office, No. 117.5, April 5, 1951, p. 17.

2 Ibid p.19.

3 For examples of some of the writers who have questioned the sincerity of Gairy's interests in the peasantry, see Jacobs, Ian and Richard *Grenada Route to Revolution* (Havana: Casas de las Americas, 1981), Dabreo, S. *The Grenada Revolution* (Casteries, St. Lucia: Girl Friday Publishing, 1981), and Amburseley, F. and Cohen, S. *Crisis in the Caribbean* (London: Heineman Books, 1983).

4 The oil boom in Trinidad attracted many Grenadians to the island during the 1950's and 1960's. The prominence achieved by Grenadians such as Uriah "Buzz" Butler, the leader of the oil field workers in the 1930's, and internationally famous calypsonian Slinger Francisco (more commonly known as the Mighty Sparrow), attracted many others to the island. See *The Grenada Revolution* by Sinclair DaBreo (Castries, St. Lucia: Girl Friday, 1979).

5 For all his years in politics, Gairy was never able to develop a base on Carriacou. The labor unrest of 1951 never spread to Carriacou and the GMMWU was never strong there. Herbert Blaize was elected from Carriacou in 1957 to serve on the Legislative Council. Even during the height of Gairy's power on the island in the early 1970's, the GULP was never able to win a seat in Carriacou.

6 Grenada Council Paper Report of the General Elections, No. 3, 1962.

7 Commission of Inquiry Report on the Control of Public Expenditures in Grenada, October 1961.

8 Ibid. p. 9.

9 Ibid p. 12

10 Ibid. p.14.

11 Grenada Council Paper Report of the General Elections, No. 3, 1962.

12 Grenada Council Paper Report on the General Elections, 1967.

Chapter 5

The Limits of Power and the
Rise of Opposition 1967-1979

The years spent outside of government were hard on Eric Gairy. Loosing political power also meant a loss in the stature and prestige he had acquired from serving in elected office. Access to money and resources was also reduced and limited to what he could muster from his post as union president. Even more difficult to accept was the gloating of his many enemies, who derived a tremendous sense of satisfaction from their belief that his last defeat at the polls signified an end to Gairy's renegade political career. That, of course, proved to be wishful thinking. Holding true to past patterns, by the end of his fifth year as chief minister, Blaize and his ruling GNP had thoroughly alienated most of the lower class with their pro-business policies. In the election of 1967 the GNP was soundly defeated by the GULP, receiving only 45.5% of the votes cast and losing seven out of ten seats on the Legislative Council to the GULP (Brizan: 363).

Constitutionally, the election of 1967 was significant because it brought with it Associated Statehood, a change in Grenada's colonial status which granted substantially greater powers to the elected local government.[1] With the frustration of the past five years fresh in his mind and a recognition of the opportunities created by the new powers he acquired, Gairy was now more determined than ever to retain political power. Writing about the Gairy regime during this period, Grenadian historian George Brizan has identified three strategies adopted by Gairy to retain control over government after 1967. These were: 1) increasing the number of people who were economically dependent on government for employment and income; 2) crushing dissent and making it difficult for the Parliamentary Opposition to operate and perform; and 3) creating a highly centralized bureaucracy where decision making was concentrated in cabinet, which was dominated by Gairy himself (Brizan:329). The strategy was clearly intended to enable Gairy to exert total control over government and to expand his influence over economic and political affairs throughout the country. During the first few years of his return to office, Gairy complimented his efforts to consolidate power with a variety of measures which helped foster the image that was serving the interests of the lower classes. The combination of tactics employed by Gairy and his government over the next five years proved to be a highly effective means of insuring regime survival within an unstable economic and political environment.

Perhaps the most controversial of the measures adopted by Gairy was the seizure of private lands from large estate owners, most of whom had actively opposed Gairy before. Under a scheme entitled "Land for the landless," the Gairy regime acquired estates, often those owned by his opponents and which were deemed idle, and had the land turned over to peasants for residence and cultivation. By 1978 over thirty estates were acquired under this plan (Brizan: 321). In most cases, land acquired by government was then handed over to peasants who were given permission by government to squat and work the land indefinitely. This tenancy was tied directly to Gairy's land reform policy and was used by Gairy as patronage to reward constituents and guarantee their political loyalty.

Through such measures, Gairy was able to deal a severe blow to his enemies among the elite, while simultaneously deepening his support among the lower classes through his apparent benevolence. His move to abolish the statutory bodies governing the production and sale of the primary exports, cocoa, nutmeg and bananas in 1972, had a similar effect. The Grenada Cocoa Industry Board, the Banana Cooperative Society and the Grenada Cooperative Nutmeg Association, were all brought under government control. These governing boards, which had traditionally been dominated by the owners of large estates who had been opposed to Gairy, were replaced by government-nominated interim boards. Though his opponents charged him with interfering and mismanaging the affairs of the boards and creating problems for the crucial agricultural sector of the economy, Gairy's takeover did not result in a decline in production or profits for the growers. His critics could only point to an increase in wages for employees of the boards who Gairy had incorporated into his union, the GMMWU, as the sole evidence of any negative impact caused by his usurpation of authority (Jacobs: 94).

The importance of such an action was threefold: 1) it neutralized the opposition by seizing control over their resource base; 2) it provided the regime with another independent base for patronage; 3) it provided the regime with the power of economic sanction which could be employed as a means of punishing opponents and rewarding supporters. Furthermore, the takeover of the boards was overwhelmingly supported by lower class Grenadians, who perceived the move as yet another example of Gairy taking on the large land owners. Accompanied by Gairy's populist rhetoric, such actions contributed further to Gairy's popularity and his image as the hero of the masses.

With the status of Associated Statehood, the Governor now became largely a symbolic figure. Though he officially retained the power to veto legislation and possessed ultimate military authority on the island, it was clear from the actions taken by the British elsewhere in the region that the change marked the beginning of a gradual end to colonialism. For the first time, Gairy had the freedom to run the domestic affairs of government with limited interference from the colonial authorities. Members of the civil service who had previously obstructed much of what Gairy attempted to accomplish were now less able to avoid compliance with his wishes if they wanted to retain their jobs.

With the government and the union under his personal control, Gairy was able to develop a broad and extensive system of patronage. Gairy cultivated a style of personal rulership which placed him at the center and the top of the system.[2] Individuals seeking employment would often approach Gairy directly and, in many cases, were granted jobs after making direct appeals to him. Businesses that wanted concessions from government on taxes or import levies were often instructed to register their employees with the GMMWU as a precondition for government cooperation.[3] In some cases, Gairy rewarded his supporters in the private sector by granting monopolies on government contracts or control over the importation of certain consumer goods (Jacobs: 52-55; Debreo 1980: 74).

In addition to patronage, Gairy utilized his power to acquire a number of hotels, nightclubs and restaurants, which provided him with an independent source of wealth. He also took control over the *West Indian* newspaper, which together with the government controlled radio station, were the primary sources of news information on the island. By 1972, the year of the next election, Gairy wielded power over most aspects of political and economic activity in Grenada.

Popular Mobilization Against the Gairy Regime

Throughout most of the period between 1967 and 1972, Herbert Blaize, the Leader of the Loyal Opposition, and the constituents of the GNP were largely ineffective in challenging Gairy as he proceeded with his efforts to increase and consolidate his power. Aside from criticism of the regime's policies delivered in long, dull speeches by Blaize at meetings of the Legislative Council, there were few signs of resistance. The *Torchlight* newspaper, which was controlled by GNP supporters, continued its outspoken criticism of Gairy and his policies, but this apparently had little impact upon the electorate. In 1972, Gairy won an even more decisive victory at the polls, capturing 59% of the votes cast and thirteen of the fifteen seats on the expanded Legislative Council. The GULP's resounding victory at the polls helped to bring about the decline of the GNP as the major opposition party in Grenada. After the election of 1972, it became clear that Gairy was the dominant political figure on the island and his former enemies were faced with the choice of either complying with his program for the country or becoming one of the victims of his regime.

Buoyed by his recent victory at the polls, Gairy announced early in 1973 that the recent elections had given him a mandate to obtain independence from Britain. The move had been expected because several other West Indian colonies in the region had already become independent or were taking decisive steps in that direction. However, Gairy's announcement was met with vocal opposition from the GNP and others who insisted that a public referendum be held before proceeding with negotiations with Britain. As evidence of popular support for their position, the GNP collected 14,000 signatures on a petition calling for a referendum on independence. In a barely veiled threat to his opponents, Gairy responded by warning that "your signature today may bear witness against you tomorrow" (Commission of Inquiry, 10/27/75). Ignoring their protests, he departed for London on May 12, 1973 with Herbert Blaize, the Leader of the Opposition, to finalize arrangements for independence. While Gairy was out of the country, the Chamber of Commerce and other anti-Gairy elements staged a shut-down of all businesses on May 16 to protest Gairy's plans for independence (*Torchlight* 5/19/73).

With the GNP in decline, opposition to independence and to the Gairy regime began to emerge from a younger, more radical group of activists. The first sign of their presence came in 1970 during the Black Power protests in Trinidad and shortly after the mutiny by the First Battalion of the Army at Teteron Bay, in Trinidad.[4] That incident, which took place amidst an atmosphere of tremendous social upheaval in Trinidad as the radical student-led NJAC (National Joint Action Committee) staged massive demonstrations for Black power on the island, ignited protests in Grenada and other Caribbean islands. On May 10th, a large group of Grenadian youth staged a demonstration in sympathy with the Black Power protests in Trinidad, demanding "more jobs now" (*West Indian* 4/27/70).

Though the protest was relatively small, Gairy responded immediately to what he perceived as a potential threat to his authority. Undoubtedly, the type of racially charged, radical rebellion that was occurring in Trinidad appeared particularly ominous to Gairy. His traditional opposition had come from the middle class, the local elites and the colonial authorities. None of these groups had the ability to mobilize elements of the lower class against his regime. The prospect of a small group of radical intellectuals attempting to mount such a challenge represented the first serious threat to his base among the constituency that had delivered him to power on the island.

On May 21, Gairy responded to the handful of Black Power protesters with what appeared to been an extreme over-reaction. Taking advantage of his political dominance on the Legislative Council, the Emergency Powers Act was adopted empowering the police to search private premises for subversive literature, guns and ammunition without a legal warrant (Brizan, 1987). Two days later, Gairy delivered an address to the nation, broadcast on the radio, to issue the following warning:

> Power in Grenada is already in the hands of the Blacks. The Governor is Black, the Bishop is Black, the Chief Justice is Black . . . If Grenada wanted any power at all it would certainly not be "Black Power", it would be Work Power for the few who are unemployed, Money Power to meet the cost and standard of living, and Brain Power for the youth, so that they would become more responsible to hold positions in the state . . . (*West Indian* 5/23/70).

Gairy went on to inform the public of his intention to establish a "special police force", which would be used against his opponents.

> I can not boast of having the patience of Dr. Eric Williams (Prime Minister of Trinidad at the time). It is said that when your neighbors house is on fire keep on wetting your own house. We are now doubling the strength of our police force, getting unlimited supplies of modern equipment and weapons. The opposition has referred to my recruiting criminals in a reserve force. To this I shall not say yea or nay. Does it not take steel to cut steel? I am proud and ready to call on Grenadians, regardless of their background, to come and join in defence of my government and in the maintenance of law and order in the country . . . I know hundreds have come and some of the roughest and toughest roughnecks have been recruited . . ."(*West Indian* 5/23/70).

Proof that Gairy would indeed back up his threat to "nip in the bud" any protest against his government did not become evident until November of 1970. Following a protest by nurses from the General Hospital in St. George's for higher wages and improved working conditions, Gairy responded by deploying police to break up the protest and later firing and transferring some of the workers who participated. In response, a larger protest was organized by a group calling itself MACE (Movement for Advanced Community Effort), headed by Maurice

Bishop and Kenrick Radix, two young barristers who had recently returned from their studies in England. This time the government responded with even greater force, ordering the police to disperse the demonstrators with tear gas. Several of the demonstrators were later arrested under the provisions of the Emergency Powers Act. In the ten month legal battle that followed, Bishop and Radix, who served as legal counsel to the defendants, were able to win their acquittal, and in the process gained national recognition for their opposition to the regime. This victory established a pattern for Bishop and his associates, who would utilize the courts to challenge the Gairy regime on numerous occasions in the future.

Following the December protests, Gairy stepped up his pressure on those he perceived as hostile to his regime. Arbitrary dismissals and transfers of workers employed by the government, such as teachers, police, and other civil servants, were carried out against those who were viewed as antagonistic to Gairy (Jacobs: 97). The irregular security units set up by the regime increased the pressure on Gairy's opponents. As a consequence of their harrassment and intimidation of poilitical activists, the security forces became popularly referred to as the Mongoose Gang (Sunshine: 63), a name given because Gairy claimed the men were working on a World Health Organization project to eradicate rabies among mongoose on the island (Interview with Gairy 9/17/87). The March 1972 issue of *Torchlight* reported that opposition elements were being beaten and victimized by gangs of GULP supporters, while "the police, though informed, reacted indifferently or not at all" (*Torchlight* 5/17/70). Not yet assured that he had convinced his opponents of his willingness to use force, Gairy took to the airwaves once again on October 20, 1971, this time announcing the formation of still more security forces called the "night ambush squad" and the "special secret police force" (*Torchlight* 5/22/70).

In response to the increased repression of the regime, Bishop and his associates sought to develop a new organization which they hoped would be more effective in opposing Gairy. In 1972, Movement for Assemblies of the People (MAP) was formed by Bishop and Radix. Inspired by the Tanzanian system of Ujamaa or African socialism,[5] MAP leaders promoted the idea that a system of participatory democracy could serve as a better form of government for Grenada than the Westminster democratic system established by the British. Aside from its ideology and vision, MAP also took pragmatic steps to increase the challenge to Gairy. In a loosing effort, four MAP associates, Selwyn Strachan, Unison Whiteman, Fitzroy O'Neale and Keith Mitchell, ran under a grouping known as "Committee of Concerned Citizens" under the GNP ticket, in a united front against the GULP.[6] Though defeated decisively at the polls, MAP activists interpreted the loss as a minor setback in what would become a protracted struggle against the Gairy regime. However, the defeat also prompted them to begin to consider means, other than elections, to oppose Eric Gairy.

Shortly after the election, JEWEL (Joint Endeavor for Welfare, Education and Liberation) was created in the rural parish of St. David's by Unison Whiteman, Teddy Victor and Sebastian Thomas. The leaders of JEWEL engaged in grassroots community organizing among peasants in St. David's, and published a newspaper, *The Jewel*, which by 1973 claimed to have a circulation of two thousand (Jacobs: 142). In January 1973, JEWEL staged a public trial at the La Sagesse Estate in St. David's. Lord Brownlow, the owner of the estate, had angered local residents when he erected a gate blocking the path that enabled the public to cross his property to gain access to the beach. JEWEL member Hudson Austin, later to become head of the armed forces of the PRG, presided as judge over a mock trial, while Teddy Victor, the editor of *The Jewel*, served as the lawyer for the plaintiffs. Lord Brownlow was found guilty in absentia by a jury of six locals for depriving people access to the beach. In an unusual departure from their traditional bias toward the wealthy, a *Torchlight* article described the incident "as a triumph of democracy," and carried the following description of events:

> The people headed for the beach. At Brownlow's house the gate was locked and fifteen policemen under the direction of Inspector Belmar were present. Belmar threatened that any act which he considered violent would be forcefully suppressed; the crowd said they would smash the gate non-violently, surged forward and threw it aside. After bathing and regaling themselves, they went home (*Torchlight* 1/24/73).

The grassroots approach to organizing adopted by the JEWEL, combined with the middle class credentials of MAP, soon became a powerful source of opposition to Gairy. On March 11, 1973, MAP and the St. David's based JEWEL came together to form the New Jewel Movement (NJM). By this time, much of the organizing against independence under Gairy was provided by the NJM, which had now eclipsed the GNP as Gairy's primary political opposition.

Prior to Gairy's departure for independence talks with the British, tension had been rising between the NJM and Gairy's various police forces. In addition to the nurses strike on April 22, Jeremiah Richardson, an NJM supporter, was killed by police in the parish of St. Andrew's. The NJM responded by organizing a large demonstration in Grenville, the second largest city on the island, to protest the killing and to attempt to shut down the island's airport. The police met the protesters with teargas and gun fire, wounding ten of the demonstrators (*Torchlight* 4/25/73). The incident touched off a wave of police brutality directed at NJM members. On April 30, Mathew Joseph, another NJM supporter, was shot by police; numerous others were beaten severely by the notorious Mongoose Gang. For many Grenadians, the most despicable and outrageous atrocity to occur during this period was the savage beating and chopping of Clarence Ferguson by members of the Mongoose Gang, and the stripping of his daughter naked before a large crowd in the coastal town of Gouyave (*Torchlight* April 13, 1973).

In early May, the NJM called a "People's Convention on Independence" at Seamoon, near the eastern port city of Grenville, where they denounced Gairy's plan to go forward with independence without the consent of the people. They also used the occasion to articulate their views on how the society should be reorganized, stressing the need for priority to be given to the satisfaction of basic needs, and calling for a replacement of the Westminster parliamentary system with a new form of participatory democracy carried out through assemblies of the people at the village and parish level. These ideas were later elaborated upon by Bernard Coard, a Grenadian lecturer at the University of the West Indies, who was enlisted by the NJM to prepare the party's manifesto.[7]

The Gairy regime responded with continued repression by the various police forces, directed primarily at members of the NJM. Despite the attacks, a call was made for a People's Congress on November 4, 1973, which drew a crowd estimated at ten thousand people (*Torchlight* 11/8/73). A People's Indictment was issued and twenty-seven charges were announced against Gairy and his government. After each charge was read to those assembled, there were resounding shouts of "guilty," culminating in the issuing of a demand that Gairy resign within two weeks or face the threat of a general strike, which they promised would shut down the entire island and ultimately bring down his government (Duffus Commission Report 1974: 8).

Regime Repression and the Loss of Legitimacy

The challenge posed by the NJM confronted the Gairy regime with a new, more threatening challenge to his authority. The NJM was building a coalition based on class alignments between the middle class, elements of the small but highly organized urban working class, and the rural lower classes. This was precisely the type of class alliance that had been established in most other parts of the English speaking Caribbean. There was an important difference however. The radical political views of the NJM and their willingness to defeat the regime through direct action protests constituted a significant departure from Caribbean norms. Interestingly, although elements within the GNP were skeptical of both the tactics and vision of the NJM, they saw an alliance with the NJM, even if only for temporary convenience, as preferable to rule under Gairy.

Gairy responded to the mounting challenge to his leadership with a two fold strategy: counter mobilization and increased repression. Demonstrating he still had the ability to mobilize supporters, Gairy responded to the anti-independence mobilization at Seamoon by staging a demonstration of his own, only a few miles away at the Grenville Market, which reports estimated drew two to three thousand people. He informed his supporters that the NJM sought to prevent the country from attaining independence in February, a challenge he would not tolerate. During the rally, Gairy saw Ken Milne, a wealthy hotelier and long time GNP affiliated opponent, amongst the crowd. Though there is some dispute over whether Gairy actually ordered the assault against him, after being identified, Milne was attacked by several individuals within the crowd and severely beaten until rescued by constables on hand (Duffus Commission Report: 141). The attack on Milne served as a sign to elites on the island that if they sided with the NJM in challenging Gairy's petition for independence, they would be treated as harshly as the radical rabble-rousers of the NJM (*West Indian* Nov. 7, 1973).

In the days that followed, Gairy and his police force prepared for what they felt would be a coup attempt by the NJM. On November 18, 1973, six members of the NJM, Maurice Bishop, Unison Whiteman, Kenrick Radix, Hudson Austin, Selwyn Strachan and Simon Daniel went to Grenville to discuss with a group of businessmen their proposal for a general strike. The police, and Gairy himself, had been informed of the meeting through their intelligence sources. At the time there were rumors circulating throughout the island that the NJM planned to take over the island on November 18, starting with an assault on the Grenville police station. In response to what was at this point a farfetched notion, Gairy called on Innocent Belmar, the Superintendent of Police, to assemble one hundred and fifty members of the so-called police aides in Grenville earlier in the day to await the NJM. Shortly after arriving in Grenville for the meeting Bishop, Whiteman and Selwyn Strachan were brutally beaten as they attempted to enter L.L. Ramdanny's cinema, the venue of the meeting. Austin, Radix and Daniel fled to the nearby home of H.M. Bhola, a local businessman and a member of the GNP, who had called together businessmen for the meeting with the NJM. These three were also arrested later and beaten by the police while being held in custody.

The beatings of the NJM leaders enraged many Grenadians, who were repulsed by the regime's use of violence against its opponents, and led to condemnation of the regime by politicians and the media on many of the neighboring islands. A few days after the beatings, an organization of businessmen, clergymen, trade unionists and professionals, calling itself the

Committee of 22,[8] passed a no-confidence motion against Gairy's government and called upon him to disband the police aides, arrest those responsible for the beatings and establish a commission of inquiry to look into the execution of justice in Grenada (Brizan, 267).

Initially, Gairy seemed to respond positively to the demands of the Committee of 22. He announced that the police aides would be disempowered and that a commission of inquiry to be headed by Sir Herbert Duffus, a well known Jamaican jurist, would be appointed. As a result of Gairy's actions, the Committee of 22 put on hold its plans for general strike. Within a few days however, the Attorney General reported that there was not sufficient evidence to justify prosecution against those responsible for the violence against the six NJM members. In response, the Committee of 22 met again and called for a general strike to begin on December 27, which would continue until "the Premier and his government resign" (Jacobs: 144). Gairy responded to the challenge of the Committee of 22 with a message to the nation, broadcast over Radio Grenada, during which he denounced the Committee of 22 as a "group of political diehards" that he had defeated repeatedly at the polls, and he threatened to "cut the leaders down to size" and charge the beaten members of the NJM with sedition and treason (*Torchlight* 12/18/73).

After the rebuff by Gairy, the Committee of 22 proceeded with its plans for a general strike. Marches and demonstrations began on January 9th. Thousands of people marched through the streets of the capital for several consecutive days, shutting down the stores of those few businessmen who complied with Gairy's order to remain open (Duffus Commission Report: 83). Marches of as many as 25,000 people under the leadership and direction of Eric Pierre, president of the Grenada Seaman and Waterfront Workers Union (SWWU) and the Commercial and Industrial Workers Union (CIWU), effectively closed the island's main port and shut down all business in the capital (*Torchlight* 1/16/74).

After several days of large demonstrations, announcements were made over Radio Grenada calling upon all police aides to report to Gairy's official residence at Mt. Royal on the morning of January 21. In the announcement, each aide was asked to bring three friends to join the force. As the tension increased and the probability of violent confrontation grew, Governor Hilda Bynoe left Grenada unexpectedly, a move that was interpreted as a concession to the demands of the protesters that she resign (Vigilante and Sanford, 1984). Later that day, as thousands of protesters marched through the streets of St.George's, Gairy met with three to four hundred police aids at Mt. Royal. Following the meeting, the police aides marched down from Mt. Royal, many carrying clubs and chains, singing: "Jewel behave. They going to charge we for murder" (Duffus Commission Report: 27). Upon reaching the port in downtown St.George's, a riot broke out between the two groups. Several of the anti-Gairy protesters were beaten and Rupert Bishop, father of the NJM leader, was shot in the back while attempting to provide refuge for women and children who had entered the SWWU headquarters during the melee.

Even after the riot, the strike continued while independence negotiations with Britain proceeded. February 7th was set as the date for independence, and both Gairy and the British were determined to go forward despite the turbulence on the island. When the event finally took place it was neither the grand ceremony that Gairy had envisioned nor the catalyst for the movement against Gairy as the NJM had hoped. Instead, Independence Day took place amidst power outages and shortages of basic foodstuffs on the island. In describing the event, British journalist Hugh O'Shaughnessy writes: "What had been planned as a glittering occasion turned out to be a miserable affair . . . the ceremonies were a sad farce" (O'Shaughnessy 1984: 53). With the support of Trinidadian and Barbadian dockworkers, who refused to handle cargo enroute to Grenada, the NJM still believed the strike could succeed in toppling the Gairy regime, particularly as the supply of petrol on the island dwindled. However, even with the government near bankruptcy and with his legitimacy on the island seeming to be at its lowest, Gairy was saved by an independence gift of one million pounds from Britain, and a loan of two million dollars from the governments of Jamaica, Trinidad and Guyana. This last minute aid, combined with Eric

Pierre's decision to call on the dockworkers to return to work, saved the Gairy government. It also clearly showed the critical role of foreign support in ensuring regime survival.

The strike of 1974 represented the greatest challenge ever faced by the Gairy regime. For the first time his political opponents had successfully made inroads into his lower class base and mobilized a large number against him, threatening to undermine his support among his most important constituency. More importantly, the NJM, which was comprised largely of middle class intellectuals, had gained credibility among local businessmen and some members of the local elites, in spite of their radical ideology and rhetoric. In fact, the strike itself was largely made possible by businessmen who closed their stores rather than by the refusal of workers to show up at their jobs. The NJM had demonstrated its ability to form a multi-class alliance against Gairy by combining elements of the landed elites, the middle class, and the lower classes. This combination of forces proved so threatening to the Gairy regime that its only recourse for retaining power was the unabashed use of state sanctioned coercion. For the time, police repression proved relatively effective as a means of obstructing the efforts of the opposition, but such tactics also had the effect of eroding some of the regime's legitimacy, both domestically and internationally.

The Isolation of the Gairy Regime and the Rise of the NJM

In response to what they perceived to be a failure of their efforts, the NJM held a strategy session during the month of April to determine the direction the movement should take in the ongoing fight against Gairy. It was during these discussions that a decision was made to transform the NJM from a mass organization with flexible membership into a vanguard party. The decision was said to have been largely based upon the conclusion drawn by the NJM cadre that the rebellion of 1973-1974 had failed because it had been led by the middle class establishment which dominated the Committee of 22 (Vigilante and Sandiford 1984: 37). The NJM leadership concluded that a disciplined, vanguard party, equipped with the

ideology of Marxism-Leninism, was the only type of organization that could succeed in removing the Gairy regime from
power. Information pertaining to the change in structure and
orientation of the party was not released to the NJM's membership, nor to the public. Henceforth, the NJM functioned as
a vanguard party, operating on the principles of democratic
centralism, and committed to the task of leading the Grenadian
people in a struggle to overthrow the Gairy government. This
change did not alter the way in which the NJM operated externally, but internally it formalized the structures of authority
and gradually led to greater discipline among the cadre.

Gairy continued with his efforts to further consolidate his
power on the island. The Duffus Commission of Inquiry held
hearings related to charges of police misconduct and released
its report in May of 1974. The Duffus report called for the
complete disbandment of the police aides, most of whose members it noted possessed criminal records for violent behavior.
It recommended the removal of certain magistrates who had
failed "to discharge their judicial duties with fairness and com-
petence" (Duffus Report: 148). Most importantly, the report
also recommended the dismissal of Innocent Belmar, the Chief
of Police, and called for sweeping changes in the administration of law enforcement and the courts.

The beatings of November 1973 and the general strike and
riots of 1974 generated considerable publicity for Grenada
throughout the Caribbean. Under the spotlight of media attention, Gairy responded positively to the Commission's report and expressed his willingness to comply with its recom-
mendations. Gairy realized that the actions of his government
damaged its reputation and he sought to restore some measure of legitimacy, both domestically and internationally, to
his regime. However, even as he acknowledged the misdeeds
of his regime Gairy argued that primary responsibility for the
violence on the island lay with his opponents who attempted
to topple his government. In remarks made after the release of
the report, Gairy said that he would "rebuild the economy that
was badly damaged by an organization which craftily misled a
number of organizations into creating a crisis in the early part
of last year." He added that he would develop measures to "ensure that any attempt in the future to create disharmony and

thereby further increasing the already high cost of living will be nipped in the bud" (*West Indian* 3/12/74).

Gairy quickly followed through on his warning by enacting a variety of laws to restrict the ability of the opposition to act against him and by attempting to restore control without relying upon naked repression. The Newspaper Amendment Act was passed which required anyone publishing a newspaper to deposit twenty thousand dollars with the government. The Act was intended to shut down the *New Jewel* newspaper, which by 1975 had a circulation of 10,000 (Jacobs: 155). This provided a legal basis for the continued harassment, arrests and beatings of NJM members, who continued to sell their newspapers throughout the island (Brizan: 345). Much of this was perpetrated by the now infamous Mongoose Gang, which continued to operate freely despite Gairy's pledge to eliminate them. Several other police aides were simply hired as regular members of the police force, while Innocent Belmar was removed from his post as head of the police force and promoted to a higher position in government. He was later selected by Gairy to contest a seat in the general elections from Gairy's electoral stronghold in the parish of St. Andrews, which he won, enabling Gairy to appoint him to serve as a minister in his government (Jacobs: 159; Brizan: 365).

Gairy's increased reliance on coercive measures served to further undermine the legitimacy of his regime at home and abroad. In 1975, Gairy attempted to recover some of the credibility he had lost during the strike by calling for a Caribbean Easter Water Parade to be held in Grenada. The event, which like the Exposition he sponsored in 1969, was another attempt at counter mobilization, designed to enhance his prestige. However, by this point, the underdog image which had distinguished him in the past had faded. His charismatic appeal, which had been rooted in his work as a labor leader and champion of the poor, had gradually been transformed to what George Danns has described as "mesmeratic" leadership, which substitutes real feats of leadership with sophistry and gimmicks (Danns 1984: 116). His address at the opening of the Easter Water Parade was indicative of the style of personal rulership he had cultivated and his attempt to adorn his regime with spiritual prowess. He stated:

God blesses the projects he has directed me to initiate. He inspires
me in whatever I do. I claim that I am simply an instrument through
which God works, fulfilling a plan for his country and people (*Torchlight* 4/25/76).

By 1976, prominent businessmen and other traditional GNP
supporters began calling for the creation of a coalition between the NJM and GNP to contest the elections which were to
be held in that year. Though many of the local elites were somewhat paranoid of the radical proposals called for by the NJM,
their overwhelming desire to defeat Gairy compelled them to
forge an alliance. In many respects, they were far more comfortable with the middle class leadership of the NJM than they
were with the working class upstart, Gairy. The pro-GNP *Torchlight* newspaper expressed the arguments for the united front
in the following editorial:

The politicians do not seem to realize that the people do not care
about ideology, or about Blaize or for that matter Whyte. (Winston
Whyte, who was the leader of the United People's Party, which was
also being considered for inclusion in the NJM-GNP alliance.) They
are concerned about bread" (*Torchlight* 10/6/76).

While the call for unity was issued to all three parties, the
UPP (United People's Party), NJM, GNP, it was clear to all that
the NJM was the most important partner in any successful coalition. Since the strike of 1974, the NJM had grown in prominence and stature on the island. Its efforts at organizing among
youth, urban unionized workers and rural peasants was beginning to provide it with a popular base that rivaled Gairy's.
The NJM accepted the need to work with the GNP, but refused
to coalesce with the UPP, whose leaders they accused of working for the C.I.A.

Finally, the three parties formed a coalition called the
People's Alliance in time for the elections. The campaign was
waged with intensity by the Alliance, whose members felt confident that the timing was right for the electoral defeat of Gairy.
In response, the Gairy forces resorted to the campaign tactics
that had worked for them in the past, providing plenty of food
and drink at campaign rallies, while harassing and intimidating his political opponents on other occasions. Gairy used the
government controlled radio station to attack his opponents,

calling them "politically malnourished miscreants" and com-
munists (Jacobs: 101). During the campaign the opposition
accused him of tampering with the voter registration process
and harassing civil servants affiliated with the opposition parties. When the election finally took place on November 7,
GULP had won again, capturing 52% of the popular vote and
nine seats in the legislature. The Alliance won six seats with
48% of the vote, and the seats were divided such that NJM
received three, the GNP two and the UPP one. As a result of
their success at the polls and growing political influence,
Maurice Bishop was selected by the coalition to replace Herbert
Blaize as Leader of the Opposition (Brizan:345; DaBreo: 112).

Despite the additional prestige it received from its status
within the Parliament, the NJM proceeded with its plans to
organize clandestinely, and continued its efforts to establish a
base among urban workers and the peasantry for an eventual
takeover of government. NJM leaders believed that any successful attempt to unseat Gairy would have to effectively undermine his support among the peasant majority, many of
whom continued to remain loyal to him due to his record as a
champion of their interests. Bernard Coard, who had recently
returned to Grenada, and who had been selected by the NJM
to contest the St. George's Town seat in the 1976 election, which
he easily won, was placed in charge of the ideological development of the party. Coard organized a study group for young
party members called OREL (Organization for Revolutionary
Education and Liberation) that trained young party supporters in the principles of Marxism-Leninism and provided them
with a radical critique of capitalism and imperialism (Sandiford
and Vigilante: 127). Meanwhile, the NJM persisted in its criticism of the Gairy regime, ridiculing him for calling upon the
United Nations during a speech to the General Assembly to
set up a committee to investigate UFOs, which Gairy claimed
to have seen on several occasions (Sunshine: 86). They also
attacked his government for the deterioration of the economy
and infrastructure, and the poor quality of education and
healthcare services.

Gairy's repression at home had increasingly isolated him
from other leaders within the Caribbean. Eric Williams, the
prime minister of Trinidad, was said to have refused to have

been seen with him publicly, while Errol Barrow, the Prime Minister of Barbados, referred to him publicly as a "political bandit" (Jacobs: 168). The People's National Party of Jamaica led by Michael Manley and the ruling People's National Congress in Guyana openly associated themselves with the NJM. Regional isolation prompted Gairy to develop diplomatic relations with rightwing dictatorships such as the Pinochet regime in Chile and the military government in South Korea. The ties with Chile were intended primarily to provide the Grenadian police force with training in counter insurgency and the use of modern weapons (Jacobs: 172). There had also been discussion in the press of Gairy making a trip to Uganda on the invitation of former head-of-state Idi Amin, but the visit never took place (*Torchlight* 11/2/77).

By 1978, Gairy's support on the island had severely eroded. The many years in power contributed to complacency and a lack of interest in his base among the peasantry. Moreover, functioning as head of state provided Gairy with little time to pay attention to the affairs of the GMMWU, and since he trusted none of his subordinates to fill in for him, the union faded in significance. At the same time, Gairy was becoming increasingly repressive. In 1977 he issued a ban on loud speakers to restrict political protests. In the same year, he issued threats against the leadership of the Public Services Association when they became involved in a dispute with the government over wages. Early in 1978, Innocent Belmar, a government minister and the former police chief, was shot and killed. NJM member Kennedy Budhlall and two others were accused of the killing, but were successfully defended by Radix and Bishop, who won their acquittal (O'Shaughnessy, 1984: 117).

Increasingly, Gairy was losing influence among his traditional base of support, the rural peasantry, particularly as his contact with the masses via his union and party had decreased. The steady decline in Gairy's support came at a time when the NJM's influence and support among the lower class was growing. Among urban workers, the NJM's influence was substantial, as most of the union leadership positions came to be held by NJM members or sympathizers. Since the strike of 1974, Gairy had relied heavily upon coercion against his opponents and his repressive tactics only served to further disaffection from his regime. Meanwhile, the NJM rose in stature and legitimacy and was able to become more effective in its efforts to undermine Gairy. All signs pointed to an eventual show down between the two parties over control of the island and leadership of the nation.

Notes

1   The powers of associated statehood generally included all matters related to domestic policy. For a detailed description of these, see *Grenada
Island of Conflict* by George Brizan (London: Zed Books, 1984) p. 327.

2   The term personal rulership was developed by Reinhard Bendix and
Guenther Roth to describe a style of leadership which cultivates ties
with elites through "an intricate web of reciprocities" in which the leader
serves as chief patron at the center of these social networks. See *Scholarship and Partisanship: Essays on Max Weber* by Bendix, R. and Roth, G.
(Berkeley: University of California Press, 1971) p. 46-62.

3   Two of the businessmen I interviewed confirmed the allegation that
Gairy coerced private businesses to recognize the GMMWU as the exclusive bargaining agent for their employees. One claimed that his workers were required to join the union even though they had held an election and voted to join another.

4   For a description of the Black Power protests in Trinidad and its impact
on political events in Grenada, see *Grenada: The Route to Revolution* by
Richard and Ian Jacobs (Havana: Vasa de las Americas, 1980) p. 94-96.
See *Crisis*, (Edited by Owen Baptiste St. James, Trinidad: Imprint Publishers, 1976) for a detailed discussion of the factors which led to the
Black Power protests in Trinidad.

5   The concept of Ujamaa, or African Socialism, was formally advanced
by Tanzanian president Julius K. Nyerere beginning in 1967 with the
Arusha Declaration. The essential premise of Ujamaa was that socialism should be based upon traditional African cultural and political
practices. As such, the village was seen as the primary level of government and through village councils it was believed that participatory
democracy would be achieved. For a discussion of the development of
socialism in Tanzania, see Coulson, Andrew *African Socialism in Practice*
(Nittingham, England: Spokesman Press, 1979).
   The formation and conceptualization of MAP (Movement for Assemblies of the People) by Bishop and Radix was clearly influenced by
Nyerere's views on participatory democracy. When the NJM took power
in 1979, it attempted to implement the idea through village and zonal
councils. For a discussion of the connection between the NJM's approach
and the Tanzanian model, see Marable, M. *African and Caribbean Politics* (London: Thetford Press, 1989) p. 210.

6   The collection of individuals who ran with the committee of concerned citizens is historically significant because of the paths their political careers later on. Strachan became a minister in the PRG government, later siding with the Revolutionary Military Council (RMC) against Maurice Bishop in a internal power struggle. White served as the PRG's Foreign Minister and was later executed with Bishop on October 19. Returning to Grenada after the U.S. invasion, Mitchell joined forces with Herbert Blaize and became a minister in the New National Party (NNP) government. Mitchell eventually turned against Blaize, leading a move to unseat him from leadership of the NNP while he was serving as prime minister.

7   Coard was born in Grenada and educated in Britain. While employed as a lecturer at the University of the West Indies in St. Augustine, Trinidad, Coard was contacted by Bishop and other NJM members who sought his input during the early period of the party's organizational development. While in Trinidad, he delivered a paper opposing independence for Grenada under Gairy. He was later asked to write the NJM Manifesto which was released at a mass rally organized by the NJM at Seamoon in May of 1973. See "The Meaning of Political Independence in the Commonwealth Caribbean" by Bernard Coard, presented August, 1973, St. Augustine, Trinidad.

8.   The Committee of 22 was a coalition of trade unions, professional organizations, businesses and churches. Though many of its members had traditionally supported the GNP, others did not. For a discussion of the Committee of 22, see Jacobs, R. and Jacobs, I. *Grenada: Route to Revolution* (Havana, Cuba: Casa de las Americas, 1980) p. 56.

Chapter 6

1979-1983: Revolutionary Grenada

Seizure of State Power

By 1979, tension between the Gairy government and the NJM had become especially high. Rumors were circulating widely across the country of plans for an armed take over of government by the NJM. There were also reports that Gairy planned to have the NJM leadership killed (DaBreo, 1979: 113). In February of 1979, two NJM members, James Wardally and Chester Humphry, were arrested in Washington D.C. on charges that they had been shipping weapons from the United States to Grenada. The impending investigation, combined with threats upon the lives of the NJM leadership, prompted the NJM leadership to act decisively in a move to topple the Gairy government on the morning of March 13.

Gairy had departed from the island the previous day for meetings at the United Nations in New York City. On the morning of the 13, NJM forces, armed largely with handguns and rifles, attacked Gairy's army at the True Blue barracks, catching the soldiers completely off guard. At approximately the same time, Hudson Austin led a group which captured the radio station, while another group headed by Kennedy Budhlall seized Pearl's Airport and the Grenville police station. Within hours, NJM supporters had taken control of police stations throughout the island, and most of the ministers of the regime had been captured and arrested, along with the leaders of the Mongoose Gang (Dabreo: 124).

While the island was being secured, Bishop spoke over the radio to explain what had taken place to the population:

> At 4:15 this morning, the People's Revolutionary Army seized control
> of the army barracks at True Blue. The barracks were burned to the
> ground. After half an hour of struggle, the forces of Gairy's army
> were completely defeated and surrendered.
> I am now calling on the working people, the youth, workers, farmers,
> fishermen, middle class people and women to join our armed revolu-
> tionary forces at central points in your communities and to give them
> any assistance they call for (Maurice Bishop Speaks, 1983: 37).

Later that day, in an attempt to allay the fears of those who
wondered about the orientation of the new government, Bishop
announced that:

> . . .all democratic freedoms, including freedom of elections, religious
> and political opinion, will be restored to the people. The personal
> safety and property of individuals will be protected. Foreign residents
> are quite safe, and are welcome to remain in Grenada. And we look
> forward to continuing friendly relations with those countries with which
> we now have such relations . . . this revolution is for food, for decent
> housing and health services, and for a bright future for our children
> and great grand children (Bishop Speaks: 38).

Immediate reaction to the take over was overwhelmingly
supportive, even among conservative organizations such as the
GNP, the Chamber of Commerce and the Rotary Club (*Torchlight* 3/21/79). To add to the feelings of goodwill on the day of
the take over, Cynthia Gairy, the wife of the former Prime Minister, voluntarily addressed the public over the radio, calling
on all Grenadians to cooperate with the new government. The
GNP issued a statement commending the "care which is being
taken by the Provisional Revolutionary Government to ensure
proper maintenance of public order and the protection of personal and property rights" (*Torchlight* 2/25.79). The *Torchlight*
newspaper, which had never been particularly friendly toward
the NJM, was also supportive of the takeover in its editorial
which appeared shortly after.

> There is a noticeable lack of panic in a somewhat volatile community,
> which could be interpreted that a majority of the people were disen-
> chanted by the one time hero of the masses, Gairy (*Torchlight*, 3/25/
> 79)

During the first few weeks after the coup, criticism and ridicule were heaped upon Gairy and the manner in which he ran

the government. Reports were released of secret rooms discovered at Gairy's residence at Mt. Royal which were allegedly used to practice Obeah and other occult rituals.[1] Also reportedly discovered was a picture album containing photographs of women who were said to have been sexually involved with the former Prime Minister (*Torchlight* 4/7/79).

As news of Gairy's secrets were leaked to the public, the *Torchlight* used the occasion to unleash its disdain for Gairy and his supporters whom they believed had been duped into following him.

> The gullible Grenadian never understood Gairy's uncommon devotion to religion as a political weapon. It was precisely because of this that he was able to hold sway for so long . . . there were many Grenadians who believed Gairy was a god. And are there not still some who believe that he can work miracles, like walking on the sea? (*Torchlight* 4/14/79)

Even a former Minister of Communication and Works under Gairy, Albert Forsythe, claimed to have been blackmailed by Gairy through the threat of witchcraft should he have turned against him (*Torchlight*, 4/16/79). Gairy became the object of scorn and ridicule and his regime was maligned and denigrated, forcing many of those who had once supported him to distance themselves and deny all claims of past support. Meanwhile, the NJM sought to assert its own legitimacy and defend the methods it had employed to obtain power through their persistent attacks against Gairy. Within a relatively short period of time, Gairy's image had been transformed from that of working class hero to that of a brutal and arbitrary dictator.

International Response to the NJM Takeover

For the NJM, securing support at home was only a part of what was needed to establish the legitimacy of the new government. Just as important was the need to win support internationally and regionally, particularly among the nations of Commonwealth Caribbean, as well as among Grenada's traditional trading partners, Britain, Canada and the United States. According to an internal policy document developed by the NJM on the subject of establishing diplomatic ties between the new government and the international community, the first major policy statement issued would seek to reassure foreign governments, by emphasizing "moderation and non-alignment and the human rights abuses of the Gairy government" (Grenada Documents, 1984:67). Bishop's early statements essentially accomplished this with its promise for free elections and the restoration of constitutional rule. ·

The regional response to the NJM takeover was initially mixed, with Jamaica and Guyana being openly supportive, while most other Caribbean governments adopted a critical, if not hostile, posture toward the new regime. As the first armed takeover of a government in the English speaking Caribbean, the Grenada revolution was perceived as a threat to the stability of its neighbors, particularly the other small islands.[2] Though Eric Gairy had long been viewed as an eccentric and incompetent leader by other leaders in the Caribbean, his government had repeatedly been elected back into office by the Grenadian people, and as such, it was recognized as a legitimate member of Caricom and other regional organizations. Moreover, the ease with which power was seized in Grenada alarmed its neighbors and awakened them to the realization of their own vulnerability to similar insurrections. Nonetheless, the initial moderation of the NJM and the pledge to restore democracy led to early recognition of the People's Revolutionary Government (PRG), as the new regime called itself, by Caricom and the Organization of Eastern Caribbean States (OECS).

Recognition from the United States was not as easily obtained. Although an early assessment by U.S. ambassador Ortiz warned that "any sanctions at this stage could be counterproductive" (Sandiford and Vigilante: 127), the radical ideology of the NJM and the anti-imperialist rhetoric of its leaders was treated as a matter of grave concern to the U.S. State Department. Initially, the official line from the U.S. State Department was to "continue the friendly and cooperative relations our two countries have enjoyed since Grenada's independence in 1974" (Sandiford and Vigilante: 132). Later, when Bishop met with Ambassador Ortiz, he was pressed for a date on which elections would be held. When the two met again on April 10, Bishop stated his concern that Gairy might attempt to enlist mercenaries to retake the island, and requested arms from the

U.S. to defend the country from such an attack. The request for arms was rejected, and in response to reports that Bishop was planning to approach Cuba for military aid, Ortiz stated that "we would view with displeasure any tendency on the part of Grenada to develop closer ties with Cuba" (Sandiford and Vigilante: 134). He also told Bishop in response to his request for development aid, that Grenada would have to follow standard procedures in applying for aid, which the U.S. channeled to the region through the Caribbean Development Bank (CDB). Following the meeting with the ambassador, Bishop delivered his memorable "Nobody's Backyard" speech, during which he declared that "no country has the right to tell us what to do or how to run our country or who to be friendly with...we are not in anybody's backyard, and we are definitely not for sale" (Bishop Speaks: 52).

Undoubtedly, the posture adopted by the U.S. State Department toward the revolutionary government was also influenced by events which were occurring elsewhere in the region. Cuba's prestige in the region had risen sharply as its ties with the Manley government in Jamaica and the Burnham government of Guyana had already provided it with greater credibility and acceptance in the rest of the Caribbean. There were major insurrections underway in Central America and left-of-center parties on other English speaking islands (St. Lucia and Dominica) were enjoying higher levels of support than they had in the past. Amidst such an atmosphere, the armed takeover in Grenada represented a significant and unwelcome development to U.S. interests.

Consolidation of the Revolution and the Emergence of Domestic Dissent to the PRG

Despite some disappointment and concern over what appeared to be a bad start in the relationship between the PRG and the U.S. government, the atmosphere of goodwill toward the new regime continued to prevail within Grenada. This was enhanced by the decision of the PRG to repeal Gairy's ban on loud speakers and newspapers that could not afford the $20,000 deposit with government. Such actions were seen as a sign that the new government would respect civil liberties and extend the political rights which had been denied by the Gairy regime. Allister Hughes, a well known Grenadian journalist and writer for the Associated Press, utilized his column in the *Torchlight* to chastise the new U.S. ambassador to the region, Sally Sheldon, advising her that she and "her Washington bosses must rethink their attitudes. West Indians have tasted independence, and we're not going to be pushed around . . . we demand to be treated with dignity and respect" (*Torchlight*, 7/1/79). The *Torchlight* itself remained cautiously supportive of the PRG; praising it for announcing its decision to return the Banana, Cocoa and Nutmeg Boards to independent control, a promise that the regime later reneged upon.

Meanwhile, the PRG was actively cultivating a relationship with Cuba. The Cubans had been invited by the PRG to assist the regime in carrying out several development projects in health, housing construction and adult education. The fact that Cuban advisors were already engaged in similar assistance projects in Jamaica, Guyana and other Caribbean nations, did not quell the opposition by the U.S. to their presence in Grenada. Similar concerns about the PRG's relationship to Cuba were expressed locally by the *Torchlight*. The newspaper also expressed concern over the new powers of the People's Revolutionary Army (PRA), following altercations between some citizens and soldiers. As further evidence of its growing unease, the paper issued the following warning: ". . . each act of indiscipline and bravado is like a breaking device on the government's progress. Unerring guidance is essential in order to prevent open hostility and to avoid the dubious pleasure of the sobriquet of "Green Beasts" (*Torchlight* 7/4/79).

The PRG took advantage of its popularity at home to launch innovative and unconventional policies in the area of foreign affairs. In July of 1979, the PRG held a summit with the Prime Ministers of St. Lucia and Dominica, to discuss the prospects for regional integration among the Caribbean Commonwealth. A few days later it was announced that relations had been established with Vietnam. At the meeting of Commonwealth nations held in Lusaka, Zambia, Bishop received international acclaim for his bold statements against apartheid in South Africa and his support for the liberation movements in Zimbabwe and Namibia. Later, at the Summit of Non-Aligned nations in Havana, Cuba, Bishop received international attention once again for his outspoken criticism of the United States and its foreign policies toward the Third World (Marcus and Taber 1983: 48-59).

Support at home remained high with rallies and various types of mobilizations organized regularly to maintain the enthusiasm that had been generated toward the revolution and to create avenues for participation. Attempts were made to deepen that support through the development and implementation of social programs designed to improve the quality of life for the poor in the rural areas. In education the government moved quickly to subsidize primary education and thereby make it free to all children for the first time. Secondary school fees were reduced through additional government subsidies, as were the cost of school books. Scholarships were made available to Grenadians for study in Cuba, Kenya, Tanzania, and several Eastern European nations, and access to the University of the West Indies for Grenadians, which had temporarily been stopped due to non-payment of fees by the Gairy regime, was once again restored.

One of the most ambitious efforts undertaken by the new government was a national adult literacy campaign, launched under the direction of the newly formed Center for Popular Education (CPE). The campaign set out to eradicate illiteracy on the island, which was estimated at 20%-25% of the country's population (Center for Popular Education Report, 1980). As in Cuba and Nicaragua, the literacy campaign involved the mobilization of large numbers of people into roles as voluntary teachers and students. Such projects provided the regime with an additional boost in its base of popular support by creating an opportunity for active participation in the revolution through the effort to educate adult illiterates (Noguera, 1992).

New construction within the first year of the PRG's rule created eight hundred new jobs. Laws were passed guaranteeing women equal pay for equal work, as well as time off and compensation for pregnancy. The nation's economy appeared to be in good shape as well, with a budget surplus of EC 2.6 million registered at the end of 1979, compared with a EC 8.3 million dollar deficit left over by the Gairy regime from the previous year. The government took advantage of its good fortune to launch its most ambitious project, the construction of an international airport. Discussions about the need for a modern airport to boost the tourist industry had been held between World Bank officials and the Gairy government years before, and Pt. Salines, located on the southern tip of the island, had been identified as the most appropriate location. The PRG now sought to realize that objective and successfully secured aid from a number of governments, in particular the Cuban government, which offered to provide much of the labor and materials needed to carry out the project (Report on the National Economy, 1981).

As the PRG moved forward with its ambitious development projects and social programs, pockets of dissent toward the revolution began to emerge. Perhaps the most visible and vocal of these appeared in the pages of the *Torchlight* newspaper. Managed and controlled by individuals with ties to the GNP, the *Torchlight* had been a constant critic of the Gairy regime. At various times it had expressed support for actions taken by the NJM in its protests against the Gairy regime, though it stated clearly that it "carried no brief for the NJM" (*Torchlight* 11/2/1973). Its initial response to the takeover had been guarded but supportive; however, it maintained its independence from government, at times praising it for actions it supported, while at other times warning of the danger of developing close ties with communist nations such as Cuba.

In August of 1979, the *Torchlight* ran an article which had appeared in the West German newspaper *Bundt*, which claimed that the Soviets were constructing a missile base on the island. Although the article contained the qualifier that "it had been unable to substantiate the report" (*Torchlight* 8/1/79), the editors of the newspaper came under heavy criticism from the PRG for printing what it considered "libelous and provocative" stories. Its editors attempted to defend their right to publish the article by arguing that Grenadians had a right to know what was being said about the island in other countries. A few weeks later, the *Torchlight* published an article about the residents of Calivigny, a village located in the southern part of St. George's parish, who were complaining about noises in the area that appeared to have been caused by military activity at PRA nearby. In response to the article, a forceful warning was issued by Hudson Austin, now the commander of the armed forces, that any publication "which reveals facts or speculation on national security information, will result in immediate detention of the individuals involved" (*Free West Indian* 9/16/'79).

The *Torchlight* responded to this threat by accusing the PRG of being overly sensitive. Meanwhile, letters complaining about the continued detention of persons considered to be a threat to the national security by the PRG began appearing in the newspaper. The GNP, the Grenada Council of Churches and numerous foreign newspapers, including the Trinidad *Express*, also appealed to the PRG for the detainees to be brought to trial or released. At a September 1979 press conference, Bishop attacked the *Torchlight* for reprinting "scurrilous and libelous material from overseas" (*Free West Indian* 10/3/'79). He also claimed that the paper was controlled and manipulated by foreign and minority interests. The *Torchlight* responded by calling on the PRG to "turn its gaze from so-called destabilizers, fascists and imperialists. The real danger to the PRG springs not from the lack of funds, trained technicians, or even unemployment. The fear which they must never allow to creep up on them is the fear of failure to create the just society" (*Torchlight* 10/23/'79).

Finally, in late October 1979, following the publication of an article which charged that Rastafarians were being mistreated by the government, the *Torchlight* was shut down by the PRG. With its closure, the only significant source of internal opposition to the government was eliminated. The regime's growing intolerance also spread to opposition political parties, which previously had operated freely. The GNP had effectively been prevented from functioning as an independent political party by NJM supporters who disrupted their meetings and threatened its leaders and members.[3] On the day after the *Torchlight's* closure, the government launched a wave of arrests and detentions, rounding up several Rastafarians who had previously supported the NJM but had recently become vocal in their criticisms of government policies. Also included in the arrests were several GNP members and others who were regarded as political opponents. Several former members of the PRG who had become disaffected from the party, including the former editor the the *New Jewel* newspaper, Teddy Victor, were also detained (Sandiford and Vigilante: 136).

These actions brought on a barrage of criticism from regional governments and newspapers. Even the left-leaning Barbados-based *Caribbean Contact,* which had previously praised the PRG, reacted to the *Torchlight* closure and the wave of arrests with an editorial in its November 1979 issue entitled: "What Has Gone Wrong with Mr. Bishop?" The following warning was issued:

> if that government chooses by its own actions and policies to squander the tremendous goodwill that accompanied its rise to power, then it must not expect that uncritical support for its revolution or foolishly think that all voices of dissent belong to the enemy camp (*Caribbean Contact* November 1979).

The Maintenance of Popular Support Through Mass Mobilization and Social Reforms

With the internal opposition silenced, the PRG was able to weather the storm of protest over its actions toward dissident elements with little difficulty. It was still able to retain a large measure of goodwill and popular support on the island by adopting measures that were seen as beneficial to the majority of the population. Programs providing free milk for those in need were set up, and provisions for no-interest house repair loans were implemented. The Marketing and National Importing Board was also established to provide local farmers with markets for their fruits and vegetables. And, with the assistance of Cuba, efforts were made to extend medical services to rural areas. As a result, the availability of doctors and nurses to the population increased significantly. During the 1970s Cuban doctors had been sent to Jamaica and Guyana, and several Caribbean nations took advantage of Cuban scholarships to send their students to Cuban medical schools. However, Grenadian contacts with Cuba were pointed to as evidence of growing communist influence by opponents of the revolution, even though the expanded medical services were highly popular among Grenadians generally.

Through these measures the PRG was expanding the welfare apparatus of the state. Though the programs themselves were described by the PRG's leadership as the "fruits of the revolution," and were seen by them as part of the strategy for constructing socialism in Grenada,[4] the social reforms enacted by the regime were not unlike the state-run welfare programs that existed in Trinidad, Jamaica and other parts of the Caribbean. Nonetheless, their adoption represented a significant development for a poor country such as Grenada, given that the resources required to maintain such programs were not easily secured. Through the adoption of social reforms such as these, the PRG won substantial support both domestically and internationally.

The challenge faced by the PRG was how to obtain the financial resources to support and maintain the expanded public sector. During the first three years of PRG rule, grants from overseas were sufficiently available to provide support to the international airport, by far the largest of the projects initiated, and to a variety of other undertakings. In fact, the regime was so successful in attracting such support that it made plans for future development based upon the notion that foreign aid would continue to be available. Pryor has characterized such a strategy to development as "foreign aid socialism," because it required such a heavy reliance on outside financial assistance (Pryor, 1984: 12).

Within the first two to three years, the strategy proved to be extremely successful. According to government statistics, unemployment had been reduced from approximately 44% to 14%, largely through increased employment in the public sector and the enlistment of several hundred young men into the military. The numerous construction projects made possible by the infusion of several million dollars in foreign aid generated considerable economic growth in 1980 and 1981. During that period the economy grew at a rate of 2% to 5%, the highest rate of GNP growth recorded in the region. Interestingly, even the World Bank issued a favorable prognosis on the Grenadian economy in 1982, thereby opening the doors for Grenadian access to loans from the International Monetary Fund (World Bank Report on Grenada, 1982).

The approval of the World Bank, a significant accomplishment for a small, poor nation like Grenada, was attributable to pragmatic approach followed by the PRG with respect to its economic policies. Ironically, Bernard Coard, the Foreign Minister who was viewed by many as the most hardline communist among the NJM leadership, was the primary architect of the PRG's prudent fiscal policies. Under his leadership, the PRG deliberately avoided any actions which might discourage capital investment, foreign or domestic. It consciously attempted to maintain supportive relations with the private sector and made it clear that its plans for the future called for the development of a mixed economy, consisting of a state sector, private sector and cooperative sector. The state sector was expected to be dominant, but efforts were made to encourage the private sector to grow and expand its operations, particularly in tourism. Private business had several representatives in government, including hotel owner and businessman Lyden Ramhdanny, the Minister of Tourism. Moreover, during his first visit to the United States as the Grenadian head-of-state in May 1983, Bishop was accompanied by some of the island's largest businessmen. The hope was that their presence might show the U.S. government that the PRG had friendly and cooperative relations with the island's private sector, with the hope of reducing the ideological hostility of the Reagan administration toward the regime.

The social reforms and the acts of regime coercion were, therefore, the only clear indication that the PRG was embarking on a development path which differed significantly from that of the previous regime. Gairy had undertaken his own initiatives to increase foreign investment in the economy, and he too had expanded the civil service in order to create more jobs for his supporters. He also had been the first leader to implement land reform on the island, although he largely used it as a means to punish his opponents and expand his web of patronage. Similarly, when the PRG considered its own version of land reform, the initial targets for land seizure were individual landowners who had been most adamantly opposed to the PRG, and Gairy himself, who had acquired substantial amounts of property prior to his overthrow. Its reforms in health, education, housing and social services were, therefore, the most significant departures by the PRG from the course of economic development charted by Gairy.

However, to Grenadian citizens, changes in policy were in some ways less important than changes in style. Shrouded in the revolutionary image it had ushered and cultivated, the PRG was able to recapture a sense of populism that had not been seen since the 1951 labor uprising. Following Gairy's example, the PRG supplemented its reform measures by focusing on ways of mobilizing the population to defend the revolution from internal sabotage and foreign aggression. In June of 1981, there was a bombing at Queens Park which appeared to have been intended as an assassination attempt on Bishop and other government leaders, but had instead resulted in the killing of three children at the scene. In response to the attack, hundreds of Grenadians were recruited to the People's militia under the premise of safeguarding the nation against future attempts at destabilization and terrorism. The PRG also used the assassination attempt as a justification for clamping down on several known opponents of the regime, including Strachan Phillips, a former high ranking NJM member, who was killed for alleged involvement in counter revolutionary activities.

Throughout the four and one half years of its rule, the PRG used the threat of foreign intervention as an effective means of rallying support for the revolution. At the time, there was substantial evidence that suggested that the fear of such an attack was well founded. Foreign intervention from either the United States or mercenaries organized by Gairy was a real possibility, particularly given the demonstration of U.S. hostilities toward Nicaragua, and the failed coup attempt by American mercenaries in Dominica in 1981.[5] The threat of foreign attack was used by the regime to generate mass mobilizations and collective involvement in defense of the nation. Rallies, marches, public meetings and ceremonies were also used as a means of mobilizing the population. A Ministry of Mobilization headed by Selwyn Strachen was set up to provide continuity and leadership in the undertakings of the mass organizations. Included under its wing was the National Youth Organization, National Women's Organization, the Center for Popular Education, and the People's Militia.

Over time, popular mobilization became an integral component of the regime's survival strategy. Faced with hostility from its neighbors in the region and from the United States, the PRG increasingly relied upon capacity to mobilize the populace to bolster its credibility. Mass mobilizations also enabled the regime to accomplish the following objectives: 1) to demonstrate that it continued to have mass support and legitimacy among Grenadians; 2) to use the mobilizations to undertake major development projects which required vast amounts of labor (ie. road construction, the national airport, national literacy campaign, etc.); 3) to counter the negative consequences stemming from its reliance upon repression against the internal opposition. Furthermore, because the regime had never held an election, successful mobilization of large numbers of people, served as an indication of its support among the population and provided the regime with an alternative source of legitimacy.

The combination of social reforms and mass mobilization were, therefore, essential components of the regime's survival strategy. However, maintaining the ability to mobilize large numbers of people over time became an extremely difficult task. Because the social reforms were made possible largely through foreign aid, the PRG found itself in constant pursuit of grants from overseas to continue funding for the programs it had created. The weak Grenadian economy, with its reliance on agricultural exports and tourism as its primary source of foreign exchange, did not have the wherewithal to sustain such a massive public sector on its own. Since the reforms had come to be seen as the essence of the revolution, both in the words of its leaders and in the eyes of many Grenadian people, the PRG found itself in the bind of being unable to sustain the reforms that many now expected as a condition for further support.

Similarly, the mass mobilizations had come to serve as evidence to the PRG's foreign critics that the revolution had strong popular support. Within the NJM leadership, it provided the reassurance that the population was still largely in support of the government. However, the task of maintaining mass mobilizations over an extended period of time became increasingly difficult. The volunteerism, widely demonstrated during the months immediately after the takeover through the literacy campaign and other national development projects, had gradually become more difficult to elicit. For example, cynicism and apathy had increasingly become evident during the second phase of the adult education program in 1982. In my own assessment of the campaign, carried out during my visit to the island in 1982, I found that participation in the program was often exaggerated in official reports, particularly with regard to its operation in rural areas. The inertia that had developed in the aftermath of the revolution was beginning to fade, and enthusiasm for the government's various mobilization schemes was on the wane. Moreover, the threat of foreign attack, which was the major driving force for the continuation of mobilizations, was becoming less and less effective as Grenadians began to grow tired of preparing for an attack that had not yet materialized. The PRG had developed a standard for maintaining its legitimacy which had become increasingly difficult to preserve.[6]

Emergence of Divisions Within the NJM and the Decline of the PRG

The decision to shut down the *Torchlight* newspaper in October 1979 exposed some important tactical differences among the leadership with regard to the regime's response to dissent. As the *Torchlight's* criticism of the NJM increased, the central committee of the NJM became increasingly worried about the paper's influence among the population. Following publication of the article concerning the Soviet missile base, Bishop delivered a public statement chastising the paper's editors for printing what it regarded as libelous accusations. When the central committee met in late October to decide upon the fate of the *Torchlight*, it was Bernard Coard who led a majority faction in calling for a clamp down, while Bishop voiced weak dissent but failed to take issue with the heavy handed approach advocated by Coard (Grenada Documents: 51-1). The final decision to shut down the *Torchlight* was made by Coard, the Deputy Prime Minister, and second highest ranking party official, while Bishop was outside of the country. Though he maintained his disagreement with the decision, Bishop did not criticize it upon his return, nor did he seek to distance himself from it in the eyes of the population.

This pattern of acquiescence on the part of Bishop to Coard's constant urging for a hardline response to internal critics and dissenters re-emerged in 1982 over the decision to shut down yet another independent news publication, the *Grenada Voice*. A single issue of the *Voice* had been published by a number of former supporters of the NJM, including Lloyd Noel, the former Attorney General of the PRG. Once again, the central committee discussed how to deal with this organized expression of dissent. The publishers of the *Voice* had gone to great lengths to comply with the PRG's policies concerning the publication of newspapers, and according to Leslie Pierre, the newspaper's editor, they took the action to test the regime's stated commitment to the principle of free speech. When the matter was discussed by the central committee of the NJM and the decision was made to shut down the paper and imprison its principle sponsors, it was Coard once again who was urging the hard line, with Bishop expressing mild dissent.

These tactical differences over how to respond to the internal opposition were indicators of more deep-seeded differences existing within the party leadership. Since his return to Grenada in 1976, Coard had been generally recognized as the ideological authority in the party. Central Committee members, including Bishop, looked to Coard for political analysis and often for political direction when making decisions on most important matters pertaining to the direction of the party or government. As has been mentioned earlier, Coard had set up a body known as OREL (Organization for Revolutionary Education and Liberation) within the party, which served as the body through which political education of younger party cadre was carried out. As leader of OREL, Coard actively cultivated the second tier leadership within the party and was seen by many of them as the ultimate figure of authority in the party.[7]

Although a formal distinction was drawn between the government and the party, all major decisions pertaining to the the economy, foreign policy and the overall direction of the country were made by the central committee and the political bureau. The government, which included several non-NJM members in key leadership positions, took responsibility for the technical and logistical affairs of the state, but most insiders acknowledged that all important decisions were made by the party. The NJM remained a very small party, its membership never exceeding two hundred, and most Grenadians knew very little about the internal discussions or decisions of the party until they became implemented as government policy. The blurred distinction between the roles of the party and the government contributed to a sense of confusion about the orientation of the government. While its policies seemed relatively moderate, the party continued to function as a vanguard on the basis of Marxism-Leninism. As pressure on the government increased and foreign aid became more difficult to obtain, the dual nature of the NJM/PRG would eventually lead to paralysis within both.

During the course of the four and a half years in power, there was a gradual shift in the make-up of the central committee and political bureau which favored Coard. Though there was no open hostility or competition between Bishop and Coard, several party members who have commented on the party's leadership in the aftermath of the invasion have described a subtle rivalry that developed even prior to the revolution between the two men based largely on Coard's envy of Bishop.[8] Beginning with the ouster of Kenrick Radix, one of Bishop's closest allies, from the two leadership bodies in 1982, Bishop's supporters were gradually removed from leadership positions within the party. In almost every case, these individuals were replaced by the second tier leadership, mostly from the ranks of the military, and most of whom had been trained by Coard as members of OREL. Many of these younger men had been sent to Soviet Bloc countries for ideological and military training, and now held high ranking positions in the People's Revolutionary Army (Marable, 1987: 145-149).

Discussions with former party members and a review of the central committee minutes reveals that the basis of the differences between the two factions were largely not political or ideological. There have been numerous explanations for the rift between Bishop and Coard. Some have suggested that Coard was a hardline Stalinist, while Bishop was more of a moderate social democrat (O'Shaughnessy: 163). While there is some evidence to support this, it must be noted that Bishop consistently went along with the decisions of the party and at times spoke strongly in defense of its more repressive actions.

Others have claimed that foreign influences from the Soviet Union and Cuba contributed to the development of the split within the party (Vigilante and Sandiford: 172). None of these explanations have withstood close scrutiny of the actual positions adopted by the two sides, leaving open the possibility that personality differences based on the psychological profiles of the two men may have been a primary factor in the fomenting of the split, as has been suggested by Jorge Heine (Heine, 1990: 183). Whatever the cause, most observers agree that internal factors played a far greater role in ushering in the collapse of the PRG than external ones.

The Decline and Collapse of the PRG

To cite the internal divisions within the leadership of the NJM as the cause of the decline and fall of the PRG or to say, as many have, that the revolution imploded or self-destructed should not diminish the significance of other factors that also contributed to its demise. Much of the analysis of the fall of the PRG, carried out by scholars seeking to explain its abrupt demise, has focused almost entirely on the differences between Bishop and Coard, and how the struggle between them resulted in the ultimate downfall of the government. Such a focus might seem to be entirely appropriate, given the significant role played by the two men in managing the government and the ruling party in Grenada. Yet, though an analysis of the internal conflicts which contributed to the PRG's collapse is important to understanding or explaining this episode of political change in Grenada, at this time no objective account of what transpired within the party is available. While the Grenada documents are useful for understanding the internal dynamics of the NJM, their reliability is questionable, given that the U.S. State Department continues to control access to material it regards as sensitive. For that reason, rather than engaging in speculation over the factors influencing the internal conflicts, the decision to execute Bishop and others at Fort Rupert on October 19th, or other actions taken by the PRG's replacement, the Revolutionary Military Council (RMC), my analysis will examine the socio-economic factors which contributed to the regime's demise.

The Grenadian economy and the limitations which are created by the small size of the island and its relative underdevelopment have posed a significant hindrance to the development efforts of all political parties and regimes that have held power on the island. Prices for the three major exports, cocoa, nutmeg and bananas, fluctuate according to prices set by the foreign markets. Moreover, Grenada's agrarian economy has been constrained by the small size of most land holdings, which limit the possibilities for mechanized cultivation. In addition, Grenada's rugged topography, of which only 6-7% of the total land area can be used for intensive agricultural production is yet another hindrance to agricultural development (Ambursely: 212). Tourism, the only other significant source of foreign exchange besides remittances from relatives abroad, also fluctuates depending upon the state of the economies in the western nations and the degree to which Grenada's image is favorably perceived by foreign travel agents. Finally, even in the best of times, capital is in short supply due to low rates of personal savings and a high demand for imported products by consumers. For this reason, the potential for economic development through locally based financing has historically been extremely limited.

As a consequence of these structural constraints, foreign assistance has been viewed by all three regimes as the only viable means for developing and maintaining the local infrastructure and promoting commercial and residential development. Fredrick Pryor suggests that obtaining a steady supply of foreign aid was the center piece of the economic development strategy advanced by the PRG, an economic development strategy which he has termed "foreign aid socialism." While this was certainly true for the PRG, it was also true for the Gairy and Blaize regimes, though neither was not nearly as successful in obtaining aid. Although the Blaize-led NNP government established in 1984 actually received more foreign aid than the PRG, the circumstances under which that aid was given were quite unique. The role of foreign aid in the NNP government headed by Herbert Blaize shall be discussed in greater detail in the following chapter.

Pryor defines foreign aid socialism as the "attempt to introduce socialism by a government completely dependent on foreign grants and concessionary loans of like-minded nations to achieve its economic ends" (Pryor: 32). He argues that this is essentially what the PRG attempted to do during its four and one half years in power, and that its subsequent collapse came about largely as a result of the failure of this strategy.

Though Pryor fails to explain how what he calls foreign aid socialism differs from the heavy reliance on foreign aid in market oriented economies, certain aspects of his arguments are compelling. Much of the domestic and international support which had been generated by the PRG was related to the charisma of Maurice Bishop and by the advances which had been made in the economy and the successful implementation of social reforms. Internally, many Grenadians were greatly impressed by the "fruits of the revolution" (ie. the international airport, though not completed, the agro industrial plant, the cement and gravel plant, the fisheries school, etc.), and as the survey that I conducted indicates (see Chapter 7), a large number of Grenadians based their support for the PRG upon their belief that economic progress had been achieved. Externally, foreign observers, (even those who were not favorably disposed toward the socialist orientation of the government such as the EEC and the World Bank) were also impressed by the PRG's economic advances. Prudent fiscal management of the economy combined with effective packaging of aid proposals resulted in huge pay-offs for the PRG in the form of grants and loans. In fact, while the PRG was in power, Grenada received the second highest amount of aid per capita among Third World countries from a variety of donor nations (Pryor: 67).

While much of the economic assistance obtained by the PRG came from socialist countries aligned with the Soviet Union (approximately 60% of the aid received) the PRG was also very successful at obtaining aid from a variety of other nations and international development agencies. Even Western governments such as the United Kingdom and Canada were among the countries which provided financial support in the form of loans or grants to the PRG. Pryor attributes the PRG's success in obtaining foreign aid to its pragmatic diplomacy and effective aid packaging proposals. Most governments and international agencies which provide foreign aid tend to support projects which yield tangible results and clearly demonstrate the impact of the assistance. The international airport was perfectly suited for meeting this criteria, although there were also several smaller projects in agriculture, the fishing industry and education, which also fulfilled the requirements of donor nations and agencies. However, even with effective packaging, countries in need of economic assistance are often unsuccessful in their bids to obtain aid largely because they lack the appropriate diplomatic personnel and skills. The PRG was particularly adept in this regard, and managed to pull off impressive diplomatic feats, such as obtaining financial support from both Iraq and Iran while the two countries were at war.

However, Pryor also suggests that the PRG began to rely too heavily on foreign assistance to implement its economic development plans. Much of the PRG's success in reducing unemployment, developing the island's infrastructure and creating social services were made possible by the influx of foreign aid. The expansion of the state sector of the economy, which began under Gairy, who had taken control over several enterprises, utilities and estates during his period in power, was greatly escalated by the PRG. By 1983, approximately 30% of the the labor force was employed in the public sector (Pryor: 147). This does not even include the army which received a large portion of the national budget for arms, supplies, living expenses and salaries. While the state sector expanded during the four and one half years of PRG rule, prices for Grenada's primary exports fell about 40% from 1978 to 1983, due to the appreciation of the EC dollar and the relative decline of the U.S. dollar to which Grenada's currency was tied. Despite the decline in foreign exchange earned from exports, the PRG's success in obtaining foreign aid enabled the country to experience a small but significant growth in the GDP (Pryor: 75).

However, by mid-1982, the PRG'S earlier success in obtaining foreign aid could no longer be sustained. Whereas prior to 1982 the PRG had been able to reduce the balance of payments deficit to the point where an equilibrium had been achieved between imports and exports, by 1982 the situation had reverted back to a significant shortfall. Short term debts increased to approximately thirty million dollars, and the deterioration of the overall balance of payments situation forced the PRG to borrow heavily in order to continue financing its capital projects and to pay the salaries of civil servants and other public sector employees. Additionally, as Grenada's indebtedness increased, the PRG began experiencing greater difficulty in obtaining new loans. Increasingly, countries which had pledged aid to the PRG were either reneging on their promises or extending aid in the form of in-kind services or commodities. This was the case, for example, with a six million dollar loan from the GDR which could only be used to purchase goods from that country. The war between Iran and Iraq compelled the Iraqi government to renege on an earlier pledge of seven million dollars in aid for construction of the international airport. Moreover, actions on the part of the PRG to silence dissent on the island made it increasingly difficult to obtain economic assistance from Western nations. By 1983, the sources of foreign aid were drying up and the PRG found itself confronted with tremendous economic problems that had ominous political ramifications.

The economic problems experienced by the PRG in mid-1983 created the conditions for the political crises which came to a head in the fall of that year. From the time of the government take over in 1979, the PRG had based its claims on legitimacy on two criteria: 1) that the revolution it had initiated was popularly supported, as evidenced by the large numbers of people who could be mobilized by the government and who participated in the various mass organizations set up by the PRG; and 2) that the revolution had been successful in satisfying the basic needs of the population and had generally improved the living conditions and quality of life of its citizens. Because the government had not held elections, sustaining this standard of legitimacy became essential to the maintenance of political power by the PRG.

While the criteria used to demonstrate popular support did not completely satisfy Grenada's critics in the region or in the West generally, it did provide the government with some time to prove that its experimental form of participatory democracy combined with a socialist oriented economic policy could work. Because its predecessor, the Gairy regime, had been discredited both externally and internally, many nations were willing to extend a grace period to the PRG so that it would have the time to carry out its political and economic reforms. Through large mobilizations, the PRG demonstrated that it had the support of large numbers of Grenadians, even without calling for elections. It had made significant advances in the performance of the economy and as a result, many of its critics, both foreign and domestic, were willing to adopt a wait and see attitude during the first three years of its tenure.

The demonstration of support through mobilizations and/ or a successful reform program was not only intended to satisfy the critics. The leadership of the party and the government had implicitly accepted the two criteria itself as the basis for evaluating their success in power. On numerous occasions, the NJM leadership made it clear that its goal was to improve the living standards of the island's lower classes, and to maintain the active support of the population through what it called grass roots democracy. In a speech given on the second anniversary of the revolution at an outdoor rally in St. George's, Bishop emphasized both of these points as two of the primary goals of the revolution:

> . . . we see it as essential that in a situation as difficult as this one that we take an approach to building our country that stresses the basic needs of our people . . . We say that it is possible even with limited resources, even with limited capital formation, even with a limited population, to go forward and bring benefits to the people . . .
> . . . We feel that the only way forward for our people and our country is for us to continue with the mobilization of our people, for us to deepen further the people's grass roots democracy and their grassroots democratic organizations where on a daily basis . . . our people must be involved and have a large part in continuing to build our revolution and push it forward (Bishop Speaks: 133).

Minutes from several central committee meetings indicate that the sentiments expressed above were taken seriously within the party, though articulated differently. As the government began experiencing greater difficulty in mobilizing support for mass activities, such as the adult education program and the militia in 1983, there was a growing sense of crisis on the part of party leaders. Through the month of July 1983 for example, several members of the Political Bureau commented with evident concern that ". . . the state of the masses was at low point, and the possibility of disintegrating support for the revolution . . ." was increasing (Grenada Documents: 112-22).

Though much of the discussion within the higher organs of the NJM over the causes of the declining level of support on the island was couched in ideological criticism of cadre who were responsible for directing and overseeing the mass work, the economic problems which were becoming more serious in 1983 were recognized as a key hindrance to reversing the situation and renewing confidence in the national leadership. A July report from the Central Committee on the state of the economy provided a gloomy forecast of future trends:

> While our economy has continued to grow we are experiencing extreme difficulties in mobilizing external finance and receiving already promised amounts. This has led to a serious cash flow problem which has slowed down and is even threatening to halt key capital investment projects, caused limited lay-offs and shaken the confidence of broad sections of the masses (Grenada Documents: 101-3).

The fact that the PRG had to approach the International Monetary Fund in 1983 for loans to compensate for the capital shortages was yet another indication that the economic outlook of the country was worsening.

Yet, despite an apparent awareness on the part of the NJM leadership of the serious nature of the economic problems faced by the government, a review of party documents reveals little in-depth discussion over how these problems were going to be addressed. Since direction on most government matters, including economic policy, came from the party, one gets the impression that little if any economic planning was taking place at this time aimed at devising solutions to the economic crisis.

Instead, the primary focus of party discussion and debate during this critical period was on making an ideological evaluation of the leadership to determine the causes for the faltering state of the revolution. It was during the course of these intense party sessions that criticisms of Bishop and his remaining allies in the party leadership came to the forefront. Pryor suggests that some of the attacks on Bishop emanating from Coard may have been a tactic used by Coard to divert attention away from his failures as the Finance Minister to address the economic problems (Pryor: 157). Others, such as Jorge

Heine and Manning Marable, see the attacks on Bishop by the Coard faction of the party as the culmination of a prolonged strategy aimed at replacing Bishop with Coard as the primary authority figure in the party leadership. Regardless of what the motivation might have been for the attacks on Bishop, it is clear that the party and government were in a state of paralysis by the fall of 1983 and were incapable of devising solutions to the economic and political problems faced by the country until the internal crisis was resolved.

Having nearly established its own form of welfare state through a heavy reliance on foreign aid, the PRG managed to win the support of vast sections of the Grenadian populace during the first three years of the revolution. However, once the flow of aid was curtailed, it became more difficult to sustain the high level of government spending on public sector employees and government sponsored services. Reductions in these areas had an almost immediate impact upon the degree of support for the government, and it became increasingly difficult for the regime to mobilize the population to support its initiatives. The decline in mass participation in government sponsored activities led to a sense of impending crises on the part of the party's leadership, who had come to base their legitimacy upon their ability to mobilize the population in support of their goals. This in turn provided a basis for an escalation of the attacks on Bishop's leadership. Increasingly, he was held to be ultimately responsible for both the economic and political crisis on the island.

Many observers have said that the PRG self destructed. Such a characterization of the regime's demise would appear to be largely valid, given what occurred during the month of October prior to the U.S. invasion. However, the effects of the constant threats and intimidation emanating from the United States should not be underestimated as a factor adding to the pressure within the ruling party, and influencing the possibilities for obtaining foreign aid. However, it is also clear that the criteria that had been established by the PRG as its basis for its legitimacy, also sowed the seeds for the eventual demise of the regime. Few governments can consistently rely upon their ability to mobilize the masses as a means of establishing and asserting its credibility domestically and internationally. Moreover, very few developing nations have been successful in creating a social welfare apparatus controlled by the state which adequately provides for the basic needs of the population over an extended period of time. That the PRG was able to accomplish both of these during the first few years of the revolution is an accomplishment for which it deserves credit. However, its inability to sustain these programs over an extended period of time could have been predicted and undoubtedly should have been expected by the national leadership.

The U. S. Invasion of Grenada

Tension within the ranks of the leadership of the NJM continued to escalate. At a meeting of the Central Committee on September 15, 1983, Liam James, a high ranking officer of the PRA, proposed that the problems experienced by the party were due to ". . . the quality of leadership provided by Comrade Maurice Bishop, who lacked a Leninist level of organization and discipline and brilliance in strategy and tactics" (Grenada Documents: 111-4). According to James, the only way to address these shortcomings in the party's leadership was to establish a joint leadership structure. Under the plan which was proposed by James, Coard was to be placed in charge of the Political Bureau and Organizing Committee, and Bishop would remain as Prime Minister and be responsible for supervising the "structure of popular democracy." The motion was approved by the Central Committee and later passed on to a meeting of forty-eight full party members on September 25th, who voted in favor of the proposal.

On September 26, Bishop left the island with George Louison, the Minister of Agriculture, and Don Rojas, the Press Secretary, for Eastern Europe. While traveling in Europe, the proposal for joint leadership was discussed with NJM party members studying in Czechoslovakia, who, along with Louison, encouraged Bishop to reject the proposal. News of these discussions and Bishop's hesitation about the decision reached Coard and other Central Committee members prior to his return to the island. This grouping met in Bishop's absence to discuss how to handle the situation.

On October 12 there were rumors circulating throughout the island that Coard and his wife Phyllis (Minister of Women's Affairs and member of the Central Committee) were planning to murder Bishop. On October 13, Bishop was accused by the central committee majority of circulating the rumor through his body guard Cletus St. Paul. He was then condemned as a 'rightwing opportunist' and placed under house arrest. While in custody, attempts were made to negotiate an agreement between Bishop and the Central Committee majority over the joint leadership proposal, but none of these were successful. On October 15, Kenrick Radix, Bishop's long time associate and co-founder of the NJM, organized a rally in downtown St. George's, demanding the release of Bishop. Radix was then placed under arrest by PRA soldiers and held in custody until he was released by the U.S. The following day five hundred students protested in Grenville, Grenada's second largest city, demanding Bishop's release, chanting "No Bishop, no Revo" (Marable: 259).

Finally, on October 19, approximately fifteen thousand Grenadians assembled at the Market Square in downtown St. George's, where they were led in a march by Unison Whiteman, the Foreign Minister, to the house where Bishop was being held. After overcoming the guards at the residence, Bishop and Jacquelin Creft, the Minister of Education who was also being held with him, were freed by the crowd and taken to Fort Rupert, a small army installation overlooking the Port of St. George's. Crowds assembled at the fort to inquire about the state of Bishop, and within a short time, thousands of people had gathered. Individuals present at the scene described it as a "carnival-like atmosphere". Merle Hodge, a Trinidadian educator who was working for the Ministry of Education in Grenada, described the sentiment of the crowd in the following manner: "With the whole country coming to town to support Maurice, you wouldn't think that it would enter anybody's head to try to take power in the face of all of that. Because you would be fighting the whole nation" (Payne, Sutton and Thorndike, 1984: 135).

A few hours later, two army personnel carriers were dispatched to reclaim the fort. One of these was led by Cornell

Meyers, a Grenadian who had served in the U.S. armed forces prior to joining the PRA. Shots were exchanged between Bishop's supporters and the PRA soldiers, resulting in the death of Meyers. During the fighting, several of those present attempted to flee, stampeding to their deaths over the side of a cliff. Eventually, Bishop called upon his forces to cease fire, anguishing at the thought of the army turning its guns on Grenadian citizens. Shortly after their surrender, Bishop, Creft, Whiteman, and two others were executed.

Two hours later, General Hudson Austin announced over Radio Free Grenada that a new government had been set up called the Revolutionary Military Council (RMC), which would have full legislative and executive authority. In his speech, Austin declared that: "Today our People's Revolutionary Army has gained a victory over the right opportunist and reactionary forces . . . the friends of imperialism were crushed. Bishop and his petty bourgeois friends had deserted the working class and working people of Grenada" (Payne, et al.: 135). He later announced that a shoot on sight curfew was imposed, during which "anyone found outdoors will be shot" (Sadiq, 1984: 31).

Though the RMC attempted to assure the population that it would adhere to the course previously pursued by the PRG, it was soon clear that it could not establish any legitimacy among the population in the aftermath of the murders on October 19. Perhaps even more important was the reaction of Grenada's neighbors and the United States, who promptly condemned the new regime. On Saturday October 22, an emergency meeting of Caricom was convened, which led to the imposition of economic and political sanctions against the RMC (Payne, et al.: 152). At the same time, plans were being made by the United States for a full scale military invasion of Grenada by the Reagan administration (*Sunday Times* 10/30/83). Discussion over U.S. plans for the invasion took place at the Caricom meeting, however, because they were unable to achieve consensus over the decision to invade. Approval for the assault was finally obtained from the Organization of Eastern Caribbean States (OECS), of which Grenada was a member.

The invasion took place on the morning of October 25th. Fighting lasted for approximately four and a half days, resulting in the deaths of eighteen U.S. soldiers, twenty-four Cubans and sixteen Grenadians. Another one hundred and thirteen U.S. soldiers, fifty-seven Cubans and two hundred and eighty Grenadians were wounded. Over twelve thousand U.S. troops had taken part in the operation. When it was all over, President Ronald Reagan declared in a televised address to the U.S. public that "We got there just in time" (United States Information Service, 10/27/83).

Notes

1 Obeah consists of a set of spiritual beliefs and practices which origi-
nate in West Africa. For a discussion about Obeah and other African-
based religions practiced in the Caribbean, see *The Rastafarians* by
Leonard Barrett (Boston, MA: Beacon Press, 1997) p. 12 -27.

2 Other small islands in the eastern Caribbean were particularly concerned
about the ease with which the NJM was able to defeat Gairy's forces. In
April of 1981, a small group of white supremacist mercenaries from the
United States and Canada attempted to invade the island of Dominica.
In an interview conducted after their arrest with the *Toronto Globe and
Mail,* the leaders of the plot explained that their plan was to use
Dominica as a launching point for an invasion of Grenada. See Sun-
shine, C. *Grenada the Peaceful Revolution* (Washington, D.C.: EPICA, 1982)
p. 123, 124.

3 Shortly after the revolution, the GNP attempted to hold public meetings on the island. At one point, Blaize even offered to participate in
the provisional government since he assumed that elections would be
held in the near future. According to media reports, NJM supporters
disrupted GNP meetings and, thereby, prevented the party from functioning. See *Torchlight* 9/16/79.

4 The expansion of the state sector for the purpose of increasing employment on the island and expanding the state's control over the economy
was a key element of the PRG development strategy. The goal was articulated by the PRG as the need to ". . . raise the cultural, scientific
and material levels of living for the mass of people . . ." and in their
view would be accomplished primarily through an expanded state sector. Other sectors, namely the cooperative sector and the traditional
private sector, were envisioned as having an on-going role in the
economy, but the state sector was to become dominant. For a discussion of the strategy and its articulation in public policy, see *Is Freedom
We Making* (St.George's, Grenada: Grenada Government Information
Service, 1980) p. 24-28 and "Socialism Via Foreign Aid" by Pryor, F. in
Heine, J. *A Revolution Aborted* (Pittsburgh, PA: University of Pittsburgh
Press, 1990).

5 In 1981, the U.S. launched a large scale military maneuver in the Caribbean called Ocean Venture '81 or "Amber and the Amberines." The
exercise involved 120,000 troops from fourteen countries. As a part of
the war game scenario, an island in the eastern Caribbean which was

under Soviet control was to be seized and a regime "favorable to the way of life we espouse" was to be installed. For Bishop and the PRG, it was clear that the exercises were intended as an actual dress rehearsal for military invasion of Grenada. See United Press International, August 2, 1981.

6   For an analysis of the role of the literacy campaign in the PRG's efforts at attaining regime legitimacy, see "Mass Literacy As A Political Strategy" by Pedro Noguera, *Journal of Adult and University Education*, vol. XXXI, No. 2 July, 1992.

7   The Organization for Revolutionary Education (OREL) functioned as an ideological training school for young members of the NJM. Its leader Bernard Coard provided instruction on Marxism-Leninism and general political education. Many OREL members later became leaders of the People's Revolutionary Army, and several including Liam Jones, Ewart Layne, Tan Bartholomew and Chalkie Ventour became members of the Central Committee. OREL members, along with Coard's wife Phyllis, became Bishop's primary ideological opponents in the party conflict that resulted in the call for joint leadership, and later Bishop's house arrest. See the *Grenada Documents* , section on the Central Committee minutes and Marable, M. *African and Caribbean Politics* (London: Thetford Press, 1987) p. 211-215.

8   Heine (1990), Clark (1987) and Marable (1987) have written about the factors behind the split in the party. All three have focused on the differences between Bishop and Coard. Clark argues that Coard's motivation was ideological: "Stalinism destroyed the Grenada Revolution. Bernard Coard was trained in its brutality, rigidity and bureaucratic decisiveness." He argues that Bishop was a populist democrat who was eliminated by Coard and his supporters because of their ideological differences. See Clark, S. "The Second Assassination of Maurice Bishop" in *New International* (New York: Pathfinder Press, 1987) p. 37.

Marable argues that Bishop went along with the "statist oriented Marxist-Leninist" dogmatism of the NJM leaders, even though he privately opposed them. He writes "...on the decisive questions of the deteriorating relations between the factions inside the NJM and the growing contradictions between the party and the state, he (Bishop) was taciturn and 'shut up within himself.'" See Marable, M. *African and Caribbean Politics* (London: Thetford Press, 1987) p. 271.

Finally, Heine argues that the ideological differences between Bishop and Coard were minor, and that the more critical differences between the two men were based on personality. See Heine, J. *The Hero and the Apparatchik: Charismatic Leadership, Political Management and Crisis in Revolutionary Grenada* (San Juan, Puerto Rico: University of Puerto Rico Press, 1987).

Chapter 7

Foreign Intervention and the Return of Herbert Blaize

Transition to Democracy: Preparations for the December 1984 Elections

Herbert Blaize served as the leader of government on two occasions prior to his election in 1984. He was first elected to the Legislative Council in 1957 with the newly formed Grenada National Party. By working in coalition with independents on the Council, he was able to form a majority voting bloc, and thereby wrest control of the Council away from Gairy and the GULP. The GNP lost the election of 1961 to Gairy and the GULP but returned to office in 1962, following the dismissal of the Gairy-led government by the colonial authorities under allegations of "Squandermania." Blaize served as Chief Minister (1957), and later assumed the title of Premiere (1962) as constitutional changes implemented by the British ceded greater authority over the affairs of the island to local government.

After being soundly defeated by Gairy and the GULP in the election of 1967, Blaize began a long career as Leader of the Opposition in the Legislative Council, which later became the Parliament, following independence in 1974. The strong anti-Gairy sentiment in Blaize's constituency, the island parish of Carriacou, enabled Blaize to retain his seat in government in the successive elections of 1967, 1972, and 1976, even when others in the GNP and NJM were unable to prevail over GULP candidates elsewhere in Grenada. Following the election of 1976, when the GNP formed the People's Alliance with the NJM and Winston Whyte's United People's Party (UPP), Blaize was replaced as Leader of the Opposition by Maurice Bishop and seemed destined to drift slowly into political oblivion as the NJM eclipsed the GNP as the primary opposition to the Gairy regime.

During the four and one half years of PRG rule, Blaize was largely invisible in political affairs on the island. After making an initial offer to the PRG shortly after the March 13, 1979 takeover to play a role in what he thought would be a provisional government with national elections pending, Blaize returned to private life in Carriacou. Unlike several other conservative politicians who opposed the regime from abroad, Blaize remained in Grenada but did not become actively involved in the opposition to the PRG.

The collapse of the PRG, followed shortly thereafter by the U.S. military invasion, created the opportunity for Blaize to come out of retirement and make yet another bid for leadership as the Interim Government, headed by Nicholar Brathwaite, prepared the country for national elections. The re-organized GNP entered the 1984 campaign among a field of six newly formed political parties, all of which had a centrist or conservative political orientation. To the dismay of many, particularly the U.S. officials on the island, prospects for electoral victory seemed to favor the GNP's traditional nemesis, the GULP. With Eric Gairy once again at the party's helm, many observers believed that the GULP would do well in rural areas where support for Gairy appeared to be strong even after four and a half years of denigration by the PRG. The other parties, it was assumed, would merely cancel each other out by competing for the same constituents.

However, while Gairy clearly retained a large measure of support from his traditional base among the rural lower classes, he was also intensely disliked and distrusted by a large section of the population. A public opinion poll conducted by Farley Brathwaite of the University of the West Indies in Barbados revealed that while 41.7% of the population was favorably disposed toward Gairy, 58.3% indicated a strongly negative disposition (Brathwaite, 1985). A review of letters to the editor that appeared in local newspapers during the campaign period shows that much of the resentment toward Gairy was based upon the judgement that he was responsible for the political turmoil that had occurred on the island over the last several years. The following letters to the *Grenada Voice* articulated this sentiment :

> This Satan Gairy is back. After being released from his corrupt, brutal and victimized government for several years. . . . now he is so bold face to threaten anyone who voices their displeasure with his presence here (*Grenada Voice* 4/2/84).

> Who is responsible for all of the terror we went through? All fingers point to Uncle saying: "it's you". So brother, keep out of politics, for we'll tolerate no more of your dirty tricks (*Grenada Voice* 4/15/84).

Among the U.S. officials who remained to monitor the situation in Grenada prior to the elections, the possibility of a Gairy victory was a matter of great concern. Having eliminated the Revolutionary Military Council (RMC), and successfully installed an interim caretaker government, the U.S. sought to insure that a stable, pro-American party would win the December elections, thereby making it possible for a complete withdrawal of U.S. troops, and a substantially reduced U.S. presence on the island within a year of the invasion.[1] The U.S. officials overseeing operations in Grenada were extremely worried about the possibility of a Gairy victory, fearing that the eccentric leader would recreate the conditions for another leftist takeover at some point in the future. Moreover, U.S. officials did not want to be accused by critics of the invasion that it had been carried out for the purpose of installing the authoritarian Gairy, whose image remained tarnished even after four and one half years of quiet exile. They were also concerned about the remnants of the NJM mounting a serious electoral challenge. However, they knew that the NJM remained deeply divided between those who had sided with Bishop and those who had aligned themselves with Coard. Even when some of them entered the race under the newly formed Maurice Bishop Patriotic Movement (MBPM), they were still poorly organized and barely able to mount an effective campaign. Still, the uncertainty of the political climate created by so many relatively unknown parties competing for similar constituencies heightened U.S. fears over the possibility of a Gairy victory at the polls.

Having achieved an easy military victory, the U.S. found itself in a bind. In order to make the intervention a complete success, they had to make sure that a stable, democratically elected government was installed prior to their withdrawal. While they wanted to ensure that Gairy did not win the election, U.S. representatives on the island also had to avoid creating the appearance that they were interfering in the political process by openly indicating their preference for a particular candidate or party. To the Grenadian people, it was clear that U.S. blessing was critical for any future government in order to guarantee the maximum amount of aid from the U.S. to the island. Many Grenadians believed that there was a possibility that the U.S. might abandon its pledge to provide aid to Grenada if it did not approve of the government elected (*Grenada Voice*, 9/7/84). This was message subtly conveyed to the populace through the local media. In an interview with the *Grenada Voice*, U.S. Ambassador Loren Lawrence made the following comment in response to the question: "What kind of government are you trying to build in Grenada?" He explained "We are not trying to build a government. That is the internal business of Grenadians. We are not supporting one party or another. We would like to see a fairly elected, honest government. Otherwise I suspect Congress would pull out of here very fast" (*Voice* 7/7/84).

To remedy this problematic situation, a meeting was convened on Union Island at which U.S. diplomatic personnel invited representatives of four of the centrist parties. In addition to Blaize and others representing the GNP, representatives from the following political parties were invited: George Brizan of the National Democratic Party, Winston Whyte of the Christian Democratic Labour Party, and Keith Mitchell and Francis Alexis of the Grenada Democratic Movement. After hours of negotiations, it was agreed that a new party would be formed which would be called the New National Party (NNP) and that its political leader and eventual prime minister would be Herbert Blaize. Though several of the leaders present were not fully satisfied with compromise that was reached, in the end all of the parties invited to the meeting went along with the proposal to form the coalition recognizing that U.S. support would be essential for the new government. The only rejection of the accord came from the CDLP (Christian Democratic Labor Party) headed by Winston Whyte, the only party official present at the meeting who was not guaranteed a leading role in the coalition or offered a ministry in the government that would be formed after the election, largely because of the small base of his party.[2]

With the marriage between the parties consummated, and the blessing of the U. S. assured, "unity" and "one love" became the campaign themes of the coalition. The NNP won the December election by a wide margin, 58.5% for the NNP compared to 36.1% for the GULP, capturing all but one of the seats in the Legislature. Gairy and supporters of the GULP immediately cried foul, charging that the U.S. had unfairly intervened in the election by providing campaign funds to the NNP, and that the Supervisor of Elections had tampered with the voter registration rolls. In spite of Gairy's objections, the new government was installed in January of 1985 and the U.S. was able to claim that it had successfully brought about a restoration of democracy in Grenada, in just fourteen months after the invasion.

Establishment of the NNP Government and the Re-emergence of H. A. Blaize

The NNP government, headed by Herbert Blaize, assumed power in January of 1985 under conditions which appeared to be extremely favorable to its success. The government inherited $164.8 million dollars of debt created primarily from the disruption in the economy caused by the invasion and the political vacuum which existed for most of 1984 (Grenada National Development Strategies, 1987). However, a pledge by the United States to provide the island with vast amounts of economic aid made the new leadership and much of the population extremely hopeful about the possibilities for the future. Even before the NNP government had been installed, the U.S. had commenced with numerous development projects aimed at restoring and improving the island's badly damaged infrastructure. The international airport, which ironically represented the source of much of the conflict between the PRG and the Reagan administration,[3] was finally completed by the

United States in 1985, and became the most tangible evidence of U.S. support to the island. Several damaged and deteriorated roads were repaved and a new highway was constructed which connected the new airport to the capitol city, St. George's. The port at St. George's Harbor was modernized with new storage facilities and machinery, and an industrial park consisting of several large factory shells was built, intended for the use of private foreign investors. The Reagan administration and the NNP government viewed a substantial increase in foreign private investment as the engine which would ultimately propel the Grenadian economy to higher levels of development and prosperity (Ministry of Finance, 1/6/87).

The United States was not alone in its support to Grenada during the months after the invasion, though it had certainly assumed the primary role as patron of the mini-state. Great Britain, Canada, the EEC, and to a lesser extent France and West Germany, contributed significant sums of aid for construction projects and newly created service programs on the island (Grenada Economic Objectives, 1987). In addition to the increase in foreign aid, once political stability was restored, tourism to the island also began to increase, prompting the expansion of the tourist sector and the construction of several new hotels and restaurants.

Perhaps the most significant area of growth in the economy was related to the rise in prices earned for nutmeg on the international market, beginning in 1985. In part, this was made possible by the economic recovery in Europe which occurred at approximately the same time. More importantly for Grenadian nutmeg producers, talks had been initiated with Indonesia, the largest nutmeg exporter in the world, to coordinate prices on the international market. A formal agreement between the two countries was signed in 1987, which brought about a sharp increase in prices, and a significant windfall in profits to local growers (Annual Report of the Grenada Nutmeg Board, 1986).

However, though the performance of the economy appeared to favor the political fortunes of the NNP, divisions within the hastily formed coalition soon began to emerge. One of the first indications of the dissension within the party occurred when Blaize selected Ben Jones, a former political ally from the GNP, to the post of deputy political leader of the party. In what his coalition partners perceived as a blatant disregard for party democracy, he made this choice even after Francis Alexis, a law professor from the University of the West Indies Cavehill campus, was elected to the post by a majority of delegates at a party convention. During the same period, there were rumors that George Brizan, the newly appointed Minister of Agriculture, and his supporters from the National Democratic Party, were continuing to hold separate secret meetings despite his membership in the coalition, and despite the fact that he was the Minister of Agriculture in the new government. As news of the growing divisions within the cabinet became more widely known, Lloyd Noel, a local attorney writing for the *Voice*, suggested that ". . . certain persons are bent on building personal empires in the false hope that they can take over the reigns in a show down" (*Voice*, 7/27/85).

In addition to the growing strains within the NNP, it was evident that the government was still very concerned about potential threats to its stability, which it believed were posed by the presence of NJM supporters on the island. Numerous students who had been sent abroad by the PRG to study in Eastern Europe and Cuba, were denied certification to practice their professions in Grenada. In the case of several doctors who had been trained in Cuba, many experienced considerable difficulty in obtaining permission to practice in Grenada. Eventually, the government found it difficult to deny their right to practice medicine on the island, given the shortage of doctors in the country, and given the fact that many other Caribbean nations sent students to medical school in Cuba for training. Increasingly, it became apparent that the government feared the ideological training which it believed the students had received, more so than their technical competency. A *Voice* article expressed that sentiment in the following passage:

> It is well known that students in communist institutions receive special indoctrination in the communist ideology and in subversion and revolution. The barrage of rhetoric to which they have been subjected may have penetrated their defenses so that they may at least be regarded as contaminated. Our ministers must proceed with caution with regard to employing them . . . (*Voice* 9/21/85).

Besides the concern about the return of students trained in communist nations, the NNP government, like the Interim Government before it, and the United States, were concerned that large sections of the populace continued to support the goals and ideology of the revolution. The island's youth were seen as being particularly likely to cling to revolutionary ideas because many of them had participated in the organizations set up by the PRG, such as the militia, and had been heavily influenced by the intense political socialization which occurred during that period. Moreover, with the upheaval in the economy created by invasion, many youth were unemployed and no longer had access to the educational opportunities created by the PRG through the provision of scholarships for study abroad. Estimates of youth unemployment (ages 16-30) from 1985 to 1987 ranged from as high as 36% (the government estimate) to 45%, the rate most often cited in the media (*Informer* 10/15/87).

The implications of such conditions were disconcerting to the political authorities. The fact that hundreds of young people throughout the island were idle and potentially frustrated could not be ignored. While many were able to emigrate during this period, the vast majority could not. Many of these young people had received military training in the army or militia. Moreover, it was widely suspected that many Grenadians had hidden their weapons in the countryside at the time of the invasion. Hence, for these reason and others, there was considerable concern on the part of the new government and its supporters that unemployed youth could become a source of instability and political violence.

To respond to this potential threat, the U.S. had initially detained large numbers of young people in the days immediately following the invasion. Because it had no way of determining who were past members of the People's Revolutionary Army and militia and who were not, the detentions were numerous and indiscriminate. Eventually, individuals within the Interim Government recognized that the vast majority of these individuals posed no immediate threat to national security, and they were released. Following their release, a new policy was put into effect which aimed at employing many ex-army personnel. According to Nicholas Brathwaite, the Chairman of the Interim Government and current prime minister (Interview, 11/15/87), it was hoped that former supporters of the PRG could be convinced or co-opted into supporting the political changes which were occurring on the island. Ironically, many were recruited to serve in the Grenada Defense Force, which was set up by the United States to preserve order and provide security on the island. Many others were later hired by the Ministry of Construction and Works that was headed by Keith Mitchell, the current political leader of the NNP. Despite these efforts however, there simply were not enough jobs available to accommodate the vast numbers of youth who remained unemployed.

Perhaps the greatest source of concern for the new government was the handling of the trial of Bernard Coard and the sixteen others who had been charged with the assassination of Maurice Bishop and other PRG ministers. From the time of their arrest during the October invasion, considerable attention was focused on the legal proceedings surrounding the case of the sixteen who were held at Richmond Hill prison. When the trial began in November 1986, huge crowds filled and surrounded the courtroom in an attempt to watch the trial and catch a glimpse of the defendants. On several occasions, the defendants were nearly mobbed by the crowds, many of whom had already judged the sixteen guilty of all charges and who seemed to desire to participate in carrying out the execution.

To some extent, the crowds hysteria had been aroused and instigated by the U.S.armed forces, which had placed Coard and Hudson Austin (the latter having served as commander of the PRA and nominal head of the Revolutionary Military Council) blindfolded and bareback on a flatbed truck and had driven them around the island. Later, the U.S. Psychological Operations Unit printed posters of the two, still blindfolded and bareback, with the caption: "'C' is for Coard and 'C' is for communism." There were several reports that Coard and the other defendants were beaten and severely mistreated while being held in prison awaiting trial.[4] Amidst an atmosphere of overt hostility toward them promoted by the NNP government, the U.S. and the local media, there was little possibility that the allegations of injustice would be investigated or impartially addressed.

Though the mood of the populace was overwhelmingly negative toward the defendants, the unresolved nature of the case perpetuated a feeling in the country that justice had not yet been attained with regard to the events of October 1983. Finally, following a lengthy trial late in 1986, fourteen of the eighteen individuals charged with involvement in the murder of Maurice Bishop were issued death sentences, and three were sentenced to prison terms of thirty to forty-five years. One defendant was acquitted of all charges in exchange for providing testimony which was used in the convictions of the seventeen others.

Following several appeals and a last minute stay of execution issued by Prime Minister Brathwaite in 1991, none of the executions were carried out. To this day, the accused conspirators remain in Richmond Hill prison having exhausted all possible channels for further appeal. They await the time when either Grenadian authorities feel it is appropriate to carry out the executions or release them, by pardoning them for their crimes as has occurred with political prisoners elsewhere in the Caribbean.[5] Their presence on the island, though less frequently mentioned by the local media, serves as a constant reminder to the population that the case has not yet been resolved. Commenting on their pending execution, a *Voice* editorial made the following statement with regard to the prisoners:

> . . . most Grenadians would prefer to put a complete and definite end to that chapter of our history . . . Considering their commitment to their adopted ideology, and the obviously unrepentant, even defiant attitude they have displayed, people will always be expecting something to happen (*Voice* 11/3/86).

Though of major political significance, the fourteen individuals on Grenada's death row are but one of many factors that have contributed to an ongoing sense of political instability on the island. After assuming office under what appeared to have been highly favorable circumstances, the Blaize-led NNP government began to experience problems within a relatively short period of time which potentially threatened its stability. Despite the factionalism however, the government believed that support from the U.S. was assured and indefinite. As a result,

NNP leaders remained extremely confident and optimistic about the prospects for the nation's future, even as conditions on the island deteriorated.

Mismanagement of Economy

During the last two years that he served as Prime Minister, Blaize and his government experienced one set back after another. As a result of numerous charges of corruption, worsening conditions in the economy, splits and defections within the NNP, the formation of competing centrists parties, and a gradual decline in the level of foreign aid to the island, the popularity of the regime plummeted and its standing among the populace became substantially diminished. Much of the blame for all of these problems was placed squarely on the leadership of Herbert Blaize. My own survey, conducted in 1987, found an extremely low approval rating for the prime minister and an overwhelming lack of confidence in his ability to the lead the nation.

How was it possible for the popularity of Blaize and the NNP to fall so quickly, given the favorable economic and political circumstances inherited by the government at the time of its coming to office? Blaize was certainly no newcomer to Grenadian politics. In fact, he was selected to head the nation in the first election held after the invasion largely because he was seen as a respected senior statesman who could provide a stabilizing influence over the society. As was true in the past, Blaize was fully supported by the local business sector on the island, and perhaps more importantly, he was supported by the United States. Most observers expected that with this kind of backing, Blaize and the NNP would succeed in their efforts to lead the country and promote development. However, this did not occur largely because of weaknesses in Blaize's leadership style that had been evident in the past.

Though saddled with a relatively large debt at the time it took office, for the most part the prospects for the economy were extremely favorable in 1984. The huge debt that the regime inherited and the interest payments that accompanied it had largely been incurred by the PRG for the construction of the international airport. Many of these loans went into arrears during the period following the invasion when there was no government managing the affairs of the nation. Within the first two years, the government succeeded in bringing the debt problem under control, largely through its receipt of large amounts of foreign aid, $157 million of which came from the United States during the five years following the invasion. With the completion of the airport and the construction of several new roads, an industrial park and a modern port facility, the government appeared to be off to a good start. In his budget speech of March 1986, Blaize predicted the perpetuation of these favorable economic trends saying: ". . . this budget was fashioned within the framework of a clearly defined development strategy, aimed at transforming the economy from a controlled, narrowly based one, to a free enterprise market oriented one" (*Voice* 1/3/87).

However, during this period of relative prosperity, the government apparently was not able to develop strategies for sustaining the growth and development that had occurred. According to Ronald Charles, Manager of the Grenada Development Bank, a subsidiary of the Caribbean Development Bank, the government was opposed to the concept of economic planning, and therefore according to Charles, there was no development plan for the country. He described the NNP's approach to economic development as a "laissez-faire" policy toward financial planning. While he acknowledged the progress which had been made in the tourist sector, in the development of the nation's infrastructure and in the nutmeg industry, he expressed a great deal of concern over the large amount of loans which had been taken out by the new government to finance its development projects. Commenting on the government's apporach to development, he said the following: "This government acts as though the money will just continue to flow. I think they will soon discover that they were mistaken" (Interview 9/12/87).

A similar concern was expressed to me by Edwin Decall, one of the larger manufacturers on the island. While he welcomed the government's proclaimed support for the private sector, he felt that the government did not have a clear sense of how to assist business in its efforts to expand and increase employment opportunities. As an example, he cited the industrial park constructed with funds obtained from USAID. Over a year after the completion of the factory shells, only one of the units was occupied. According to DeCall, the Industrial Development Council (IDC) which had been set up by the government to attract foreign investors and to encourage foreign businesses to locate in Grenada by offering tax incentives was suffering a form of bureaucratic paralysis. He suggested that part of the problem was that its former chairman, a retired judge who knew nothing about business, had no idea of how to achieve the objectives which had been set for the IDC. His primary complaint with the government, however, was with its taxation policies, which he felt hindered rather than enhanced the opportunities for business on the island.

Negative reference to the government's handling of its taxation policy was cited throughout the island, by both the rich and poor, as one of the major errors committed by the new government. In 1986, acting on the advice of an American advisors, the government eliminated all personal income tax and imposed a value added tax (VAT), a twenty percent levy on most goods and services (*Voice* 6/13/86). The reasoning behind the imposition of the VAT was that it would increase government revenue at a time when the government's budget was reflecting a substantial deficit. Although it was not perceived to be a regressive tax by its proponents, in that the twenty percent assessment would affect consumers proportionately based on the value of the goods and services they purchased, public reaction to the VAT was overwhelmingly negative.

In response to the VAT, a local calypsonian produced a record entitled: "The Ship is Sinking", a direct reference to the NNP government. The immediate impact of the new taxation policy was to impose an added cost on most consumer goods which was felt by all consumers. This resulted in the price of locally produced rum for example, for which there was almost no export market, becoming higher than that of imported rum on the local market. Meanwhile, personal income tax, which previously had not been paid by most of the island's poor due to their low incomes, was no longer paid by the rich or middle class either. The immediate result was a 32 million dollar shortfall in government revenues reported by the end of 1986, due to the inability of the government to devise an effective means of collecting the VAT from local businesses.

To address its growing deficit problems, in late 1986 the government announced plans to retrench eighteen hundred civil servants. This announcement proved to be even more politically damaging to the government than the VAT. The number of people employed in the public sector had grown considerably under the Gairy and Bishop regimes, and despite his emphasis on the free market, Blaize had initially followed a similar strategy. The government proposed to lay-off of eighteen hundred workers, an action which would have a direct impact upon thousands of people, given that many of those targeted for retrenchment were heads of households. Though the government later reduced plans for retrenchment to only half of those originally targeted in 1987, the political damage had already been done, and new calypsos, far more critical than the first, were sung once again about the failures of the NNP government and Blaize.

Collapse of the NNP Coalition and the Growth of the Opposition

As it became evident that the NNP government was growing increasingly unpopular, members of the coalition began to abandon the party and their posts in the government. Kenny Lalsingh and Phinsley St. Louis were among the first parliamentarians to leave the NNP in early 1986. Both cited as their reasons for leaving an intense dislike for Blaize's autocratic leadership style. Later that year, George Brizan and Francis Alexis, the Ministers of Agriculture and Legal Affairs, also abandoned the party and their posts in government. The two were among the more highly regarded politicians on the island, and were seen by most observers as two of the more competent ministers in the government.

Brizan and Alexis cited many different reasons for departing from the government, including a lack of democracy within the party, corruption on the part of government ministers, the government's failure to support a resolution calling for sanctions against South Africa at the United Nations, and the unwillingness on the part of the prime minister to call meetings of the parliament regularly to allow for public discussion and debate of national policies. Primary among their criticisms was an attempt to distance themselves from the unpopularity of the governments' economic policies. Many observers believed that the two had hoped that by leaving their posts, they would create a loss of confidence in the government and force early elections. In preparation for that possibility, the two teamed up with others who had abandoned the NNP coalition and formed the National Democratic Congress (NDC) in 1987, which elected George Brizan political leader and Francis Alexis its deputy.

With Brizan and Alexis gone, the NNP government had essentially reverted back into a GNP government. With the exception of Keith Mitchell, who had originally been a political ally of Alexis, the other important members of the coalition were gone. The remaining government ministers were members of the traditional GNP. The opposition attempted to use this fact to call for new elections, arguing that the voters had elected a coalition and not the GNP, and as such, the present government did not represent the will of the people. But these charges were not compelling to either the local media or to the population as a whole. The vast majority of people appeared to be skeptical and too weary to opening the door to political chaos, which many feared would occur by holding early elections.

Moreover, aside from its criticisms of Blaize and the remaining members of government, the NDC presented no clear alternative to the policies of the NNP. While its leaders pledged to be honest, and claimed that they would help heal Grenada's wounds through the promotion of "family values" (NDC Convention October 1987), there was no significant difference in the political orientation of the two parties. Moreover, even in its weakened state, the NNP still had the backing of the U.S. Brizan and other NDC members went out of their way to declare their support for American policies in Grenada and the region, with the hope of getting the U.S. to transfer its support to them, but these efforts proved largely unsuccessful. Throughout these trying times for Blaize and the NNP, the U.S. remained supportive and demonstrated its support through a steady though reduced flow of aid.

Though admired by large numbers of Grenadians,[6] Brizan was also distrusted by many others for his lack of experience in government and for his prior involvement with the NJM. Though never a member of the party, Brizan had held a relatively high post in the Ministry of Education under the PRG. Among many of the civic leaders I interviewed, Brizan was highly regarded as a technocrat; many felt that he would make a fine Minister of Finance. However, even some of his supporters questioned whether he had the "right stuff" needed to serve as prime minister. Moreover, there were doubts about the sincerity of the alliance between Alexis and Brizan. Several people I interviewed stated that Alexis was too ambitious to allow Brizan to hold the top leadership post in government, and that eventually the kind of power struggle which developed between Bishop and Coard would occur between Brizan and Alexis. Undoubtedly, such concerns influenced the NDC to select another senior statesman, Nicholas Brathwaite, the former head of the Interim Government, to serve as political leader of the party and prime minister after the 1990 elections.

As the NDC worked to consolidate itself in order to become a viable alternative to the NNP, the GULP began to make its own slow recovery from its unsuccessful attempt in the 1984 elections. Though older and now with failing eyesight, Eric Gairy remained the undisputed leader of the party. Within months after his return to the island in 1984, Gairy had begun to reorganize his supporters and made efforts to re-establish both his political party, the Grenada United Labor Party, and his union, the Grenada Manual and Mental Workers Union. After protesting what he believed was an unfair election, Gairy sought to enhance his standing in the eyes of the U.S., which he viewed as the ultimate power broker in contemporary Grenadian politics. In June of 1985, he delivered 22,000 signatures on petitions which called for the establishment of a permanent U.S. military base in Grenada. In an interview with me, Gairy stated that he had warned the United States and Great Britain about the possibility of a communist takeover of his government prior to the NJM coup. He suggested that the only way Grenada could be safe from communist aggression would be through a permanent military presence on the island (Interview 8/22/87).

Utilizing a strategy which had proven effective for him in the past, Gairy's GMMWU called for strike at twenty-nine government owned farms in October of 1985. The strike, which was reported as being "effective in varying degrees," was immediately declared illegal by the Ministry of Agriculture (*Voice* 10/5/85). Borrowing from a page out of Grenada's history, after a week of the strike, the government implemented a minor wage increase on its own without entering into negotiations with the union, hoping that this would break the strike and the union. Gairy responded by warning that "people who attempt to break the strike expose themselves to danger (*Voice* 10/9/85). The GMMWU attempted to continue the strike for four months, but in the end, most of the workers either returned to their jobs or were replaced.

Despite this set back, Gairy proceeded with his efforts to reestablish his political base on the island. In a surprise move, Gairy announced in the fall of 1987 that he would step down from his position as political leader of the GULP. In his place, Gairy selected Dr. Raphael Fletcher, the former Vice Chancellor of the University of the West Indies, to head the party. The selection of Fletcher was seen as a surprise to most observers. Fletcher was widely respected among the islands' middle class, and his rise to the leadership of the GULP was seen as a major challenge to the NNP. The combination of Gairy's charismatic appeal to the lower class and Fletcher's rational appeal to the middle class presented both the NNP and the NDC with a formidable opponent. The GULP announced its plans to amend the constitution and make Grenada a republic if it won the national elections. Under such a plan Gairy was to become the nation's first president and Fletcher would serve as prime minister. However, holding true to past patterns and his inability to work collectively, Gairy produced conflict and strong disagreements between Fletcher and himself, which eventually led to Fletcher's departure from the party prior to the 1990 elections. According to Fletcher, "Gairy hasn't given up on the idea that he can personally run everything within his union and party. It was clear to me that the arrangement would never work out" (Interview with Fletcher 10/12/87).

The maneuverings of the GULP and the NDC over two years before the next scheduled election added to the sense that Blaize and the NNP government had lost the confidence of the people. Already in 1987, the local media reported on the political affairs of the island as if the campaign for the election had already begun, often calling on Blaize to either step down from his post as leader of the party (*Informer* 10/5/87), or for the scheduling of early elections (*Voice* 11/8/87). Despite all of this, Blaize was determined to remain in office through the end of his term and, as the opposition to his leadership grew, so did his resolve to retain his control over the government.

Political Corruption and the
Gradual Withdrawal of U.S. Support

When Herbert Blaize was elected into office at the head of the NNP ticket in the 1984 elections, his support among voters was largely based on the assumption that he was an experienced politician who could bring stability to the nation. In two separate surveys conducted prior to the election by Farley Brathwaite and Selwyn Ryan, there was strong evidence that Blaize's ability to bring stability, security and order to the government, as well as his perceived honesty, were all factors influencing a positive response by voters to Blaize (Brathwaite 1984: 17). Similarly, a *Voice* editorial published a few days before the election endorsed Blaize and the NNP in the following manner: ". . . what is clear to us is that the NNP, under H.A. Blaize, offers the best chance of providing the stability and credibility that we need" (*Voice*: 12/1/84).

Two years after his election, the stability which had been hoped for and promised still had not yet been achieved. In the months after the U.S. invasion, there had been a significant increase in the number of crimes on the island. Reported incidents of violent crimes, which had been extremely rare in the past, rose dramatically during this period. Drug dealing, which had been minimal during the PRG period due to the severe penalties imposed by the government even for minor drugs such as marijuana, had substantially increased. For the first time, cocaine and its derivative crack were available on the streets of St. George's.

Critics of the U.S. invasion, such as Kenrick Radix, blamed the U.S. armed forces stationed on the island for the increase in drug trafficking and prostitution. At a press conference on October 16, 1987 held to commemorate the deaths of Bishop and the others killed at Fort Rupert, Radix said that "the only thing the United States has done for Grenada is to bring cocaine and AIDS onto the island." Others blamed the ineffective police force for the rise in crime and drug trafficking. The police force, like the Grenada Defense Force (GDF), had been specially trained by the United States in counter terrorism tactics, and once their training was complete, U.S. troops were gradually withdrawn from the island. Early in 1987, a young woman named Madonna Swan, who was alleged to have been involved with drug trafficking, was found murdered. Shortly after the incident, local newspapers began reporting that the slain woman had been a companion of the Police Commissioner. The Commissioner, who had been living in Trinidad prior to the invasion, was recruited to Grenada by the United States to head the GDF and the local police. As rumors circulated about the Commissioners' involvement with the murder victim, the Commissioner suddenly disappeared from the island. When he was later identified by reporters in Trinidad, he claimed to know who was responsible for the murder but refused to provide any information to local authorities.

Later, in the fall of 1987, there was a series of armed robberies at several of the nutmeg weighing stations in the rural areas. Men dressed in camouflage and armed with AK-47 rifles, stole several thousand dollars from the nutmeg stations and killed and wounded a number of the farmers who had gone there to sell their crops. The "Masked Men," as they were referred to in the local media, set off a wave of speculation about the possibility of armed guerillas in the countryside raising money which might later be used to launch a wave of terrorism against the government.

The government attempted to minimize the damage caused by these incidents by downplaying their significance, and despite urgings to do otherwise, Blaize refused to speak on the matter in his weekly addresses to the nation. However, as the number of violent incidents increased and rumors of government complicity in drug trafficking spread throughout the island, the government was forced to respond. In a public address to the nation, broadcast on the radio, Blaize announced that GDF troops were being dispatched in search parties to hunt down the masked men and to restore a sense of security on the island (Radio Address, 10/2/87). Despite these reassurances, violent robberies continued, several of which were perpetrated against elderly citizens, and contributed to the fear and sense of instability that was pervasive throughout the island.

At the same time, charges of corruption were being levelled at the government by the political opposition and the local press. A major focus of these charges was on the government's handling of the sale of a small airplane, which had been purchased from Brazil through a loan by the PRG for Bishop's travels abroad. Initially, Keith Mitchell, who was responsible for the plane as the Minister of Aviation, announced plans for launching a new state enterprise, Grenada Airways. Later, it was reported that the airplane had been sold to a private businessman for an amount less than the balance owed on the loan. Upon further investigation, government officials were unable to explain where the money was that had been obtained from the sale of the plane (*Informer* 9/24/87).

In the winter of 1986, another incident occurred which shook public confidence in the government. In response to calls from the opposition for an investigation into the National Insurance Scheme (NIS), it was discovered that 37 million dollars had been borrowed by the government to make up for the shortfall in government revenue created by the failure of the government to collect the VAT. The National Insurance Scheme had been set up by the government in 1985 as a retirement plan for public sector employees. Once the loan from the NIS was made known to the public, the government pledged to repay the loan by the following year.

Incidents such as these served to undermine the goodwill and confidence which had been widely held toward the regime at the time it took office. While the government attempted to dismiss its critics as being politically motivated, it was clear that by 1987 it no longer possessed the political mandate it claimed to have been given by the voters after the 1984 elections.

Perhaps the most devastating blow to the NNP government came from the United States. Throughout its term in office, the NNP had been assured of full U.S. backing, a promise which had been fulfilled on numerous occasions. According to Lloyd

Noel, a writer for the *Grenadian Voice,* the U.S. had made a pledge to the Grenadian government to "supplement budgetary shortfalls that may result in the intervening period until the new taxes take effect" (*Voice* 10/16/87). In keeping with that pledge, the U.S. had provided the Grenadian government with an 8 million dollar grant in 1986 and a 6 million dollar grant in 1987. Both of these were for the purpose of direct budgetary support, meaning that these grants were used by the government to pay for recurrent expenditures. In an interview conducted with an assistant to the ambassador at the U.S. Embassy, Phil French, I was told that it was extremely unusual for the U.S. government to provide that type of aid. In explaining the reason for the grant, French said that " Grenada has a very special relationship with the United States. We have a close working relationship with the government; they share our perspective, our commitment to democracy and free enterprise" (Interview 10/14/87).

When I later asked the official from the U.S. Embassy how long the United States would continue to provide its current level of support to Grenada, he informed me that the U.S. planned to gradually decrease its aid commitments to Grenada. In fact, he said that the United States did not intend to maintain an embassy on the island permanently, and for that reason had only rented the facility where the embassy was being housed. He added: "I don't see the aid continuing past the next five years. Eventually Grenada will be treated just like any other OECS (Organization of Eastern Caribbean States) country." In other words, once the threat of destabilization from leftist insurgency was clearly past, the "special relationship" between the U.S. and Grenada would become ordinary and the aid which had accompanied that relationship would no longer be forthcoming.

This prospect perhaps more than any of the domestic challenges faced by the NNP assured its eventual demise. Throughout its past, Herbert Blaize's GNP had relied quite heavily upon foreign support to enable his party to obtain control over the national government. In every case in the past Blaize's ascendancy to power had been made possible, at least in part by foreign intervention. Despite this assistance, Blaize was never able to retain political power in successive elections.[7] His anti-populist, pro-business policies consistently undermined his efforts to retain political power and resulted in his loss of political support on the island.

Shortly after the 1984 elections, there were several clear indications that the regime headed by Herbert Blaize would not survive beyond the next election which was scheduled to occur some time in 1990. The long expected palace coup, about which rumors had circulated for some time, wherein Blaize was to be replaced by one of the government ministers, eventually was attempted. In an unprecedented move, Keith Mitchell, the only prominent non-GNP member of the NNP coalition to remain in the government, was elected political leader of the party at a party convention in 1989. His ascendancy to party leadership, a post that is traditionally held by the prime minister, signified a crushing defeat for Herbert Blaize. At this point, not only was he under attack from the NDC, the GULP and the MBPM, but now his own party had turned against him. Following his election as party leader, Mitchell appealed to the NDC for a no-confidence motion in the government, an action he hoped would force early elections. Fearing that such an action might boost Mitchell's and the NNP's chances at the polls, the NDC refused to comply, preferring to contend with the beleaguered Blaize for the time being. The death of Herbert Blaize in December of 1989, three months prior to the national elections, finally brought an end to what had become a major political crisis and stalemate on the island.

Under the circumstances that prevailed during the post-invasion period, foreign support coming from the U.S. was largely responsible for Blaize's re-emergence in Grenadian politics. Had the coalition of centrists parties not been forged together by the U.S., under the threat of withholding its aid, it is quite possible that Blaize would have been elected to head the government. Having returned to private life during the four and one half years of PRG rule, Blaize's career as a politician had for all intents and purposes come to an end. Were it not for the U.S. fear of a Gairy victory in the 1984 elections, Blaize's retirement would undoubtedly have gone on uninterrupted.

There were many in Grenada who thought that the failure of the NNP government would allow history to repeat itself once again. As one shopkeeper in Birchgrove St. Andrew's said to me:

> Blaize is Gairy's best campaign manager. Every time we get Blaize in office, Gairy is bound to follow. The people always get so damn fed up with Blaize that they is happy to have Gairy come back again. You watch and see what go happen in the next election. Uncle Gairy going to come back into power in Grenada, and all those that mocked him when he was out, is going to catch hell when he return.

History did not repeat itself, however, and Gairy was unable to obtain victory in the 1990 elections, even in his own constituency. It now seems that the strong following that he enjoyed for many years in the rural areas has been irreversibly diminished. The death of Blaize and the fading of Gairy have finally created the opportunity for a generation of new leadership to rise to the forefront of Grenadian politics. Whether or not they will be able to handle the challenges and problems that confront the nation is a question that can only be answered in the future.

Notes

1 In my interviews with officials at the U.S. embassy, I was informed that the U.S. did not intend to maintain a permanent embassy in Grenada. Staff member, Phil French, informed me that the U.S. State Department wanted to gradually reduce its role and presence on the island as political calm and stability returned.

2 In an interview with a political leader who attended the Union Island conference, I was informed that positions within the NNP government were to be based upon the perceived strengths of the four parties that had been invited. Although Winston Whyte had been invited to the meeting, thus indicating that he was considered a serious candidate, his poor showing in the early polls diminished his ability to negotiate for an office in the new government.

3 The construction of the international airport at Point Salines became the focal point of heightened hostilities between the Reagan administration and the PRG. The U.S. government maintained that Grenada did not need a runway as long as the one that was being constructed by the Cubans, and postulated that the airport would be used for military purposes by the Cubans and Russians. Ironically, construction of the airport was completed by the U.S. and the controversial runway was built even longer than had originally been planned. For a discussion of U.S. opposition to the airport, see *Grenada The Peaceful Revolution* by Cathy Sunshine (Washington, D.C.: EPICA, 1980).

4 For a discussion of the treatment of Coard and the others accused of executing Bishop, see Ferguson, J. *Revolution in Reverse* (London: Latin America Bureau, 1990) p. 95, 96.

5 The most recent example of a political prisoner being pardoned and released from prison came in the case of Abu Bakhar, the leader of the Muslimeem, which attempted a coup against the Trinidadian government in 1990. For a discussion of the legal proceedings surrounding his pardon and release, see *Caribbean Week*, January 1994 Vol. 5. No. 6.

6 Brathwaite found that prior to the election, George Brizan enjoyed a 58% approval rating, according to his polls. This was the highest rating among the field of candidates at the time. See Brathwaite, F. "The 1984 Grenada Elections" (Cavehill, Barbados: University of the West Indies Press, 1985).

7   The closest that Blaize ever came to winning successive elections was in
    1962. Actually, there would not have been an election in that year had
    the Chief Administrator Lloyd not suspended the constitution, follow-
    ing charges of "Squandermania." Gairy won the election of 1961, fol-
    lowing four years of a Blaize-led government (1957-1961).

Chapter 8

The Basis of
Regime Support in Grenada

Survey Research Methodology

While a review and analysis of Grenada's political history provides one method of explaining the dramatic shifts in political leadership that have occurred since 1951, history alone can not tell the whole story. The rise of Gairy through his leadership of the uprising of 1951, the jockeying back and forth between the GNP and the GULP during the late 1950's and 1960's, the gradual rise of the NJM as the primary source of opposition to the Gairy regime, the 1979 NJM takeover followed by its collapse due to divisions within the party, and then the return and eventual decline of Herbert Blaize and the NNP all can be understood through an examination of history. Such an examination makes it possible to explain how and why the dramatic changes in political leadership that have occurred on the island were possible. It also makes it possible to explain why Grenada has deviated from the political patterns evident in other Commonwealth Caribbean countries.

However, even a thorough assessment of the island's political history leaves several questions about the reasoning and political behavior of the Grenadian people unanswered. For example, even after a review of the island's political history one is still left wondering whether the rise and fall of the three regimes was accompanied by fundamental changes in the allegiances of the populace? That is, to what extent has the ascent and decline of the three regimes been linked to changes in popular sentiments and preferences? Do the dramatic fluctuations in leadership reflect significant shifts in political values and attitudes? Moreover, given the differences with respect to the ideological orientation and leadership styles of Gairy, Bishop and Blaize, how do Grenadian citizens interpret these dramatic changes in political leadership? Finally, after experiencing life under the three regimes, how do Grenadians evaluate in retrospect the three leaders and the regimes that they led, and on what basis have the individual leaders been evaluated and judged by Grenadian citizens?

To find the answers to these questions I undertook a survey of one hundred and twenty Grenadians (N=120). Actually, my approach to the data collection involved more than conducting a simple survey because each individual was interviewed by me in person for approximately forty-five minutes to an hour. To get at the opinions, beliefs and personal evaluations of Grenadian politics from each respondent, I had to spend a considerable amount of time probing their responses to questions and analyzing the personal stories and anecdotes they recounted about experiences they had with the three regimes. Through the interviews I hoped to gain insight into the political values of the populace, particularly as it pertained to their attitudes toward politics and government generally. Were Grenadians simply a passive people who were susceptible to being misled by fast talking politicians or were they cynical, apathetic, and alienated from the political process? Were their political decisions influenced primarily by a coherent ideology or was self-interest the major factor at work? What differences were there among the population, with respect to age, social class, gender, area of residence, level of education, etc., in their views of the three leaders? And finally, how did the people explain the upheavals that had occurred on the island, particularly since the revolution of 1979, which had so profoundly altered the character of politics in Grenada?

From the start I knew that the interviews would be necessary because I was not going to be satisfied with developing an explanation of political change in Grenada that was based exclusively on an historical analysis. My personal experience in Grenada led to me to realize that most histories do not incorporate the actions, experiences and responses of ordinary folk. Even newspapers and government documents, the primary source material from which I constructed the contemporary political history of the island, typically limit their accounts of events to the actions taken by politicians, businessmen, the clergy and other "important actors" within society, while the role and views of the common folk remain largely invisible. Given my interest in understanding how the Grenadian populace responded to the changes in leadership that had occurred since 1951, I had to find some way of gaining access to their evaluations of the three leaders and the regimes that they led and incorporate these perspectives into my analysis.

To answer the questions I had posed, I created a sample of two hundred and fifty potential interviewees from a list of voters which I obtained from the voter registration rolls maintained by the Parliamentary Office on Elections through simple random sampling techniques. Through the use of random numbers, subjects names were selected from the registration rolls which are organized according to residence (village and parish). Once I had obtained an adequate sample that included names from across the island, I commenced with my effort to conduct the interviews by making personal contact with the individuals whose names appeared on the list.

Early on I encountered two problems. First, I experienced considerable difficulty locating the individuals whose names had appeared on the voter registration rolls. In most cases, I was able to find the household in which the individual lived, but often, the individual who had been identified was not at home. In such cases, I typically conducted an interview with a family member or a neighbor. Randomness and the anonymity of the respondents was maintained by my inability to predict or determine who I would end up being able to interview at any given household.

Secondly, in many cases my possession of a list of names for interviews raised suspicion on the part of prospective interviewees and others, who were concerned about my motives and wondered why their names had been selected. In most cases, these concerns were allayed by my willingness to interview whomever I contacted first and by my assurance of protecting their anonymity and the confidentiality of the data obtained. The fact that I was asking general questions about their political views and not about particular individuals also made the interviewing easier. Also, the presence of my five year old son, who accompanied me on most of the interviews, also allayed fears that I might be a spy or C.I.A. agent.

The questions I used in the survey were designed to test some of the broader theoretical propositions which had prompted me to undertake this research at the outset. In keeping with my desire to learn as much as possible about the thinking of those I interviewed, I decided to use questions which were open-ended and non-leading. This was in keeping with my inductive approach. I did not want to impose my categories upon the respondents nor did I want the concepts and categories that I was using to be artificially injected into my dialogue with them. The open-ended approach also allowed the respondents to speak freely, in a manner that felt natural and non-suggestive. The questions were kept relatively simple and straight forward, to reduce the possibility of misinterpretation. In most cases, I would pose a question and then follow up with an explanation of what I was trying to find out, in order to ensure that the respondent understood the intent of the question.

The first thirty interviews were used to formulate and refine the theoretical propositions I would use later to carry out my analysis of the three regimes. The five explanations of political support that I mentioned earlier (ideology, charismatic leadership, patronage, coercion and foreign support) all appeared in the literature as relevant explanations of regime survival. One of my objectives in using the survey was to test the theoretical propositions found in the literature on political behavior and regime survival in developing societies. The survey allowed me to probe the validity of these hypotheses as they pertained to the political attitudes of the respondents. Once I conducted the interviews, I sought to determine the extent to which these theoretical propositions were relevant to the responses that I had received. For example, in asking an individual which leader they felt had done most to help the country and why, I used the response to provide me with some indication of the political values of the respondent. If a respondent stated that the reason why s/he felt that Eric Gairy had done the most to help the country was because s/he had gained materially as a result of a policy or action taken by the Gairy regime, then it could be inferred that Gairy's strategy of using of patronage to court constituents may have influenced the respondent's feelings of support for that particular regime. Similarly, if a person stated that s/he felt Bishop was the best leader because of certain personal qualities he possessed (i.e. sincerity, intelligence, etc.), then such an answer could indicate that the promotion of Bishop's charismatic personality by the PRG had influenced this particular individual to support Bishop and the PRG.

While such an approach relied heavily on my interpretation of responses and, therefore, might seem to have been easily influenced by my own prejudices, the open-ended nature of the questions employed provided ample opportunity for elaboration. I recognized that the evaluations of the three leaders expressed by most individuals could be influenced by a variety of factors. For that reason I hoped that by providing each respondent with the opportunity to fully articulate their reason for taking a particular position, I could have more confidence in my ability to codify their responses with accuracy. Moreover, I believe that the cumulative effect of interpreting and codifying responses across a range of cases proved effective as a means of revealing patterns with respect to the values held by the Grenadian population. In presenting the data collected in the following pages I have not allowed my need to categorize the responses of those interviewed to dilute the complexity present in their political thought processes. My approach in presenting the data is to allow the voices of those interviewed to come through clearly, so that their sensibilities, priorities and concerns are not lost in my analysis.

In almost every interview, the respondents spoke as though they were very familiar with Grenadian politics, often expressing opinions which were well thought out and developed as a result of previous discussion and thought on these and related topics. Rarely were the questions posed unanswered. More often than not, I was forced to ask the respondents to limit their answers to my questions because time did not allow for a completely open-ended articulation of their views on politics and government. The topic was clearly one of great concern to most of those questioned, and for that reason the survey did not create opinions where none existed previously, it merely drew them out.

The interviews provided me with a means of ascertaining how ordinary Grenadians made political choices and formulated their political opinions. The interviews lent themselves to a discourse about many aspects of Grenadian politics: what constitutes good political leadership; what citizens should rightfully expect from their government; and, the political values of the individual and the society as a whole. To ensure that the complexity of opinions obtained is accurately conveyed, I have made very limited use of descriptive statistics to present a picture of Grenadian political attitudes and values in my analysis of the data collected through the survey. Instead, I have made extensive use of direct quotations extracted from the interviews. These, I believe, provide a more vivid picture of Grenadian perspectives because they convey the depth, complexity and diversity of the views I encountered. They quotes presented also enable the research to be enhanced by the substance of Grenadian ideas in a way that is often not possible in typical survey research or political opinion polls.

There have been other surveys of public opinion conducted in Grenada since the U.S. invasion. These polls are referenced in the final chapter as I attempt to draw conclusions from this study. In this chapter, however, I will use quotes obtained from the surveys to illustrate how the three regimes have been viewed and to ascertain on what basis they have been evaluated. When appropriate I will supplement the quotes with my own observations. The thirteen months that I spent in Grenada in 1982 and 1987, and the various experiences I have had there, provide me with yet another source of information that influences this analysis. The combination, I believe, shall provide the reader with a more in-depth perspective on Grenadian values and enable us to answer the questions that inspired this research.

Eric Gairy—Liberator or Dictator?

While I have never adhered to the notion that it is possible to engage in social research from a truly impartial and objective standpoint, particularly given that the process of selecting and framing questions always involves some assignment of priority based on the values of the inquirer, I consciously approached my research in Grenada with the goal of not prejudging my subject. I did so not because I hoped to shroud my research under the pretext of objectivity, but rather because I simply had no way of explaining the changes that occurred in Grenada during the five years that had lapsed since my last visit. As I have stated previously, I was a partisan, a supporter of the revolution and an outspoken critic of the invasion. Still, I did not want my prior knowledge of the country to limit what I could discover through my research. I was committed to allowing Grenadian voices to be heard distinctly and separately from my own, even if I strongly disagreed with what I heard. I believe that my approach worked, and on several occasions I found myself actually surprised by what I discovered.

Perhaps my greatest surprise during the course of the research was the depth and breath of support and respect that I found for Eric Gairy. Having lived in Grenada during the time of the revolution, the only references to Gairy that I had previously heard were negative. During that time period Gairyism had been equated with every possible social malady, from all aspects of underdevelopment, to repression, corruption and evil. Gairy himself had been elevated to the status of dictator by the revolutionaries, and even Grenadian-born calypsonian, The Mighty Sparrow, sang a song entitled "Dead or Live," in which Gairy was listed along with the Shah of Iran, Anastacio Samoza and Idi Amin as one of the great tyrants of the world after he had fallen from power. Such negative references to Gairy in the popular culture led me to believe that Gairy was completely discredited throughout the island.

However, during the course of conducting the interviews, I found that large numbers of people still expressed support for Eric Gairy. Almost all of the individuals interviewed possessed strong feelings about Eric Gairy; in most cases, they either loved him or they despised him. Of the 120 respondents to the survey, 22% identified Gairy as the person whom they felt had done the most to help the country. Slightly more, 25%, regarded Gairy as the leader who had been most supported by the people. (See Chart #1) Conversely, a higher percentage of 38% of the respondents identified Gairy as the leader they liked the least. (See Chart #3)

What was perhaps most interesting about those who liked and disliked Gairy was the degree of variance based upon age.

Among those who identified Gairy as Grenada's best leader, 69% were over the age of 55, while among those who regarded Gairy as the leader who had done the least to help the country, 72% were below the age of thirty. (See Chart #2) This sharp contrast in the political attitudes of Grenadians of different generations can be explained in two ways. First, Gairy's reputation as a champion of the poor was based upon his efforts in the trade union movement of the 1950's. Several of the elderly people I interviewed participated in that movement, or felt that they benefited directly from the labor movement led by Gairy. In the eyes of many of these individuals, the legacy of that movement continued to have tremendous meaning to their lives, and for that reason, they continued to view Gairy in a positive light.

Conversely, many of the younger people interviewed received their first exposure to politics during the late 1970s, at the time when the Gairy regime was in a period of decline. Many of them supported the NJM during the 1970s in their electoral campaigns and their protests against the Gairy regime. Furthermore, many of these respondents claimed to have been active during the period when the PRG was in power, and their memory of Gairy was based primarily on the vilification, blame and ridicule that had been heaped upon him by the PRG and its supporters. Certainly they had heard of his past heroics in the labor movement, but for many youth, Gairy's abuse of power during his years in office had completely negated any positive contribution he may have made.

Yet, despite the PRG's efforts to destroy any positive memory of Gairy, many persons on the island continue to hold him in high regard. Among those who identified Gairy as the leader

Chart #1
Which leader has done the most to help the country?
(N=120)

Leader	All Ages	N
Gairy	22%	(26)
Bishop	66%	(79)
Blaize	12%	(15)

Chart #2
Leader regarded as having done the most to help the
country by age of respondent

Leader	Age		
	under 30 (48%=58)	30 - 55 (34%=41)	over 55 (18%=21)
Gairy	22% (12)	27% (11)	69% (15)
Bishop	72% (41)	46% (18)	28% (5)
Blaize	6% (3)	27% (12)	3% (1)

who had done the most to help the country, many based their support for his leadership on the historic role he had played in leading the labor struggles of the 1950s. Many cited his courageous role in leading the "small man", as poor people are often called in Grenada, in the struggle of 1951. One forty-five year old teacher from Grande Anse described Gairy's role in this way:

> The emergence of Gairy in 1951 to lead the workers struggle against the rich land owners set the stage for the people's revolution in 1979. Gairy made it all possible by showing poor people that they could stand up for their rights in Grenada. It was really Gairy who brought an end to slavery, mental slavery.

Other Gairy supporters, or Gairyites as they are often referred to in Grenada, emphasized Gairy's commitment to providing for the interests of the poor, and his desire to ensure that the poor had an opportunity to participate in the politi-

Chart #3
Which leader did you like the least?

(N=120)

Leader

Gairy	38%	(46)
Bishop	12%	(14)
Blaize	50%	(60)

cal life of the nation in ways that had previously been reserved to the elites and the middle class. Many respondents mentioned his efforts to raise the wages of estate workers, and to provide them with holidays and sick leave. Others pointed to Gairy's interest in the residents of rural villages who had often been neglected by the colonial government, due to a tendency to place greater emphasis on the Town of St. George's and the Grande Anse tourist area located south of the capital.[1] One sixty-two year old woman from Happy Hill, a small village in the northern part of the parish of St. George's, described Gairy's role in developing the country in this way:

> Before Gairy came to power the poor people didn't have nothing. We could barely clothe we children or find the money for gas to cook we food. Gairy looked out for the little people. He put on the Easter Water Parade which was a big thing that made all Grenadians proud, and the Expo. He tried his best to give the poor man a chance to feel as though Grenada was his home too and not just the place for the big shots and tourists.

Another seventy-two year old man from Caliste, a small village located at the south western tip of the island, described the accomplishments of the Gairy regime in Caliste:

> Under Blaize, Caliste was least. We didn't get nothing from his government and he didn't give a damn about us. He knew we loved we Uncle Gairy, cause he was the one who brought us a school, he fixed we road and he put in a little post office. Gairy never forgot us in Caliste.

For the most part, however, Gairy supporters explained why they believed that Gairy had done most to help the country by citing personal benefits they received when he was in power, which they attributed to his regime or to Gairy himself. Some of the poorest people I interviewed in the southern part of St. George's parish (Grande Anse Valley, Woburn, etc.) told me that Gairy had given them the houses they were living in or at least had allowed them to build a home for themselves on government owned land. One mother of eight children in Grande Anse Valley, who was threatened with eviction by Blaize's NNP government, told me that her home had been built by Gairy's "Green Beasts." (Many Grenadians referred to the armed forces

Chart #4
Why did you like him the least?

Leader	too much corruption	too much repression	economic hardships	personality of leader	other
Gairy	16% (7)	52% (24)	9% (4)	12% (5)	11% (5)
Bishop	–	31% (5)	17% (2)	–	52% (7)
Blaize	9% (5)	5% (3)	73% (44)	8% (5)	5% (3)

under Gairy as the "Green Beasts," based upon their reputation for using violence against known opponents of the regime.) She went on to state that:

> Gairy sent his "Green Beasts" here to build a home for me and my children and this blasted government ain't goin to take it from me. Gairy has done so much to help the poor people in Grenada, and now this damn Blaize is trying to take what he didn't give.[2]

Many mentioned that they had received jobs during the time that Gairy was in power. In some cases, the respondents claimed that Gairy was personally responsible for their employment at a government job. One forty- eight year old woman from the village of Brizan told me that she had gone to see Gairy personally at one time, to request that her daughter who had recently completed secondary school be hired at the state-run General Hospital. Two weeks after her visit with Gairy, her daughter was hired. In her response to the question, the woman said:

> Gairy has done the most to help this country because I know for myself that when I went to him for help, asking for me daughter to get a job at the hospital, Gairy listen. He was always a good man if you was good to him. Uncle would never leave you with nothing if you went to him to ask for help.

Several others cited similar experiences of appealing directly to Gairy for financial assistance and being given gifts of ten or twenty dollars. Others said that Gairy had helped them with the courts and prison system, when members of their family had gotten into trouble with the law.

The responses of those who identified Gairy as Grenada's best leader or as the leader who had done the most to help the country indicate that personal, material benefit was by far the most salient factor influencing an individuals opinion. Of the 28% who cited Gairy as the best leader, 76% cited personal material benefit in their explanation of their opinion. Another 18% mentioned Gairy's historic role in leading the agricultural workers in the 1950s, while the remaining 6% made reference to the populist ideology of the regime (its commitment to helping the poor and willingness to take on the rich, etc.) as their reason for citing Gairy. (See Chart #7)

Among those who regarded Gairy as the leader who had done least to help the country, the reason given most often was the use of violence against opponents of the regime (52%). A significant number mentioned corruption (16%) as the primary factor, while several others (12%) made negative reference to his personality, using phrases such as arbitrary, unfair, malicious, wicked, etc. to describe him. Finally, many of the respondents (20%) said that they disliked Gairy because he was an embarrassment to the country. His belief in witchcraft, known as Obeah in Grenada, his belief in unidentified flying objects, his associations with individuals allegedly involved in organized crime, rumors of his exploits with women, and his lack of formal education were all mentioned as reasons for viewing Gairy negatively.

Most notable among Gairy's detractors were young people under the age of thirty, 58% of whom identified Gairy as the leader who had done least to help the country. Typical of the reasons given for such a negative view of Eric Gairy was this response by a twenty-four year old carpenter from the Town of Gouyave in the parish of St. John's:

> Gairy was a very vindictive man. If he knew you was against him, he would try to make it so that you couldn't work. Or, he would get his men from the Mongoose Gang to beat you. Eric Gairy never do nothing for Grenada except to victimize the people and make himself rich. The amount of people who has been hurt by Gairy is so high. There was a little girl living here in Gouyave . . . the Mongoose attacked her father and then they pulled off she clothes in front of the whole village. Is this type of thing that Gairy and his men do. That is why I hope he would go blind now. It would serve him right for all the wickedness he has done in Grenada.

In addition to the use of repression or coercion by the Gairy regime, several respondents also cited efforts which they believed were directed by Gairy to deprive them, their family or village of basic services or employment, based upon their political opposition to Gairy. As was mentioned earlier, Gairy's use of patronage involved a system of punishment and rewards; those who were loyal to Gairy received direct or indirect material benefits, while those who opposed him were denied material benefits and/or were also subjected to physical intimidation and violence. Only 6% of those who identified Gairy as the leader who had done the least to help the country mentioned the use of violence by the regime as the reason for their negative evaluation. However, 18% of those who disliked Gairy claimed to have been denied employment, harassed at their jobs or deprived of basic services in their villages as a result of opposition to Gairy.

One thirty-five year old woman from Boca village, located near the Grand E'tang rainforest in the parish of St.George's, described what she claimed was harassment carried out by the Gairy regime against her and her family:

> When Gairy was in power you had to support the GULP if you wanted work. I sent my daughter after she finished secondary school at St. Joseph's Convent to the Ministry for a job. She was a smart girl and I felt she should get work. Well, Gairy wanted to sexually exploit her, and when he find out who her father was, there was just no way she could get a job in government. My husband was with the JEWEL, and there was many times when the Mongoose would come here looking for him and end up destroying something at my home because they couldn't find him.

Another interesting pattern observed through an analysis of the survey data was the fact that 82% of those with more than secondary education identified Gairy as the leader who had done least to help the country. While such persons constituted only 6% of the entire survey, the results are revealing nonetheless. Nationally, individuals possessing more than secondary level education comprise less than 4% of the population. However, such persons tend to be concentrated in positions of influence, such as the churches, the media, business, education, higher ranking civil service positions and the professions. The fact that such respondents in the survey were

Chart #5
Leader liked best by educational level of respondent

Education (completed or partially completed)

Leader	primary (76%=91)	secondary (18%=22)	post-secondary (6%=7)
Gairy	42% (38)	17% (4)	–
Bishop	47% (43)	74% (16)	56% (4)
Blaize	11% (10)	9% (2)	44% (3)

overwhelmingly biased against Gairy is consistent with the fact that traditionally the middle class has supported Blaize and the Grenada National Party. (See Chart #5)

The reasons most typically given for disliking Gairy were often highly subjective, having to do with his style, personality, lack of formal education and manner of conducting political business One St. George's businessman I interviewed expressed his contempt for Gairy in the following way:

> Gairy was an ignorant buffoon. He was much more interested in lining his pockets and receiving meaningless honorary degrees than he was in solving the nation's problems. Gairy knew that he was inferior that is why he worked so hard to be accepted by Grenada's leading families, but he never could . . . The only reason why he was able to hold on to power for so long was because he had charmed so many of the ignorant people on the island, who to this day continue to call him Uncle Gairy . . .

Perhaps what was most interesting about the respondents that held positive attitudes toward Eric Gairy was that a significant number of those who identified Maurice Bishop as the leader who had done the most to help the country also spoke highly of Gairy. Such comments were unsolicited for there was no follow up question in the survey regarding who was Grenada's second best leader or who, in their opinion, was next in line as the leader who had made the greatest contribution to the development of the island. On their own, several respondents stated that while they felt Bishop had done the most to help the country and had been the leader most supported by the people, Eric Gairy had also made a significant contribution. Given the ideological differences between the two leaders, particularly as exemplified by their foreign policies, and given the constant vilification of Gairy carried out by Bishop's PRG, it might appear contradictory that some Bishop supporters would recognize the positive contributions made by Gairy during his years of leadership on the island. In the pages ahead, these and other perplexing questions which emerge from the survey shall be explored in an effort to understand the political reasoning of the respondents to the survey and, hopefully, of Grenadians generally.

The Appeal of Maurice Bishop

Since his death at the hands of members of the People's Revolutionary Army, Maurice Bishop has attained the status of martyr and national hero in the eyes of supporters and opponents alike. Bishop is highly regarded as a political leader by all sectors of Grenadian society, including his ideological opponents, and even some of those who were imprisoned by the PRG for activities that were once considered counter-revolutionary. At least part of this pervasive respect toward Bishop is due to the perception that he made the ultimate sacrifice for his nation, giving his life, and that his motives in leadership were genuine and sincere, even if considered misguided by some.

Among the respondents to the survey, Maurice Bishop was the leader most often identified as having done the most to help the country (66%), as having been the best leader (64%), and as the leader who was most supported by the people (66%). (See Chart #6) Among those who regarded Bishop as the best leader, 36% stated that it was due to his personal qualities as a leader, making explicit reference to his honesty, sincerity, concern for the poor, his unassuming persona or down-to-earth personality, and his personal warmth and compassion. 28% of the Bishop supporters expressed their reasoning in terms of the personal and societal benefits which had been experienced during the period that he was in power. Several cited the construction of the international airport, the provision for scholarships to Grenadian college students, and the development

Chart #6
Which Leader was Most Supported by the People?

(N=120)

Leader

Gairy	26%	(31)
Bishop	65%	(78)
Blaize	9%	(11)

of the Agro-Industries plant, as well as personal benefits, such as jobs and opportunities which had been created by the PRG, or the revolution, as they termed it. Finally, another 22% made mention of their support for the ideological direction provided by Bishop when he served in national office. Many of these respondents spoke favorably of the international standing achieved by Grenada while Bishop was in power, while others spoke positively of the relations with Cuba, his commitment to serving the poor and his willingness to stand up against U.S. aggression. (See Chart #7)

Typical among the answers given by those who expressed support for Bishop was a recognition and emphasis upon the personal qualities he possessed. In fact, several of the people I interviewed imbued Christ-like qualities upon Bishop, such as one forty-two year old woman from Grenville who said "like Christ, Bishop died for the sins of we Grenadians". His rescue by thousands of Grenadians from house arrest, his refusal to defend himself against the attacks by the military at Fort Rupert on October 19, 1983, and his apparently mistaken belief that the military would not turn their guns upon the people all served to reinforce the image of Bishop as a man with angelic qualities or as one Grenadian woman put it "a leader who had been blessed by God". The fact that his father, Rupert Bishop, had also attained martyr status as a result of his death by members of the Mongoose Gang while defending a group of school children at a anti-Gairy protest in St.George's added to the sense that Maurice Bishop was a leader who had sacrificed a great deal for his people.

Disproportionately, female respondents to the survey tended to emphasize Bishop's personal qualities when speaking of why

Chart #7
Why was this leader the most supported?

	personality	material benefits	societal benefits	ideology
Gairy	22% (7)	54% (16)	24% (8)	—
Bishop	36% (28)	28% (22)	14% (11)	22% (17)
Blaize	12% (1)	12% (1)	64% (6)	12% (1)

they felt he was Grenada's best leader or why they felt he had done the most to help the country. 67% of those who expressed support for Bishop in the survey were women. (See Chart #8) This is particularly significant because women comprised only 58% of the sample.[4] Several mentioned Bishop's good looks and his physical features, such as his height, when describing what it was that they liked about him. More often, their comments were filled with emotion and grief about his death and overwhelming feelings of dismay about the prospects for Grenada's political future in the aftermath of his assassination. One thirty-four year old female shopkeeper from Mount Moritz, a rural village in the north part of the parish of St. George's, described her feelings about Bishop in this way:

> Bishop was our only real leader. Grenada has never had another like him and we never will. Bishop was a special man, a loving man. He cared for the people of this country, and he died because he loved this country too much. Bishop gave the people of this country hope. It was

Chart #8
Which leader was liked the best
by gender of respondents
Gender

Leader	Female (58%-60)	Male (42%=51)
Gairy	24% (17)	20% (10)
Bishop	63% (43)	72% (37)
Blaize	13% (9)	8% (4)

Chart #9
Grenada Population by Gender[5]

Male   48%
Female   52%

> a real thing to see how the youth became excited by Bishop, and how
> all the people would go out to hear him at the rallies and functions.
> There could never be another leader like him.

Similar sentiments concerning the irreplaceability of Bishop
were expressed to me by men and women alike. One forty-four
year old fisherman from the town of Sauters, located on the
northern tip of the island, explained the people's love for
Bishop to me in the following way:

> The way the people of Grenada loved Bishop makes it hard for an-
> other leader to come now to take his place. It is like a woman who has
> a good husband, one who takes care of her, buys her what she needs,
> provides for his family, loves his woman. If that man is to die, another
> man can't just jump in there and take his place. The woman will al-
> ways be thinking about the husband she lost. The next man must be at
> least as good as the last one, otherwise it would never work. That is
> like us in Grenada now. Bishop is gone, and all these different jokers
> trying to become the next leader. But the people don't even want to
> hear them, cause they still bad for Bishop, and they just can't forget
> so easy.

Without question, the strongest base of support for Bishop,
as evidenced through the survey but also widely acknowledged
throughout the society, is among the youth. Of those who identified Bishop as Grenada's best leader in the survey, 72% were
under the age of thirty. (See Chart #1) Many of the young
people I interviewed told me that they had served in the militia or army, were members of the National Youth Organization or in some way had actively participated in activities which
were created by the revolution. Several claimed to have taken
up arms in defense of the island against U.S. servicemen during the invasion, while many others claimed to have been involved in the armed takeover of the Gairy government of March
13, 1979. The young people interviewed were also far more
likely to express support and approval for the ideological di-

rection of the nation under Bishop's leadership. They were also much more likely to use the language adopted by the leadership of the revolution in expressing themselves, using terms such as bourgeois to describe elites on the island, imperialists to describe the U.S., and people's revolution to describe the period from 1979 to 1983.

The young people interviewed were also much more likely to defend the socialist orientation of the PRG and its relations with Cuba and other socialist countries. One twenty-seven year old laborer from Grande Anse explained his support for Bishop in the following way:

> As the leader of the Revo, Bishop understood that he would have to do things to benefit the masses if the country was to progress. Gairy took us a little way, but then he get mixed up in the Obeah thing and start to like the power too much. It was Bishop and the Jewel who wanted to take the country to a higher level, a more democratic level, where the poor people, who is the majority in Grenada, would have a better life. All the other governments was run for the benefit of the bourgeoisie. Only the PRG was truly committed to the masses.

Of course, there were also respondents who did not feel as positively about Bishop's role as leader of the country. Only seven of the thirty professionals, business people and ministers interviewed ranked Bishop as Grenada's best leader. This appears to have been largely due to their belief that Bishop was anti-business and placed unnecessary hardships on the private sector.[6] Among respondents fifty-five years old and older, only 28% expressed support for Bishop and the PRG. Among people between the ages of thirty and fifty-five, there was a nearly even split, with 46% supporting Bishop, and the remainder supporting either Blaize or Gairy. (See Chart #1)

The reasons given for not supporting Bishop varied among the respondents. Respondents with higher income and more education tended to emphasize Bishop and the PRG's negative posture toward business and government infringements on activity within the private sector. While several of these acknowledged some of the positive steps taken by the PRG in the area of fiscal management, particularly with respect to the approach taken toward the World Bank, for example, the overall sentiment expressed charged Bishop and the PRG with unfairly interfering with the operations of private business through the imposition of tariffs on imports and other measures. Here is an example of how one Grenadian businessmen expressed his criticisms of the PRG:

> The communists didn't know nothing about business, yet still them was always trying to tell the business people what they can and can not do. One minute them is encouraging tourism and telling those of us who run the hotels that we must expand so more tourists can come to Grenada. The next minute them telling us how much we must pay the maids and people working for the hotel. You can't do business like that.

Most frequently, the criticisms expressed by those who identified Bishop as the leader who had done the least to help the country emphasized the denial of basic freedoms such as detention without trial, the lack of elections, and the lack of freedom of press, association and speech. While only 12% of the respondents identified Bishop as the leader who had done the least to help the country, similar sentiments were expressed by others who cited either Gairy or Blaize as their least favorite. Interestingly, even some of those who expressed support for Bishop also mentioned their disapproval for the way in which political freedoms were handled.

For example, one thirty-two year old shoemaker from Caliste that I interviewed told me that he felt Bishop had been Grenada's best leader even though his brother had been unfairly imprisoned by the PRG. He explained his reasoning to me like this:

> I feel that Bishop was the best of the leaders Grenada has had, but I didn't like all of the things that went on when Bishop was in power. A lot of people from Tivoli and other villages in St. Andrew's were locked up by the PRG. My brother was one of them, and the thing is that I know my brother loved the revolution. He loved Bishop too. But if you talk to him about it now you will find that he is still bitter. A whole lot of people loved the revolution, but they didn't like the way some things went on.

Several of those who expressed criticisms of Bishop and the PRG mentioned their disapproval of the militarization of the country which took place while Bishop was in power. The formation of the militia and the military training received by many civilians, including many young people, was cited by a number of Bishop's critics as an aspect of the revolution that repulsed them. Several of the older respondents expressed their concern that exposure to the use of weapons and military life had deteriorated the values of the youth and led to greater disrespect by the youth for the seniors on the island. One fifty-eight year old grandmother expressed her feelings on the matter like this:

> During the revo, every little boy and girl had a gun. The PRA (People's Revolutionary Army) was teaching all of them how to shoot and warning them all the while to look out for counters (counter revolutionaries) Meanwhile just who do you think the counters are that them was talking about? It was we, the parents and grandparents of the children, who was trying to send them to church to teach them Christ's way. This is the thing I didn't like about the revo; too much guns!

Despite the criticism, however, most of those who did not support Bishop expressed some form of respect for him and his leadership. It is significant that several of the respondents who identified either Gairy or Blaize as the leader who had done the most to help the country cited Bishop as the leader who had been most supported by the people. In many cases the respondents themselves were strong partisans of either Gairy or Blaize, but when asked for their objective assessment regarding which leader was most supported or most loved by the people, many grudgingly admitted that Bishop had generated the strongest following. One seventy-two year old man from Caliste explained Bishop's appeal to me in this way:

> I will always believe that Eric Gairy was Grenada's best leader, because if it were not for him most of the poor people in Grenada wouldn't have nothing. But these young people in Grenada don't understand that. They like Bishop because the man could talk so well. He fooled them, because they did not know that he was a communist. But I knew it. I knew all along that the man was a thief. But the young people in this country was bad for Bishop, even some of the old. That is the honest to God truth.

Blaize supporters made similar acknowledgements, though they too were openly critical if not hostile to Bishop and the regime he led. One of the lawyers I interviewed, who was a member of Blaize's NNP, said the following about Bishop:

Bishop set this country back a lot by bringing the Cubans in here. He drove out the foreign investors and caused a lot of problems for the businessmen on the island. But, I must say this, the man had vision. Everyone had talked for years about how Grenada needed an international airport, but it was Maurice who started to build the thing. Bishop was a doer, he didn't just talk about things. If you look at all the things them boys in the PRG accomplished in just four and a half years, you would have to admit that they did a lot. A lot of it was shit, yes, but them did some good too.

Overall, the respondents expressed respect for Bishop, if not overwhelming admiration. Undoubtedly, the fact that he was assassinated has added to the respect and appreciation expressed for Bishop. Even the NNP government, which went to great lengths to erase the memory of Bishop and the revolution, did not engage in a propaganda campaign directed at the legacy of Maurice Bishop. In part, their avoidance of any denigration of Bishop seems to be due to their recognition that there is still a reservoir of support for him on the island. Other leaders of the PRG, particularly those who are still in prison, as well as those who have left the country and those who remain active politically within the country, have all been the objects of political attacks. But there appears to be a degree of reverence subtly displayed toward Bishop which even his most bitter opponents maintain.

To this day, there is no official memorial in honor or recognition of Maurice Bishop. The absence of such a symbol is a sore point to many Grenadians. There has been an effort led by the Maurice Bishop Patriotic Front to designate his birthday as a national holiday. However, this is unlikely to occur in the near future. Despite the incredible amount of support for Bishop revealed through the survey and acknowledged by other opinion polls, rapprochement will probably not occur until the population and the ruling political parties have come to terms with the trauma created by the events of October 1983.

The Re-emergence of Herbert Blaize

Like an old prizefighter making a comeback from retirement, Herbert Blaize returned to the center stage of Grenadian politics in 1984. The NNP easily won the election in that year, although Gairy and his GULP partisans cried foul play and accused the United States of unfair interference. At sixty-seven, Blaize was selected over several younger political aspirants because it was generally believed that as a former leader of the country, Blaize would have the credibility to pull the country together in the wake of the traumatic events of 1983. According to one leader who attended the Union Island conference, Blaize was selected because it was felt that he could be most easily manipulated by the United States:

> Blaize has always been the pawn of the wealthy elites on the island. He is a known quantity. They felt they could rely on Blaize to do the things that Uncle Sam wanted to see get done in Grenada. The rest of us went along with it because the U.S. representatives told us that we wouldn't get no U.S. aid if we didn't (Interview 11/4/87).

Even for an experienced politician such as Blaize, the task which confronted him at the time of his election was formidable. The island's agricultural economy, which had been disrupted by the invasion, was in total disarray. Loan and trade agreements that had been made by the PRG were discarded, particularly when those involved communist nations. The coalition government that had been forged together by the U.S. was fragile, and by 1986, George Brizan and Francis Alexis, two important ministers in the government, defected to form their own opposition party. Then there was the matter of the PRG supporters, in particular the former members of the People's Revolutionary Army, most of whom were now unemployed. Concerned with the potential threat posed by these idle young men, the government sought to find ways to incorporate them into the workforce.

At the time the survey was conducted, August 1987 through February 1988, public opinion toward the Blaize regime was at a low point. 64% of the respondents identified Blaize as the leader who had done the least to help the country. Only 12% cited him as the leader who had done the most to help the country. A mere 11% mentioned him as Grenada's best leader, and only 9% as the leader who was most supported by the people.

The most frequently expressed complaint about Blaize and his leadership of the government concerned his handling of the economy. References to the high rate of unemployment, which at the time was said to be as high as 40% of the labor force, were a common source of resentment and frustration. Although few respondents to the survey stated that they were unemployed (8%) when asked about their occupation, several claimed to have lost their jobs and were engaged in activities such as fishing or farming. These are largely subsistence activities and seldom generate adequate income for the average Grenadian.

In addition to the high unemployment, the government announced a plan to retrench a large number of government workers in 1987. Several of the respondents to the survey cited unemployment and retrenchment as an indication of Blaize's insensitivity to the poor. Such a charge was expressed by one thirty year old electrical worker from the village of Mt. Parnassus, located in the parish of St. George's:

> The first time Blaize ruled the country he was only interested in the business people. Now he come again with the same blasted thing. It's like he is trying to bring the country back to colonial days. The poor man don't have nothing in Grenada now. As long as Blaize stay in power he will just continue to listen to the U.S. and give the poor people hell.

Of the respondents who identified Blaize as the leader who had done the least to help the country, 73% based their answer on his treatment of the poor. (See Charts #3 and #4) Additionally, a majority of those respondents stated that Blaize was merely carrying out policies which were designed by the United States. Chief among those policies cited by the respondents as evidence of U.S. manipulation was the VAT (Value Added Tax). The VAT had been implemented by the Grenadian government in 1986 following a recommendation by a U.S. economic advisor who suggested that the government eliminate personal income tax and impose a value added tax on all goods and services. At the time of my field work, the most prevalent response to this change in policy was one of outrage. Whereas the majority of Grenadians had previously paid little or no income tax due to the small salaries they earned, the new VAT was felt by everyone in the society. Several of the respondents cited the VAT as an example of Blaize's contempt for poor people and evidence of his interest in serving the needs of the wealthy on the island.

Relatively few of the respondents perceived Blaize's relationship with the United States negatively. That is to say, most of the respondents welcomed U.S. aid, although some expressed concern that Grenada's sovereignty was compromised by its subservient relationship to the United States. The majority of those respondents who characterized Blaize as a pawn of the U.S. stated that Blaize was not taking full advantage of the help that the United States was willing to offer Grenada. They felt that Blaize was allowing himself to be manipulated by the U.S. without reaping adequate rewards for his favors. This was particularly true of the business people I interviewed. Edwin DeCall, one of the larger business owners, claimed to have originally been a supporter of Blaize and the NNP. He expressed his criticism of the NNP government in this way:

> No matter how much money and assistance the United States gives to Grenada it will not make one damn bit of difference. This government has no fiscal plan. It has no plan for economic development which will guide its policies. If you ask them for a copy of their plan they will tell you that they don't believe in planning. What kind of nonsense is this! How can you call yourself leading a country without a plan for the economy? You must know what it is you want to do if you are going to see some progress. I don't blame the U.S. for this. It's not their fault. It is the fault of this blasted government which don't know what the hell it's doing.

Other respondents felt that the United States must share the blame for the failures of the Blaize government. One thirty-eight year old seamstress from the Town of Victoria in St. Mark's parish explained the failure of the Blaize government in the following manner:

> After the invasion, Reagan was watching out for Grenada. He wanted to see the country recover and achieve progress. But he choose the wrong man to lead the country. I must blame them for the problems that we are seeing now because it is they who put Blaize back in. He is the man in charge, yes, but they is the ones who put him there.

Blaize's poor health and age was often cited as a factor to explain the reason for problems experienced by his government. Many of the respondents said they felt that Blaize was too sick and too old to lead the country. A number stated that younger leadership was needed to address the problems facing the country. Even in Blaize's home parish, the neighboring island of Carriacou, several of the respondents stated that Blaize had outlived his usefulness as a leader. One twenty-five year old taxi cab driver from Carriacou made the following point when describing Blaize:

> The last time Blaize was in Carriacou not one of the cab drivers would pick him up to carry him to his house. He had to call a friend on the phone to come for him. We are tired of the man. All he has done is to make promises to the people of Carriacou. We have not seen one tourist boat here yet. The man is just too old and feeble to be Prime Minister. It is time for him to go on and retire and let a younger man take his place. His mind and body ain't functioning right any more.

Among the respondents who were critical of Blaize, there was also a general feeling that he had not taken advantage of the many opportunities that were available to his regime. Not only was his government the recipient of several millions of dollars in U.S. aid, but several of the respondents felt that Blaize was in a position to build upon the projects that had been initiated by the PRG. One twenty-seven year old laborer from the village of Crochu, located in the parish of St. David's, made the following analogy:

> Bishop set up everything for Blaize. It's like Blaize come to the kitchen to find that the food is all prepared. All he have to do is set the table and dish out the food. Bishop had done all the work before he came. But still, the old man is messing up the meal for the people.

While the overwhelming sentiment expressed by the respondents was one of dissatisfaction with Blaize and his government, there were those who praised him. Typically, those who expressed support for Blaize cited the role he played in providing stability for the country following the coup and invasion. Even some of those who were not to be counted among his admirers stated that Blaize was an honest man, that he had never personally been involved in any corruption, and that he was one of few leaders that could be trusted following the invasion. The fact that he led the NNP to victory in the election of 1984, capturing over seventy percent of the votes, also sug-

Chart #10
Which leader did most to help the country
by occupation of respondent

Occupation

Leader	farmer (26%)	prof. (4%)	unskilled laborer (27%)	bus. (6%)	skilled fish. (13%)	craft (9%)	unem. (15%)
Gairy	42%	0	48%	14%	38%	26%	44%
Bishop	47%	8%	46%	32%	55%	64%	52%
Blaize	11%	92%	6%	54%	7%	10%	4%

gests that many of the voters trusted his leadership and per-haps if the survey had been conducted earlier, different re-sults would have been obtained.

As was true in the past, most of the business people, profes-sionals, and individuals in high status occupations expressed support for Blaize. Though such individuals accounted for only 5% of the respondents, the fact that many of them held influ-ential positions in the society suggests that Blaize continued to enjoy support in a very important sector. People with more than secondary education comprised only 6% of the survey, and 76% of them ranked Blaize, Grenada's best leader. (See Charts #5) Such results are not surprising, given Blaize's and the GNP's traditional base of support among the urban middle class, business sector and estate owners. It should be noted that while support for Blaize among other categories of re-spondents was largely negligible, the fact that he is supported by influential groups and individuals such as businessmen, clergymen, estate owners, and professionals provides Blaize with a very important base of support, whose influence in Grenadian politics and economy far exceeds their numbers.

Several of the businessmen I interviewed expressed criti-cisms of Blaize even though nearly all regarded him as the best of Grenada's three leaders. Several criticized the lack of economic planning and the government's policies toward taxa-tion on imported goods. Others criticized him for his auto-cratic manner in dealing with members of his party and government, and blamed him for the defection of Brizan and Alexis. Yet, nearly all of the businessmen interviewed held Blaize in high regard, particularly in comparison to Gairy and Bishop. Largely, their reasoning seemed to be motivated by self interest, as can be seen from this comment made by one of the island's car dealers:

> Every government understands the importance of a strong private sector to the economy. And every leader that has ever held power in Grenada has promised to work with the private sector to make our job easier. But each and every time, all the politicians do is to interfere with business. The best thing is for government to stay out of business altogether. Leave business to the businessmen, and we'll leave politics to the politicians. Blaize is the only man who understands this. He has tried to leave us alone, although he too has made some stupid mistakes. But when judged next to Gairy and Bishop there is clearly no comparison. Blaize has been our man.

One disclaimer which must be made regarding the survey is that because it was conducted while Blaize was serving as Prime Minister, attitudes toward him and his regime may have been more negative than if the survey been conducted a few years after his term in office, particularly after his death. Under the leadership of Blaize, the NNP clearly won the election of 1984 by a landslide. Hence, at some point there must have been a higher degree of popular support for him earlier on during his last term in office. It may be that Grenadian voters viewed a vote for Blaize as a means of ensuring continued financial support for Grenada, since he clearly was the candidate favored by the U.S. It is also true that political attitudes toward a leader or government are not static; they change depending upon a number of factors, primary among which is the degree of prosperity in the economy. In the succeeding pages I will explore some of the reasons for changes in political attitudes, in an attempt to explain how and why leaders have fallen from grace with the Grenadian public and the extent to which a lack of popular support has bearing upon the ability of a regime to retain political power.

Living Conditions and Political Choices

During the course of my research in Grenada, I wanted to know the extent to which the living conditions experienced by those

I interviewed influenced their attitudes toward the three regimes. To obtain this information, I asked each person I interviewed the following question: "How would you describe your living conditions during the time that Gairy, Bishop and Blaize were in power?" In responding to the question, I asked each person to describe the living conditions that they experienced during the period when each of the three leaders was in power. I followed this up with more specific questions regarding whether or not the individual was employed, at what sort of job, and whether they considered the pay they received to be adequate for their needs. Later, I attempted to determine the extent to which there was a correlation between how a person described his/her living conditions when Gairy, Bishop and Blaize were in power and how they felt about the three leaders.

Most of the answers to this question were based upon the perceptions of the respondents' personal experience. Some respondents attempted to make an overall assessment of what living conditions were like for most Grenadians during the period that a particular leader was in power. However, more typically, respondents based their answers on whether or not they were employed during the period in question or how they or members of their family fared with respect to economic opportunities under the three regimes. For those whose employment was tied to agriculture, the prices obtained for their crops on domestic and international markets was a relevant factor. Cost of living and the availability of certain goods at local retail outlets were also some of the criteria employed by the respondents in answering this set of questions.

Among those respondents who did attempt to make a more general assessment of living conditions during the three periods, there was a tendency to base their answers upon their own experience. This was particularly true for the business people I interviewed, many of whom tended to speak on behalf of the private sector generally, or for the nation as a whole. The following comment made by a St. George's shoe salesmen is an example of this kind of generalization:

> When Bishop and the PRG was in power people could hardly get the things they need. The stores were nearly empty at Christmas time because of the taxes imposed by the government. It was terrible thing man. Christmas is a very special time for Grenadians. People save their

money all year long to buy a little something for their family. The damn government was spoiling things up for everyone. They was making it real real hard on the businessman especially.

Non-businessmen also made similar generalizations, but most often these were based upon the respondents perception of what living conditions were like for others in similar socio-economic circumstances. For example, a number of the poorer respondents answered the questions about living conditions by saying that nothing had changed. One forty-four year old woman from the village of Birchgrove in St. Andrew's answered the question like this:

> The poor have always had it hard in Grenada. It don't really matter who is in power, so long as you are poor you must work hard every day. Gairy did try to help the poor folks some. Bishop did a bit too. Blaize ain't done a blasted thing for us. But always the poor people have it hard. Sometimes it is hard just to find a little something to eat. It ain't easy in Grenada.

There was also a tendency among many of the respondents to judge progress in living conditions upon the successful implementation of economic development projects. Often, the projects referred to had no direct impact upon the respondent but were cited by the respondents as symbols of national progress. This was particularly true for the Bishop supporters who often cited the construction of the airport, the development of the Agro-Industrial plant and the establishment of the Fisheries School as examples of progress. In response to the question about living conditions when Bishop was in office, one twenty-six year old male school teacher from Fontenoy in the parish of St. George's said the following:

> Living conditions have generally been good under all the leaders. There is one thing very special about Grenada; a person can always find himself something to eat. Even if its just some green fig or bread fruit, you can't go hungry in Grenada. But, we did make some more rapid progress when Bishop was in power. Bishop got the country moving for the first time. Things started to happen all over the island Roads were being repaired, even in the small villages in the country. The whole nation was mobilized to achieve some progress.

Analysis of the responses to the survey questions reveals interesting associations between how an individual felt about a particular leader or regime, and how they felt about living conditions while a particular regime held power. (See Charts #1-#15) Among Gairy supporters, the vast majority (76%) stated that living conditions were better when Gairy was in power. The majority of these based their answer upon personal benefits they had received during the time that Gairy was in office. Most often cited as an indication of better living conditions were the availability of jobs, housing and community services. In their responses to the question, Gairy supporters often credited him personally with providing the benefits that were cited. This can be seen in the response given by a fifty-three year old woman from the village of Mt. Airy in the parish of St. George's to the question about living conditions during the Gairy period:

> Things was much better when Gairy was in power. Prices was not so high, and you could always find work, especially if you was with Uncle. Gairy always took care of his people. My husband and my son had a good job with the government back then, and things were not so hard as they is now.

Gairy supporters were split in their views on living conditions under the PRG, with 28% saying they were good, 34% saying they were bad, and 38% saying they were O.K., neither good nor bad. These mixed feelings about living conditions under Bishop and the PRG, correspond with the stated attitudes of Gairy supporters toward the PRG. Only 22% of those who identified Gairy as Grenada's best leader cited Bishop as the leader who had done the least to help the country. In contrast, 78% of the Gairy supporters said that Blaize had done the least to help the country. This corresponds with the responses given by Gairy supporters to questions about living conditions under Blaize and the NNP. 72% of the Gairy supporters said that conditions had gotten worse while Blaize was in power, while only 4% said living conditions were good, and 24% said they were O.K.

Similar results were obtained through an analysis of Bishop supporters, with 84% saying that living conditions were good while Bishop was in power. As was pointed out earlier, many of the Bishop supporters cited progress achieved in the economic development of the country under the PRG as an indication of improved living conditions. There were also some

Chart #11
How would you describe living conditions during the period that Gairy, Bishop and Blaize were in power?

(N=120)

Leader	Good	Bad	Mixed/O.K.
Gairy	42% (50)	37% (44)	21% (26)
Bishop	58% (69)	34% (41)	8% (10)
Blaize	7% (8)	73% (88)	20% (24)

who spoke of the personal benefits which they had received during the four and one-half years that the PRG was in power. One twenty-eight year old man from Carriacou responded to the question about living conditions like this:

> During the revolution there was much more opportunity for the youths to educate themselves because the government provided scholarships to go abroad and study. I myself was able to go to Bulgaria to study mechanics for two years. Now I know a trade, and no matter what this government does I will always find work because I have a trade. I owe that to the revolution, and there are a lot of others like me who have skills that they learned when they studied overseas.

Bishop supporters were mixed in their statements about living conditions under Gairy and Blaize. 48% said that conditions were bad while Gairy was in power, while 35% said they were good and 17% said they were O.K. 55% of the Bishop supporters said that conditions were bad under Blaize, while another 28% said they were good and 17% said they were O.K. These results also correspond with the stated attitudes of Bishop supporters toward Gairy and Blaize. Of those who identified Bishop as Grenada's best leader, 33% cited Gairy as the leader who had done the least to help the country, while 67% cited Blaize.

Finally, among Blaize supporters, there was also a strong correlation between support for Blaize and responses indicating that living conditions were good, if not better, while he was in power. 85% of those who identified Blaize as the leader who had done the most to help the country said that they felt living conditions had improved while Blaize was in power. Since

Chart #12
How were living conditions under the three leaders?
(Gairy Supporters)

Leader	Good	Bad	Mixed/O.K
Gairy	76%	–	24%
Bishop	28%	34%	38%
Blaize	4%	77%	19%

many of these respondents were people with higher incomes and business people, there may have been a tendency on the part of these respondents to discuss favorably the state of the nation's economy during the recent period when Blaize had held power. One thirty-four year old rum factory manager from Westerhall, St. David's made the following comment about living conditions since the election of Blaize:

> When Blaize won the election he brought stability to the country, and stability is always good for business. Now people feel safer about making investments. I have some friends in England who are going to invest plenty of money in this here estate. They would not do it if the political situation on the island did not seem secure. So you must credit Blaize for bringing that kind of reassurance to the country. And once business is thriving again in Grenada, well everyone is bound to benefit because more people will be working, so they will have more money in their pockets.

Blaize supporters generally held negative views with regard to the quality of living conditions under the Gairy and Bishop regimes. The vast majority, 72%, felt that conditions were bad

Chart #13
How were living conditions under the three leaders?
(Bishop Supporters)

Leader	Good	Bad	Mixed/O.K.
Gairy	12%	65%	23%
Bishop	85%	15%	–
Blaize	28%	55%	17%

Chart #14
How were living conditions under the three leaders?
(Blaize Supporters)

Leader	Good	Bad	Mixed/O.K.
Gairy	18%	75%	7%
Bishop	12%	72%	6%
Blaize	82%	4%	14%

under Bishop, and an even higher 75% felt that living conditions were bad under Gairy. Such an overwhelmingly negative view toward living conditions under the two regimes does not relate directly to the views expressed about the two regimes. Relatively few, 26%, of the Blaize supporters cited Bishop as the leader who had done the least to help the country. However, in their comments about Bishop, positive remarks were largely reserved to respect for his personal attributes, while the bulk of the criticism was based upon disagreement with his ideological orientation and his treatment of the private sector. Since the PRG's ideological orientation was largely seen as being manifest in the economic policies of his regime, it may be that the negative views about living conditions during the Bishop period were based largely upon the respondents' feelings toward the economic policies advocated and implemented by the PRG.

Generally, the analysis of the responses to the questions about living conditions under the three regimes revealed a high correlation between how one felt about a regime and how one perceived living conditions while that particular leader held power. This does not necessarily mean that there is a causal relationship between the two attitudes. It simply confirms what most politicans know: there is a correlation between how one perceives their living conditions and how one feels about a particular regime. This is a widely known truism of politics, a bread and butter issue, but one that is nonetheless a source of considerable consternation for political leaders in poor countries like Grenada. Satisfying the needs of the population in a poor country such as Grenada is an extremely difficult task. Moreover, not all the people have the same needs. When establishing priorities, governments are forced to make choices about which interests within the population will take precedent over others. The kinds of decisions that are made by political leaders regarding these priorities often has tremendous bearing upon how they are viewed by the citizenry, and ultimately, how long they are able to hold on to political power.

Choosing Future Leaders

Having lived through the Gairy, Bishop and Blaize regimes, the Grenadian people have experienced three very different leaders, each one possessing a different style of leadership and taking a different approach to the socio-economic development of the island. At this point, with the deaths of Bishop and Blaize, and the poor health of Eric Gairy, the stage has been set for new leadership to emerge on the island. In 1990, a relatively new party, the National Democratic Congress (NDC), won the national elections, and Nicholas Brathwaite, the former Chairman of the Interim Government (1983-84) was selected to serve as Prime Minister. The NDC did not, however, win enough seats on the Parliament to form a ruling majority, and had to form a coalition with the GNP. The most recent election in June of 1995 was won by the NNP, now headed by Keith Mitchel. Although the NNP won eight seats and therefore did not need to form a coalition with another party to rule, Mitchel has already been confronted by several allegations of corruption and illegal behavior. Over a decade after the U.S. invasion, politics on the island are still unpredictable, if not unstable, and the political future of the island and the direction that will be taken in the years ahead remains unclear.

One of the questions asked during the course of the survey may shed some light on Grenada's political future. (See appendix) Question number nine of the survey asked the following: "When you vote for someone in the next election, what is the most important thing you will look for as you determine who would make the best leader?" The intent of the question was to allow the respondents to state for themselves what sorts of characteristics they considered important when making a decision regarding the choice of political leadership. This question also provided another way of getting at the basis of regime support.

Undoubtedly, there are many factors that may influence an individual when a choice about political leadership is being made. Is the candidate perceived to be honest and trustworthy? Will s/he live up to the promises made during the campaign? Will s/he look out for my interests and the interests of my community or interest group? Will s/he be able to find solutions to the problems facing the society and the economy? Should I vote at all, and why? Given the variety of considerations that may influence voting behavior, I sought to use this question to ascertain what some of the major factors influencing political preferences might be.

My impression from speaking to many Grenadians was that there was a high degree of cynicism towards politicians and politics generally. The splits within the NNP coalition, combined with the constant attacks and incriminations leveled by politicians against one another, seemed to severely undermine the credibility of many political leaders. Moreover, the shifting alliances between Grenadian politicians, such as Keith Mitchell's efforts to undermine Blaize within the NNP, and Gairy's recruitment of Raphael Fletcher followed by his prompt dismissal, has generated distrust and a lack of faith toward the existing political parties. Such a sentiment was vividly expressed by a twenty-nine year old male from Tempe, located in the parish of St. George's:

> Grenadians have had enough of politricks. We have been through Gairyism, communism and colonialism once again under Blaize. Most of the people is so damn fed up now with all of these parties and politicians that they don't want to see another election no time soon. You just don't know who to trust again. Bishop was good, but the rest of these men is just a bunch of thieves and criminals.

Similar sentiments were expressed by 16% of the respondents to question number nine of the survey. Within that category I have included those who have said they will not vote at all in the next election. Interestingly, the majority of those who expressed such a negative attitude toward all existing politicians and parties were young people under the age of thirty. 82% of those who said they would not vote in the next election or that they did not trust any politicians were thirty years old or younger. The fact that the majority of such respondents identified strongly with Maurice Bishop may indicate that they have become disillusioned with Grenadian politicians in the aftermath of Bishop's death. Particularly because he was assassinated by members of his own party, there is a feeling that even those who claim to have been his allies can not be trusted. It is even less likely that such persons could be led to support any of the more moderate or conservative parties, since they tend to express a more left-leaning ideological orientation. (See Chart #11)

Another example of such a political stance can be seen from this statement made by a twenty-five year old fisherman from the Town of Gouyave, located in the parish of St. John's:

> All of these men who are running to become the next prime minister is doing the same thing. They make promises and they tell you all the great things that they would do if they was to win the election. They make it sound like things would be as good as they was during the days of the Revo. It's so easy to tell that they are lying. Most of them didn't even support Bishop. Half of them wasn't even in Grenada when the PRG was in power. They think they can say anything they want to the people of Grenada because we is ignorant. But I'll tell you one thing: the Grenadian people know they had it good when Bishop was around, and they will not find it easy to take on one of these jokers so soon.

There were of course many others who did feel as though they would vote in the next election. There were also those who felt that there were viable leaders who would provide sound leadership in the future. In responding to the question about the type of leadership they were looking for in the next election, 33% stated that they were looking for a leader who possessed personal qualities such as honesty, integrity and fairness. 32% of the respondents said that they were looking for a leader who would provide them with some form of material benefit, or generally improve the quality of life for the society by creating more jobs or providing more housing. 14% stated their preference for a leader with whom they shared a common ideological orientation, while the remaining 3% said they were looking for a leader who could bring the country the type of foreign support it needed to strengthen the economy.

Among those who emphasized the personal qualities of Grenada's next leader, there was a tendency to expect that the leader should have more than ordinary attributes. Such persons envisioned Grenada's next leader as a special person,

Chart #15
What will you look for in a candidate when you decide who to vote for in the next election?

(N=120)

Attributes

Leadership Qualities	35%	(42)
Economic Benefits	32%	(38)
Ideology	14%	(16)
Foreign Support	3%	(5)
Will Not Vote	16%	(19)

one who could lead the nation through the strength of personality and character. When commenting on the field of candidates who would be contesting the 1990 elections, such respondents dismissed several of the hopefuls as totally unacceptable based upon personality flaws or inconsistencies between their stated beliefs and observed behavior. The implication was that these respondents were looking for a charismatic leader, that rare individual who possesses the "right stuff" with which to lead.

An example of how this view was expressed can be seen from the following statement made by a forty-three year old woman from the Town of Grenville. In response to the question of the type of leader she would support in the next election, the woman said the following:

> After all that we have went through in Grenada we need a leader who can bring us together as a nation. Someone who can unite the people so that we can achieve some progress. It must be someone who can mix among the people, who doesn't look down upon the poor people. Not someone who thinks he is too big. Not someone that will only help the people who is rich and powerful.

Based upon that criterion, the woman proceeded to discuss and dismiss many of the contenders for national leadership. As she evaluated the politicians, she emphasized their personal qualities, and on that basis, she judged them to be acceptable or not.

Brizan could never be the leader of Grenada. You can't trust the man. You can look at him and tell that he is a person who looks down upon the small people. And as for Alexis I would never vote for him. You can just see that with Brizan and Alexis you will just have another Bishop and Coard. Alexis is saying now that Brizan will lead, but sooner or later he will turn against him just like Coard turned against Bishop . . . Keith Mitchell is a blasted thief. All the people saying that he is involved with the drug business. All I know is that the man is a thief. He sell the airplane that the Cubans gave to Bishop, and he can't show where the money is . . . Raddix just don't have it. He is a good man to help you if you get into some trouble, but he can't lead this country. He don't have the mind for it.

For the 32% who said that they were looking for a leader who would provide material benefits for the population, there was a mixture of cynicism and pragmatism to their views. Many of these respondents expressed frustration over their inability to discern which of the political candidates would fulfill their campaign promises. Yet, unlike those who stated that they would not vote either because they could not believe the politicians or because they felt that all the politicians were the same, several of those who emphasized the importance of material benefits said that they wanted to see what they would be able to get out of the different parties before they made a choice. During the pre-election period in 1988, several of the parties were working hard to woo citizens for membership. Some individuals were being recruited to fill paid positions within the campaign apparatus of the various parties, while others claimed to have been promised jobs if the party they supported won the election. What mattered most to these respondents was choosing the winning candidate before the election. To support a party or candidate that was likely to lose the election could eliminate or reduce the possibility of receiving favors from the winners. It was assumed that the winning party would take care of "their people" first and ensure that their needs were addressed.

Some of those who expressed this view were already members or supporters of political parties. Gairy supporters were particularly confident that they would be taken care of if the GULP won the election. One forty-four year old man from the Town of Gouyave expressed his optimism about a Gairy victory like this:

> Is one thing I know for sure—I have been with Gairy for a long time.
> My father was one of Gairy's right hand men. If Gairy win the elec-
> tion then I going to be O.K. There will be work for me because Gairy
> always looks out for his people. That is what make the people love
> Gairy so much, he will never let us down. That is why we never let our
> leader down.

Similar views were expressed by NNP supporters, many of
whom possessed government jobs at the time that the interview was conducted. One of the NNP supporters who I interviewed was a former member of the NJM, who had been arrested by the PRG because he was accused of leading a group
of Rastafarians in the Tivoli area in counter-revolutionary activities. Since the election in 1984, he had been hired by the
Ministry of Communications and Works which was headed by
Keith Mitchell. The young man described his occupation as
that of a supervisor of construction work crews. He drove and
retained a government vehicle for his personal use, and it was
clear that he had one of the better jobs with the government.
During my interview, he made the following statement when I
asked him what he was looking for in the next political leader
of the country:

> We have been through a lot in Grenada, but since the NNP has been
> in power, I find that things have got a little better. More people is
> working, and you can see that we getting the help from the U. S. that
> we need. I will stick with the NNP in the next election. I'm not so
> crazy for Blaize, but then I hope he will be replaced by someone else
> to lead the government. They have done a lot to help me, more than
> any of the other governments. So, I am going to stick with them.

Others who were also looking for material gain from the
next regime were less partisan, and in fact, many seemed relatively uninterested in the election. They said that they would
vote, but had not yet made up their minds about who they
would vote for. They seemed generally unexcited and ambiva-
lent about the candidates who were contesting the election but
were hopeful that new leadership would bring about an improvement in their living conditions. In response to the question, they made statements like: "I want someone who will bring
jobs for the people," "Someone who is thinking about the
poorer class of people. Who will provide jobs for the people,"

"We need someone who will create opportunities for the youth, who will give the youth something to look forward to when they finish their education." Such respondents expressed no faith in a particular leader or party, but were merely hopeful that the election would lead to an improvement in the economy.

Finally, there were those who expressed a desire for leadership which promoted a particular ideological orientation. Though they constituted a mere 14% of the sample, this group seemed to possess the strongest feelings about politics generally and the importance of the coming election in particular. Most of these respondents identified Maurice Bishop as the leader who had done the most to help the country but few of these expressed support for Kenrick Raddix and the Maurice Bishop Patriotic Front as a viable leadership alternative. They were precise in their criticisms of the candidates, emphasizing disagreements with the policies they advocated as the basis of their opposition to their candidacy rather than their personalities. Often, they spoke of the political record of the candidates, citing examples of previous stands they had taken on issues as a way of providing evidence to support their opinion that a particular leader was unfit for national leadership. And when they spoke affirmatively on behalf of a candidate or in support of a particular policy orientation in government, they explained themselves with logic premised upon their ideological assumptions.

This was evident in the comments made to me by a thirty-two year old male photographer from the rural village of Annendale, located near the Grande Etang rain forest in the parish of St. George's. The man was employed as a photographer for one of the national newspapers and was very familiar with the day to day happenings in Grenadian politics. When I asked him what he would be looking for in a leader when he voted in the next election, he responded with this statement:

> Grenada is a poor country, and a very small country. We can not make it by ourselves. We must have some help from one of the larger countries. Probably, that help will have to come from the United States for the next few years because they are running things down here now. But we can not afford to have a leader who will just do whatever it is the U.S. tells them. That is what the NNP has done, and as a result, the poor people ain't have nothing here now. We need a leader who

will look out for the poorer peoples, but at the same time, keep things cool with the U.S. We must have their help, but we can not let them control the government.

An analysis of this response to the question reveals a fairly sophisticated view of politics in Grenada. This individual clearly recognizes the need for foreign aid but is cognizant of the potential for losing or compromising national sovereignty as a consequence of receiving it. He also recognizes the need for a government which is sensitive to the needs of the poor who comprise the majority of the citizens in Grenada. As the interview progressed, he let me know that he would be supporting George Brizan and his National Democratic Congress in the next election. He explained: "Brizan is the only one who can lead Grenada effectively at this time. He knows we need help from the U.S., and he knows that the poor people have it hard and that the government must try to help them. He can do the things to help the poor people without making the U.S. say: 'Hey, this fellow is a communist. We must get rid of him or he will become like another Bishop.'"

Many of the respondents who articulated an ideological basis to their political preferences expressed support for Brizan and the NDC. They tended to be people who had at least completed their secondary education, and they were generally between the ages of thirty and forty-five. For the most part, their ideological orientation consisted of a strong belief in protecting Grenadian sovereignty, a social welfare orientation toward the role of government, and a high degree of faith in the ability of intellectuals to lead. Most supported Brizan because they felt he was intelligent, competent, pragmatic and progressive with respect to his attitudes toward poor people. Such qualities were seen by these respondents as essential prerequisites for solving the many problems which beset the country. In the words of one thirty-eight year old civil servant from the Town of St. George's:

Grenada needs leaders who are well educated. People who understand the problems which face our society and who understand what it will take to solve them. We have had too many leaders who just run the government like a pappy show. We need serious leaders, who have the intelligence to do the right things.

Based on what we know about the electorate from the survey, it may be easier to understand how and why a Gairy, Bishop and Blaize could emerge as leaders in the society. However, given the mixture of political priorities among the voters, with some emphasizing personal attributes of potential leaders, others material benefits, and still others a particular ideological orientation, it is still difficult to determine what kind of leaders will be supported in the future.

Summary of Survey Findings

In several important ways, the survey findings support the historical analysis that has been presented of the Gairy, Bishop and Blaize regimes. The review of Grenada's political history provides us with the overview from which we can ascertain how each leader was able to rise to a position of power and why each of the regimes they led eventually lost power. Yet, historical analysis does not make it possible to explain the attitudes and perceptions of the Grenadian people. The data obtained from the interviews provides an avenue through which we can assess the political values, priorities and expectations of the Grenadian people. Of course, the survey is limited by its temporality, in that the opinions solicited capture attitudes at a particular time in history. The responses can not tell us how an individual may have felt about a regime in the past, why they may have changed their feelings toward a particular leader or even how they may feel about them in the future. Still, a knowledge and an understanding of their attitudes and opinions is important because it provides greater insight into the reasons behind observed political behavior.

Through the historical analysis, it was observed that all three of the regimes experienced a decline in political support during periods of economic instability. The Gairy regime was nearly toppled in 1974 following the general strike, which created numerous economic hardships and severely reduced government revenues. The economic crisis brought on by the political conflict over Grenada's independence made it difficult for Gairy to finance and maintain his extensive patronage network and, thereby, exacerbated the political difficulties faced by the regime. Moreover, the fact that Grenada's internal conflicts coincided with a major recession in the world economy and a substantial rise in the cost of energy imports contributed further to the weakening of the Gairy government. As the opposition to Gairy grew stronger the regime felt compelled to rely increasingly upon coercive measures to maintain control. Excessive reliance on coercion, in turn, further undermined the regime's legitimacy at home and abroad.

Similarly, the political crisis within the NJM was precipitated, at least in part, by the deterioration of the economy. As the volume of foreign aid was reduced in 1982, timely completion of the airport was jeopardized. Loss of foreign aid also contributed to the government's difficulty in meeting the payroll of the expanded state sector. In areas of the country where support for the NJM had already been weak, such as St. David's and parts of St. Andrew's,[7] economic problems contributed to further decline in political support. In the end, lagging support for the revolution became one of the major issues that contributed to the internal party conflict that developed between Bishop and the Coard faction and ultimately caused the demise of the regime.

Finally, the NNP government also began experiencing its greatest difficulties when a shortage in government revenues due in part to the implementation of the Value Added Tax forced the regime to lay off public employees and tap into pension monies from the National Insurance Scheme. The survey found that the growth of unemployment and the lack of economic opportunity became the major issues influencing attitudes negatively toward the Blaize-led government. Economic hardships combined with the widespread perception that Blaize was biased toward serving the interest of the wealthy contributed to a decline in legitimacy and popular support for his government.

Analysis of the survey data reveals that a majority of the respondents placed emphasis on the quality of their living conditions in making their evaluations of the three regimes. The correlation between which leader an individual thought was best and how they characterized living conditions during the time the leader was in power was very high: 76% of Gairy supporters, 85% of Bishop supporters and 82% of Blaize supporters felt living conditions were good for them when their favorite leader was in power. Conversely, 73% of those who identified Blaize as the leader who had done the least to help the country mentioned the deterioration of their personal economic circumstances as a factor.

On the other hand, while material benefits may be relevant to understanding political support, it does not explain everything. Only 32% of the respondents to the survey stated that their preference for a candidate in the next election would be based upon their ability to determine which one would provide them with the greatest material benefits. In contrast, 35% of the respondents emphasized that they were looking for a leader who possessed special qualities, such as honesty, compassion for the poor, and intelligence. This finding does not negate the fact that living conditions and material benefits are important to the political choices made by many, if not most Grenadian voters. However, it does suggest that other factors are relevant, as well, in understanding the sensibilities of Grenadian voters.

It is the way in which these other factors influence political attitudes that makes it difficult to explain Grenadian reactions to political change, much less predict the character of allegiances in the future. While many Grenadians seem to be particularly attracted to the personal qualities possessed by charismatic leaders like Maurice Bishop and Eric Gairy, under the right conditions a non-charismatic leader like Herbert Blaize can be supported. With an overwhelming desire for stability and social peace in the aftermath of the U.S. invasion, and with a strong expectation that U.S. aid would flow if their choice for leader won the election, even a leader with the history of Herbert Blaize could garner substantial popular support. However, once it became clear that his promises for rebuilding the national economy were meaningless to ordinary Grenadians, the importance of his honesty and ties with the U.S. quickly diminished.

The survey also confirms a point that was made with regard to the use of coercion: excessive coercion on the part of a regime can lead to a loss in support unless the measures are effectively justified to the population. It could be argued that the Gairy regime may have been less repressive than the Bishop or Blaize regimes, in that it imprisoned fewer political oppo-

nents and did not call upon a foreign power for military assistance in order to achieve its goals. Yet, among those who cited
Gairy as the leader who had done the least to help the country
(38% of the respondents), over half (52%) cited the use of violence by the regime against political opponents as the reason.
The Bishop regime, on the other hand, which was accused by
many of its international opponents of perpetrating numerous human rights violations, was only cited by 31% of those
who saw it as the government which had done the least to help
the country (12% of the respondents) as being overly repressive. Clearly, the extent to which government coercion is tolerated by the populace is directly related to the degree of legitimacy it enjoys. Legitimacy is in turn shaped by how the
population perceives the overall effectiveness of the regime.
The social welfare programs of the PRG for a time enhanced
its image as an effective government, despite the fact that it
was never duly constituted by way of national referendum.

Finally, the survey findings demonstrate the relative
unimportance of ideology to the Grenadian people when evaluating the three regimes. While many of Bishop's supporters
(22%) cited agreement with his ideology as the reason for backing him and his government, very few of his detractors stated
that it was because of disagreements with the ideological perspective of the regime that they opposed him. In fact, although
Gairy and Blaize have gone to great lengths to distinguish themselves ideologically from Bishop, supporters of the two leaders tend to express more support and respect for Bishop than
either Blaize or Gairy. The influence of class may help to explain this paradox. Despite his radical orientation, Bishop's
middle class origins made him far more acceptable to the
Grenadian middle and upper class. Similarly, despite his middle
class background, Bishop's track record of serving as an advocate of the poor, and the PRG's commitment to serving the
needs of the lower class majority, made Bishop far more attractive than Blaize to Gairy supporters. The fact that the vast
majority of Grenadians continue to respect and admire Maurice
Bishop, even after several years of concerted propaganda aimed
at discrediting him and a deliberate effort at erasing all
memory of his existence, carried out first by the U.S. Psychological Operations and later the NNP government,[8] attest to

the power of his personality and the relative unimportance of his ideological orientation.

These are some of the connections which can be drawn between the survey and the historical analysis. In the final chapter, I will examine the broader implications of this study with respect to the question of regime survival as it pertains to Grenada and other developing countries.

Notes

1 The development of Grenada's tourist industry, which began to takeoff during the 1960's, has contributed to the uneven development of the island. Most of Grenada's white sand beaches are located in the southern part of the island, and hence, a majority of the hotels, resorts and restaurants have been built there. As a result of this pattern, most of the jobs in construction, retail and tourism have been concentrated in this area of the island. The completion of the national airport at Pt. Salines has further exacerbated this problem by making the old airport in Grenville (Pearl's Airport) obsolete and, thereby, contributed to the decline of Grenville, Grenada's second largest city, as a commercial center. Additionally, the construction of the new highway and industrial park by U.S. A.I.D. in the southern region has compounded the problem of uneven development.

2 Both Gairy and the PRG used land reform as a means of punishing their opponents. The NNP government sought to reclaim lands which it believed were taken illegally from its rightful owners. Some of these confiscated lands have been sold to foreign investors or taken for government use. Many of these acquisitions became extremely controversial because, in many cases, the lands had been squatted by poor people who had few options for relocation. See *Informer* 10/12/87 for a story about the squatter removal controversy.

3 The reason most frequently cited by those who regarded Bishop as the leader who had done the least to help the country had to do with what they considered excessive emphasis on the military and militarization of the country by his government.

4 Women were over-represented in the sample because many of the interviews were conducted during the day, at a time when working men were less likely to be found at home.

5 This data was obtained from the 1980-1981 Population Census of Commonwealth Caribbean.

6 Although the PRG recruited several businessmen to serve in the government, none of them were members of the party. According to Bishop, their presence was intended largely to show the "imperialists" that "they have some good fellas in that thing" (Bishop's Line of March Speech) and to demonstrate the government's commitment to a mixed economy. Despite these attempts at inclusion, most of the owners of the larger

businesses on the island were firmly opposed to Bishop and the PRG. See Joefield-Napier, W. "Macroeconomic Growth Under the People's Revolutionary Government" in *A Revolution Aborted* by J. Heine (Pittsburgh, PA: University of Pittsburgh Press, 1990).

7   NJM support was weakest in rural areas where Gairy supporters were predominant. There is also evidence that NJM support was lower in areas that received less in terms of social services or employment opportunities. See Noguera, P. "Mass Literacy as a Political Strategy" in *The International Journal of University Adult Education*, Vol. XXXI, No. 2, July, 1992.

8   In the aftermath of the U.S. invasion, the U.S. Psychological Operations Unit set up headquarters in downtown St. George's from where it developed and released a steady flow of propaganda attacking Bishop, the revolution, socialism, Cubans and many of the goals of the PRG. Films were shown on the evils of communism, T-shirts which attacked Coard and Austin were produced and distributed freely, and a variety of other techniques were used to undermine support for the NJM. For a discussion of U.S. promoted propaganda in the post-invasion period, see Clark, S. "The Second Assassination of Maurice Bishop" in *The New International* (New York: Pathfinder Press, 1987) and Ferguson, J. *Grenada: Revolution in Reverse* (London: Latin American Bureau, 1990).

Chapter 9

An Analysis of the Survival Strategies of the Gairy, Bishop and Blaize Regimes

Extracting Lessons From Grenada

In 1962, Archie Singham and the research team he had assembled undertook a study on the political crisis that had occurred in Grenada in that year, following the suspension of the constitution by the Chief Colonial Administrator. Though suspension of the constitution was clearly within the realm of power held by the British over its colonial possessions, it was nonetheless a highly unusual act of intervention. This was certainly not the first nor by any means the most serious political disturbance experienced by the British within its colonial empire. However, elsewhere challenges to colonial rule were characterized by mass anti-colonial, nationalist movements often accompanied by labor unrest, as in the case of India, or by rebellions from disloyal subjects, like the Boers of South Africa who had never truly accepted British rule.[1] The constitutional crisis in Grenada was of a different sort. It was not the product of a popular uprising but the result of strained relations between a loyal and dedicated civil servant and a local political leader. Sensing that it might be possible to use Grenada as a case study for a crisis that they believed was "not an isolated phenomenon but one that is inherent in the colonial situation" (Singham, p.vii). Singham and his associates undertook their study with the hope of extracting lessons from Grenada that could be useful to the study of charismatic leadership within colonial polities.

During the course of his research, Singham discovered that it was not possible to grasp the full significance of the crisis and interpret its meaning without understanding the island's history, its social and economic character, and most especially, the importance of the labor uprising of 1951 which had brought Eric Gairy to the center stage of Grenadian politics. In developing his analysis of the society and its politics, Singham employed a multidisciplinary approach, drawing on history, economics and sociology to establish a context for explaining the events of 1962.

As a result of his efforts, Singham produced a work which has been widely recognized as one of the more significant contributions to the study of politics and culture in colonized societies. Though thorough in his investigation of the case and in his exploration of the details of the crisis, Singham managed to avoid becoming absorbed by the particulars of Grenadian society and the intrigue surrounding the lives of its colorful characters, a temptation which could have produced an interesting history rather than a useful socio-political analysis. In so doing, *The Hero and the Crowd* (1967) became essential reading for students of politics in the Third World and laid the basis for further theoretical development in what had been a largely neglected area of research in social science.

Following Singham's lead and approach, I, too, was initially motivated by my desire to make sense of a political crisis that had occurred in Grenada, this one having taken place in October 1983. By this time, Grenada was no longer an obscure island in the eastern Caribbean having gained international significance for its socialist oriented revolution in 1979 and the U.S. invasion in 1983. In the aftermath of the invasion, several writers were drawn to Grenada, most seeking to interpret the events of 1983, due to the widespread recognition that the events of that year constituted a significant development in the on-going East-West competition for geo-political influence, and a watershed in relations between the U.S. and the English speaking Caribbean.

Having been familiar with Grenada prior to the invasion, and having witnessed first hand the efforts of the PRG at transforming the society, I was drawn to return to Grenada with a different objective in mind. For me, the pictures of Grenadians welcoming U.S. marines after the invasion and news of the overwhelming victory by Herbert Blaize in the 1984 elections prompted me to question my assumptions about the basis of support for government in Grenada. My knowledge of Grenada's history led me to wonder how it was possible that a society which seemed to have been supportive of a socialist, anti-imperialist government and its charismatic leader could suddenly elect a conservative like Herbert Blaize. I also wondered how long this particular regime would survive, given its sharp deviation from the two regimes led by Bishop and Gairy before him that had held power in the recent past, both far more populist in their orientation. Armed with these questions in mind, I returned to Grenada in 1987 in search of answers.

Like Singham, I recognized and hoped that the questions I had posed and the investigation I was to undertake in Grenada potentially held significance for other societies and places. Taken in the broadest sense, the questions were neither new nor unique. For all its peculiarities, the characters and events of contemporary Grenada have counterparts and analogies elsewhere. Like Eric Gairy, there have been a number of leaders who have violated established norms and laws, but have been able to retain loyalty and support among their constituents. In the U.S., Mayors Vincent "Buddy" Cianci of Providence, R.I. and Marion Barry of Washington, D.C., are contemporary examples of political leaders who have been able to consistently win elections even when confronted with criminal charges and credible challenges to their moral conduct and character. In such cases, the ability of the leaders to appeal to the particular sensibilities and interests of their constituents outweighed the voracity and validity of charges against them. Moreover, popular distrust of those making the accusations has backfired in many cases and produced even stronger support for an embattled leader, as it did so often for Gairy in his struggles with the colonial authorities and local elites of Grenada.

Similarly, there have been other regimes like the PRG that have been able to acquire legitimacy, both internally and externally, despite having acquired power through the use of force or via other non-electoral means. The PRI (Institutionalized Revolutionary Party) of Mexico is widely recognized as a legitimate though somewhat corrupt regime, despite the fact that it has functioned as a one-party state since coming to power in

1914. Likewise, the Communist Party of China, though once treated as a renegade state, is now generally regarded as a legitimate government and has been accepted as a participant in most international arenas involving diplomacy and trade. Hence, the limited credibility attained by the PRG during its four and one half years of rule is not surprising, even given the extent to which the PRG deviated from the norms of the Anglophone Caribbean.

Finally, even the dramatic fluctuations in leadership that have occurred in Grenada find parallels in other places. The 1989 electoral victory of Violetta Chamorro and the UNO (Unified Opposition of Nicaragua) Party in Nicaragua over the Sandinistas, and the election of former associates of Manuel Noriega in Panama, less than five years after the U.S. invasion, are vivid examples of political outcomes which dramatically altered prior political trends. Such occurrences, while unique, are not particularly rare. And while radical changes in political leadership have historically been less likely among western democracies, the uncertain political and economic realities of poor nations might very well increase the likelihood of radical political change, especially in the Third World and Eastern Europe.[2]

In this final chapter we turn to the issue of regime survival in Grenada. While historical analysis makes it possible to explain the rise and fall of the three regimes, and analysis of survey data provides an opening through which we can understand the social basis of regime support, none of these approaches produce insights into the inner workings of the regimes themselves. Such a perspective is important if we are to understand how each regime went about maintaining power and if we are to learn why the efforts of each regime ultimately failed.

Each of the three regimes we have examined developed strategies that were designed to retain political power. The cultivation and maintenance of popular support, while not a requirement for retaining power, was an important element in the strategies pursued by all three regimes. Each regime employed a different strategy to secure and maintain popular support. This strategy was based on a combination of the particular assets available to the regime and its unique ideological orientation, which invariably influenced how it went about devising foreign and domestic policy. The fact that all three regimes eventually lost much of the support they had originally enjoyed suggest that none of the strategies they employed were sufficiently effective to ensure their survival. In the following pages I will examine the survival strategies pursued by the three regimes and return to the five variables discussed earlier, charismatic leadership, ideology, patronage, foreign support and coercion, as a means of evaluating the strengths and weaknesses of the three.

The Vicissitudes of Regime Survival

Throughout this study, I have made reference to five themes or strategies which are commonly employed by regimes throughout the world as ways of ensuring their survival. Grenada's political history and the survey of political attitudes suggest that charismatic leadership, ideological appeals, patronage, coercion and foreign support are all important, to varying degrees, to understanding the process of political change in Grenada. These strategies were not utilized uniformly by the Gairy, Bishop and Blaize regimes nor were they employed in the same way. Yet, to a greater or lesser degree, each of these methods served as part of the strategies employed by the three regimes to prolong their hold on political power. In a more general sense, it could be said that all three regimes attempted to retain power through a variety of measures designed to either produce or maintain popular support or to stifle the opposition. Still, the five strategies that have been identified in this study provide a basis for comparison between the three regimes and can now be used to assist in answering the last remaining question which motivated this research: how can regime survival in Grenada be explained.

The extent to which a particular approach is emphasized as a major component of a regime's survival strategy is largely related to the ideological orientation of the regime and to the particular attributes of its leaders. For example, both Gairy and Bishop possessed charismatic personalities which enabled the regimes they led to appeal to different sectors of the population. The promotion of their personalities was utilized as an important asset of the two regimes and a key element of the survival strategy pursued by the two governments. The charismatic appeal of Bishop and Gairy facilitated the mobilization tactics employed by the two regimes and proved valuable particularly when displays of mass support were needed to provide a boost to the regime's image and to thwart the efforts of the opposition. Blaize, on the other hand, was not a charismatic leader and his organizations (both the GNP and later the NNP) had to rely upon other tactics to cultivate political support and maintain legitimacy. In its place, the regimes led by Blaize relied heavily upon foreign support, first from the British colonial authorities prior to independence and later from the United States. At various times, the relationship that Blaize cultivated with foreign powers enabled him to compensate for the absence of special qualities within himself.

In the pages ahead, I shall conduct a final comparison of the three regimes that focuses on the strategies employed by each one to retain power. In so doing, I will attempt to explain both the success and the failures associated with a particular strategy. This will be done with recognition to the structural and cultural conditions on the island, which create the context for understanding political activity and political behavior.

The Use and Limitations of Charisma
in Attaining and Maintaining Political Power

Though clearly an asset to any leader or to the party or regime with which s/he is associated, Grenada's history shows that charismatic leadership is not sufficient as a strategy for building and maintaining a stable and secure government. Charismatic leaders can be very important because they serve as the spokesmen who articulate the vision of a party or regime, and, in so doing, play a key role in generating popular support. As popular figures, charismatic leaders have the ability to mobilize support among key constituencies. Often, their personality becomes the symbol of the regime itself, and their image, stature and reputation serves as the foundation upon which governments can be built and parties can be voted into office. Charismatic leaders can generate unity among constituencies that are divided and can provide vision and direction to those seeking deliverance from oppressive conditions (Wriggins 1969). They can also contribute to efforts at soliciting foreign aid, assuming of course that their appeal is not uniquely attractive to the sensibilities of the local population, as was the case with Eric Gairy.

Yet, as Gerth and Mills point out, charismatic leadership is "inherently unstable" in that ". . . if they (the people) do not fare well, he is obviously not the master sent by the gods" (Gerth and Mills, 1974: 249). Over an extended period of time, charismatic leadership can not serve as a substitute for effective government. If a government does not succeed at improving the conditions under which people live, if it fails in its efforts to satisfy the basic needs of the population, and if it is unable to fulfill or change the expectations of the people, then charismatic leaders will eventually fall, as would any other unsuccessful leader. Charismatic leaders in the Weberian sense, after all, possess more than merely a charming personality. Charisma is a quality of leadership that is considered special or extraordinary, capable of delivering rewards and benefits to a society that would be unattainable by normal men and women (Bendix and Roth, 1971: 170-175). For this reason, few regimes rely upon charismatic leadership alone. Instead, the charismatic appeal of a leader is typically used as only one of many tactics employed by a regime to retain political power (Wriggins: 123-137).

The experiences of the Gairy and Bishop regimes clearly reveal that charismatic leadership had its limitations. In both cases, the charismatic qualities of the two leaders were most important during the period when the parties they led were first making their bids for power. However, once their control over government was established, other methods had to be devised to ensure the regime's retention of power.

Gairy made use of his charismatic personality to build the GMMWU and later the GULP as mass organizations which could be used to challenge the power and authority of the British and the local elite. The appeal of his personality, complimented by his oratory skills, talents as an organizer and keen understanding of the cultural sensibilities of his constituents made it possible for him to command the loyalty and support of thousands of Grenadian peasants. His initial emergence as a political leader was made possible by the severe social and economic conditions experienced by the peasantry and by the growing resentment on their part toward the glaring inequities that existed in Grenadian society. Gairy's ability to mobilize the lower classes into a political force made it possible for their resentment to be transformed into political power, of which Gairy was the primary beneficiary.

However, because the regime he led relied so heavily upon Gairy's charisma and the personal style of leadership he cultivated, other aspects of the strategy which brought him to power tended to be neglected. This was particularly true with regard to the development of his organized base through union and party, both of which declined in importance during the times when he occupied positions of leadership in government. Singham argues that "the hero (Gairy) does not have a genuine mass party; he has supporters who are personally committed to following him but who are not controlled by him" (Singham: 176). He adds that "the essential link between the hero and the crowd is the former's ability to mesmerize crowds and canalize their emotions for short periods of time" (Singham: 176).

Gairy's ambivalence toward organization was compounded by the authoritarian manner in which he ran both the union and the party. Previously, loyal defectors often accused Gairy of running his organization in an arbitrary and dictatorial manner, and throughout the early part of his career, numerous close allies abandoned him due to his inability to work with others on an equal basis. Singham explains Gairy's ambivalence toward organization in this way:

> Any type of inner circle that did exist was heavily dependent upon Gairy's personal support in maintaining their electoral strength. He was careful not to allow any of his supporters to develop strong and viable constituency organizations; instead, he always tried to maintain direct personal contact with each such organization (Singham: 181).

Gairy's distrust toward organization led him to utilize it only when it suited his needs, which was usually during a campaign for office or during the periods when he was out of power.

Adhering to this pattern, Gairy spent considerable time attempting to reorganize his union upon returning to Grenada in 1983, in an attempt to re-establish his political base, much like he had done from 1957 to 1961 when he was banned from government by the colonial authorities. However, once again, he had trouble retaining members who were not completely subservient to him.[3]

The charismatic qualities of Maurice Bishop played a similar role in the development of the NJM as an effective force in opposition to Gairy during the 1970's. After years of competing with Blaize and the GNP for political leadership during the 1950's and 1960's, Gairy finally attained a position of nearly unchallenged authority by the early 1970's once the British, Blaize's primary sponsors, were out of the picture in domestic politics. This was particularly true during the period following his overwhelming victory at the polls in 1972. The GNP's historic dependence upon the backing of the colonial authorities, combined with its inability to appeal to the lower strata, severely restricted its potential as an effective political opponent to Gairy's GULP. However, the NJM was formed shortly after the election of 1972, and Maurice Bishop, another charismatic figure, gradually began to assume the primary role of the leading opposition to Gairy in Grenada.

Unlike Gairy, Bishop and the NJM understood the need for organization, and actively sought to create mass organizations, both before and after assuming power, as a way of increasing their influence and support among the population. Particularly during the campaign against independence under Gairy, the NJM was extremely successful in mobilizing large numbers of people and building up the ranks of their organization. After the revolution, recruitment of large numbers of people into the people's militia, women's and youth organizations, and the national literacy campaign was seen as a critical part of the NJM's strategy for sustaining popular support. Furthermore, whereas Gairy felt threatened by members of his party who possessed their own following or who potentially could challenge his leadership, Bishop demonstrated complete trust toward his colleagues within the NJM. In fact, his tendency to be too trusting has been cited by numerous writers as the reason that the conspiracy against him within the party was able to lead to his house arrest, and ultimately his assassination (Marable, 1987; O'Shaughnessy, 1984; Lewis, 1987; Heine, 1990).

Bishop also possessed talents as an orator and an organizer. However, unlike Gairy, Bishop could successfully appeal to the island's middle class. Though they were distrustful of his left-ist rhetoric, his middle class origins made them more open to his leadership than they were to Gairy, whom they regarded as a scoundrel of low status. Moreover, because Bishop, unlike Blaize, also made a concerted effort to appeal to and organize the the rural lower classes, Gairy's traditional base, he became a formidable opponent of the Gairy regime. The limited success of these inroads, combined with his support among the urban working class and the youth, enabled Bishop and the NJM to undermine Gairy's base and lay the basis for the demise of his regime.

Data obtained from the survey clearly suggests that among those respondents who supported either Gairy or Bishop, the personal attributes possessed by the two leaders were important factors influencing their support. Several of the Gairy supporters mentioned Gairy's ostentatious style and character, as well as his compassion for the poor, as qualities which they admired in him. Likewise, Bishop supporters typically mentioned attributes such as his kindness, his love for the people, his sincerity and humility. 22% of the Gairy supporters and 36% of the Bishop supporters in the sample expressed their support for the two leaders in terms of the personal qualities the leaders possessed, while this was true for only 12% of the Blaize supporters.

To a large extent, much of Eric Gairy's resilience as a politician can be explained by the strength he derived from his charismatic personality. Gairy was effectively removed from office or deprived of the right to serve in government on three separate occasions. In the wake of each of these political setbacks, which were mounted largely through attacks on his character, Gairy was able to rebound and rebuild a formidable political base. The source of his support on the island and the reason for his resilience was the unshaking support of the rural estate workers and small peasant proprietors, who Gairy led in the rebellion of 1951, and who remained largely loyal to him, even during the years when he was not in power. His opponents encountered great difficulty in their efforts at courting his rural base, despite their numerous attempts to attack and malign him. With the exception of the Town of St. George's and Carriacou, the opposition faced an uphill battle in their efforts to compete with Gairy for the support of the rural electorate.[4] As a union and party leader, Gairy was without question the undisputed leader of Grenada's agricultural proletariat.

Though viewed as more of a gentleman than a rogue, Bishop also presented himself as the champion of the lower class. His early work as a lawyer representing those who had been victimized in one way or another by the Gairy regime helped to earn him a reputation as a populist. His defense of striking nurses in 1972 and numerous others who had been victims of police brutality and other abuses, led to Bishop's becoming well known throughout Grenada and the Caribbean as a capable "people's lawyer." Bishop's image was further enhanced by the beating he experienced at the hands of Gairy's Mongoose Gang and the police. The infamous Bloody Sunday beating, combined with the murder of his father while protecting school children during a demonstration in St. George's helped to create an image for Bishop as a leader who had made tremendous sacrifices for "the people" and for his cause, the overthrow of Eric Gairy.

Charismatic leadership is also relied on heavily during the period which immediately follows the acquisition of state power. For both regimes, this was the time when the need to legitimize the government was greatest due to the challenge both leaders posed to existing structures of power, both domestic and international. This suggest that the emergence of a charismatic leader may be most important during periods of political crisis (i.e., the uprising of 1951 or the 1979 NJM takeover), at which time the qualities of the charismatic leader can be used to obtain or consolidate power through their ability to rally popular support.[5] This does not mean that political stability can not be achieved following a political crisis without the presence of a charismatic leader (i.e., the aftermath of the

U.S. invasion in 1983); however, for both the Gairy and Bishop regimes, projection of the charismatic leader proved to be a valuable asset.

It may be that it took another leader possessing extraordinary leadership talents or "gifts," as the term charisma would imply, to overthrow Gairy. Bishop's popularity as a leader began to develop at the time when Gairy had substantially reduced his contacts with the masses. Having decisively beaten Blaize in the elections of 1967 and 1972, Gairy had ceased to pay attention to the work of his labor union and no longer relied on mass mobilization to achieve his goals in the political arena. Instead, he developed and expanded his patronage system, which he previously had been unable to create due to the control exerted by the colonial authorities. He created a network of allegiances between himself and thousands of Grenadians who were personally indebted to him for employment, housing, land or contracts.

Bishop's charisma, combined with the organizing ability and determination of the NJM, enabled him to gradually undermine Gairy's base of support on the island. Beginning with those who were not integrated into Gairy's patronage system and those who had lost favor with Gairy, Bishop and the NJM were slowly able to cultivate a following based largely among middle class youth and the urban working class. Gradually, segments of the rural lower class and the middle class began to regard Bishop and the NJM as a viable alternative to Gairy. Though the NJM was never as dependent on the personality of Bishop as the GULP was toward Gairy, his stature as a leader on the island became extremely important to their efforts, for he alone possessed the ability to counter the magnetism and loyalty associated with Gairy's personality.

The differences in the charismatic personalities of Gairy and Bishop are significant and have bearing upon why they were able to appeal to different segments of the population. Raised in the rural villages of St. Andrews, Gairy emerged out of the peasantry and was entirely familiar with the values and customs of the rural lower classes. His approach to organizing relied heavily upon religious and spiritual symbols because he understood the appeal of such an approach to the peasantry. He claimed to have been on a mission from God, and to this day asserts that God selected him to lead Grenada.[6] He was well acquainted with Obeah, an African-based religion practiced widely in Grenada and the Caribbean, and the practices associated with it, and incorporated some of its beliefs and symbols into his unique leadership style.[7] Moreover, he understood common Grenadian sensibilities, the fact that Grenadians respect what they call a "bad john," someone who is audacious and bold and refuses to back down to anyone. Gairy projected this trait particularly through his challenges to the colonial authorities and the large estate owners and he did so with flamboyance and dignity.

Conversely, Bishop's image was that of a more modest leader and he generally appeared to be far less self-aggrandizing than Gairy. Partially because of his privileged background, Bishop went out of his way to demonstrate that he felt at home among the masses. During the 1970's and even during the first few years of PRG rule, Bishop made an effort to develop personal ties with common folk. When in public, he took on no airs and made easy conversation with ordinary folk. He earned a reputation as a leader with humility, as one who always displayed courtesy toward others regardless of their class position. In his analysis of the split between Bishop and Bernard Coard, author Jorge Heine points out that "Being a London-educated lawyer from a well-known and respected light-skinned St. George's family, he made his own the demands and aspirations of the black rural folk" (Heine, 1990). Whereas Gairy presented himself as the Honorable Doctor Sir Eric Mathew Gairy, having obtained several honorary titles during his tenure in public office,[8] Bishop was referred to as Brother Bish, or simply, Maurice.

Yet, these differences in leadership style are less significant when one examines how the charismatic personalities of the two leaders were used by the regimes. As the chief spokesmen for their governments, both Gairy and Bishop utilized their talents as orators and the appeal of their personalities to persuade the populace to support their policies and programs. Such direct appeals by the two men were particularly useful to the two regimes when it became necessary to justify repressive measures or to rationalize and attempt to explain the causes of economic hardships on the island. Certainly not all were appeased by the charm of either leader, but for their core constituencies the personal touch of the popular leader went a long way.

The Limits of Charisma

Yet, despite its usefulness as a means of mobilizing popular support, charismatic leadership is insufficient as a base upon which to build a government. While it was an important component of the survival strategies employed by the two regimes, neither the GULP nor the PRG relied exclusively upon the charisma of their leaders to maintain popular support. However, when other components of the strategy failed, charismatic leadership proved inadequate as a foundation for sustaining either regime. In the case of the PRG, beset as it was by internal divisions, hostility from the United States and a deteriorating economy during the final months and weeks before the invasion, the charisma of Bishop was one of the only effective components left within its survival strategy.

In fact, it could be argued that Bishop's appeal to the masses led to the ultimate downfall of the government. In reaction to the news of Bishop's arrest by members of the NJM central committee, thousands of Grenadians boldly challenged the army and freed him from captivity, thereby setting the stage for the violent confrontation which ended in the assassination of Bishop and the collapse of the government.[9] His opponents within the NJM were clearly aware of the threat posed by Bishop's popularity to their plans for seizing power.[10] To counter his appeal, General Hudson Austin delivered a speech over Radio Free Grenada on behalf of the RMC (Revolutionary Military Council), which implicitly attacked Bishop and sought to undermine his credibility.[11] The failure of this effort made it impossible for the RMC to establish political legitimacy on the island.

In summary, it can be said that while charismatic leadership is an asset to any regime, it is also limited in its usefulness. Certainly the NNP could have benefited from having a more charismatic leader than Herbert Blaize, whose conservative disposition and lack of appeal has been widely criticized throughout the population. Moreover, the lack of an effective spokesman for the regime contributed to some of its political troubles. A charismatic leader might have been more effective at explaining the economic difficulties the nation experienced in 1986 and 1987. Despite committing himself to weekly addresses over the radio, Blaize was unable to muster the support his regime needed.

In place of charisma, Blaize relied heavily on support from the U.S. and other donor nations to demonstrate that his ties to foreign powers made him an essential ingredient to the island's political future, for only he could insure that the aid would continue to flow. However, as was true in the past, Blaize's excessive reliance upon the support of foreign powers provided him with only a temporary boost, which was sufficient for winning the 1984 election but could not carry him much further.

Yet, even for the Gairy and Bishop regimes, charisma proved insufficient as a foundation for the two governments. No matter how popular the leader or how persuasive his oratory, charisma can not substitute for social and economic policies that ensure the well-being of the population. In fact, the inability of a regime to deliver on these eventually becomes proof that the leader who once was perceived as charismatic is not really so special after all.

Ideology: Its Usefulness and Irrelevance to Regime Survival

While it can be said that all three regimes were guided by some form of ideology and attempted to use ideology to both cultivate popular support and to justify the policies and actions taken by them, all of the evidence suggests that the particular ideological orientation adopted by each of the regimes was relatively unimportant, and in some cases even irrelevant to the population in its evaluation of the three leaders. This fact helps to explain to a large extent why it was possible for three regimes embracing dramatically divergent political ideologies to obtain popular support at some point during their tenure in office.

The fact that a right-wing populist like Gairy could retain power uninterrupted for twelve years, only to be overthrown by a left-wing populist such as Bishop, who in turn was replaced by Herbert Blaize, the conservative, pro-business politician, would, for good reason, confuse many an observer, particularly those not familiar with the peculiarities of Grenadian society. There are relatively few countries where such dramatic fluctuations in political leadership have occurred. The Commonwealth Caribbean has more typically followed the pattern seen in Jamaica, where the electorate has switched its allegiances every eight years from the left-of-center People's National Party, to the right-of-center Jamaica Labor Party. Of course, the Caribbean also has had its share of thoroughly entrenched oligarchies, such as Vere Byrd in Antigua and the PNC (People's National Congress) in Guyana. Still, fluctuations in the ideological orientation of the regimes that have held power in other parts of the West Indies have not been nearly as extreme as they have been in Grenada.

The Grenadian phenomenon can only be explained by the relative unimportance of ideology to the Grenadian populace. This fact is powerfully confirmed by the survey conducted by myself, as well as surveys conducted by others on the political opinions of Grenadians. For example, Brathwaite found through his survey conducted in the months preceding the 1984 national elections that while 60.3% of the respondents objected to the curtailment of freedom of speech under the PRG, 91.3% still expressed the view that the PRG was popularly supported during its four and one half years of rule (Brathwaite: 14). Apparently, while a majority of Brathwiate's respondents may have considered infringements on their political freedoms by the PRG important, such actions on the part of the PRG did not lead to popular rejection of the regime. Similarly, while he found that 79.3% of the respondents supported the U.S. invasion of the island, he also found that 93.1% felt that the Cubans had made a positive contribution to the development of Grenada. This finding is particularly significant given claims that have been made by some observers (Valenta and Ellison 1986) that the Cuban presence on the island was a source of great resentment by the Grenadian populace.

My own research revealed what might appear to be ideological inconsistencies among the populace in their evaluations of the three regimes. In response to the question that asked which leader had done the most to help the country, a surprising 13% answered that all three had made a contribution. Among the 21% who cited Gairy as the leader who had done the most, Bishop was most often named as their second choice. Similarly, for the 9% who mentioned Blaize as the leader who had done the most to help the country, Gairy and not Bishop was most often the leader cited by these respondents as the one who had done the least to help the country. These findings suggest that while the ideological differences between the three leaders may have been significant, such differences had little bearing on how the three leaders were evaluated by Grenadian citizens. One might expect that there would be some congruence between a respondent's stated preference for a particular leader and their ideological leanings. However, the fact that supporters of Blaize and Gairy, who were both staunchly anti-communist, would be less likely to identify Bishop as the leader who had done the least to help the country than one of the other two leaders suggests that the ideological orientation of the leaders had little bearing upon how they were evaluated by the respondents.

The findings of Brathwaite and myself conflict significantly with the views of critics of the PRG, both in Grenada and in the U.S., who have stressed the incompatibility of the PRG's socialist ideology with the Christian morals and values embraced by most Grenadians (Sandford and Vigilante, 1984; Seabury and McDougall, 1984). Though it may have been just a sign of wishful thinking on his part, Phil French, a U.S. embassy official whom I interviewed, stated that there would be no future for the left in Grenada due to "the rejection by Grenadian citizens of their communist ideology" (Interview 10/21/87). Similarly, in a speech delivered on the occasion of the visit by President Ronald Reagan to Grenada, Blaize asserted that "we (Grenadians) had been living in a stinking communist hole," implying that Grenadians were oppressed by the ideological orientation of PRG (*Voice* 3/17/86). Bishop Sydney Charles expressed similar sentiments during an interview with me in which he claimed that the "deeply rooted Christian values of Grenadians would never permit them to accept the form of socialism and atheism which the PRG was trying to establish" (Interview 11/9/87). The idea that Bishop and the PRG would have never been able to retain power for an extended period of time due to the inherent conflict between the ideological orientation of the regime and the values of the people is not supported by any of the surveys conducted in Grenada after the invasion.

What the surveys do suggest quite clearly is that the ideology adopted by all three regimes was of far less importance to Grenadian citizens in their evaluation of the regimes than other factors. These other factors include an individual's perception that his/her living conditions were improving, and a sense that social and economic conditions throughout the country were generally getting better. I shall elaborate on these perceptions later, when I address the use of patronage and foreign support.

Singham suggest that the absence of a firmly rooted traditional culture in Grenada and other West Indian societies leads to a type of political socialization in which the "individual finds it very difficult to develop a political value system that differentiates between rational and irrational demands for change" (Singham: 192). He contends that "such an individual does not readily respond to ideologies or ideological values but rather to leaders who can articulate his hostility . . . the object of his hostility is not clearly focused: the individual is against the state, or the economic conditions he suffers under or just 'them'" (Singham: 193). Singham's observations about the ideological ambivalence of the population are confirmed by the more recent surveys which show almost no clear patterns with respect to the ideological orientation of the population.

Yet, it is important to point out that while it may be true that the ideological orientation embraced by a regime provides no indication of whether or not that regime was supported by the populace, it does not mean that ideology was of no value or importance to the regime itself. On the contrary, whereas the citizenry may have largely based their evaluation of the three regimes upon an individual and collective sense of social and economic progress, the regimes themselves tended to measure their success or failure on the extent to which they achieved their ideological goals.

This was particularly true for the PRG, which placed all of its plans and measured all of its progress through the lenses of the Marxist-Leninist ideology adopted by its leaders. Yet, this was also true, though to a far lesser extent, for the Gairy and the Blaize regimes, both of which set goals that were largely influenced by their particular ideological leanings. Though less doctrinaire than the PRG, the Gairy and Blaize regimes perceived their success as being related to the correct applications of policies which were devised and implemented under the influence of their ideologies.

The Role and Importance of Ideology to the PRG

Most of the policies and programs enacted by the PRG were influenced by the ideological outlook of the leadership which they described as Marxism-Leninism. Because they perceived their government as one which served the interests of the workers and peasants first and foremost, they embarked upon numerous projects designed to improved the living standards of these groups. The elimination of school fees, the creation of the free milk program, the house repair program, the national literacy campaign and reforms which made health care more accessible were all products of the party's ideology, which called for redistributing the island's wealth such that the needs of the masses became the highest priority of the government.[12]

This goal was made explicit through speeches by Bishop and other leaders of the PRG, but more importantly, these goals were openly discussed in the meetings of the Central Committee and Political Bureau. In his "Line of March" speech delivered to the members of the NJM on September 13, 1982, Bishop explicitly stated the party's goal of creating a "dictatorship of the proletariat" (Bishop Speaks: 67). While this was seen as a long term goal of the revolution, in the short term this would involve the suppression of the "rights" of the island's elites and middle class when their aspirations conflicted with the perceived interests of working people. "The point is all rights are not for them, all freedoms are not for them, but all freedoms and rights are now for the majority who are no longer oppressed and repressed by a tiny minority. That is very important because that is what dictatorship or rule means" (Bishop Speaks: 62).

Beyond a general commitment to serving the needs of the lower classes, even at the expense of the middle and upper class if necessary, the PRG's ideology also influenced its policies in other ways. It's foreign policy, for example, was heavily influenced by ideological factors, as was its strategy for soliciting foreign aid.[13] Domestically, the regime's policies in the area of law enforcement, media, education, tourism, land reform and economic development all had the stamp of the regime's ideology.

What this meant in a practical sense is that policy directions on how to handle matters in these areas was developed by the party, rather than being left to the government. As has been pointed out previously, there was a sharp distinction between those individuals who held positions in the government and those who served in the leadership of the party. As part of its "united front strategy" (Grenada Documents: 51-13) the PRG had invited certain individuals who were non-party members to serve in important positions in the government. In part, this was a necessity due to the shortage of individuals in the party who possessed the skills and training to perform all of the necessary functions in the government and civil service. However, the presence of non-party members in the government was also intended to reassure foreign and domestic critics of the government that the PRG would not pursue an overly radical course. Bishop explained their inclusion in the following manner to party members:

> From the start too, comrades, we had an alliance with sections of our upper petty bourgeoisie and national bourgeoisie right from the word GO . . . I can remember well that the first set of names we announced for the ruling council was fourteen . . . and these fourteen names were made up mainly of the petty-bourgeoisie, the upper petty-bourgeoisie and the national bourgeoisie; . . . that is who the People's Revolutionary Government was. And this was done deliberately so that imperialism won't get too excited and would say 'well they have some nice fellas in that thing; everything alright' and as a result wouldn't think about sending in troops (Bishop Speaks: 63).

Beyond influencing government policy, the ideology of the party leadership also was used to plan for the future development of the country and the "revolution." While the leadership of the NJM saw the creation of socialism as the ultimate goal of the revolution, they perceived several obstacles which blocked that development, some of which were external, namely the threat of foreign intervention, but internal ones as well. For example, the leadership believed that the country was at a "disadvantage since only the working class can build socialism" (Grenada Documents: 51-16). According to the definition employed by the party leadership, Grenada had a very small working class. The many, poor, small land owners throughout the island were seen as an unreliable force for the task of building socialism since their ownership of land was believed to encourage petit-bourgeois aspirations and values (Grenada Documents: 51-17). To address this obstacle, the party leadership envisioned replacing small peasant proprietorship with wage labor on larger state-owned and managed farms, as well as cooperatives which were to be established with government assistance.

This is just an example of how the ideology of the party influenced the way in which it administered the government and planned for the future development of the society. Of course, it must also be said that ideology was also used as the basis for criticizing Bishop by other members of the leadership of the party. Couched in the rhetoric of Marxism-Leninism, Bishop was accused and found guilty of "bourgeois liberalism" and was said to have exhibited a low level of ideological development (Grenada Documents: 101-4). In the end, ideology became the basis for the split within the leadership, and provided the justification for the execution of Bishop and other NJM leaders in the final days, thereby creating the opportunity for the U.S. invasion.

The Role of Ideology in the Blaize and Gairy Regimes

The Gairy and Blaize regimes were far less concerned with ideology than the PRG, though ideology also played a role in the formulation of policies and goals pursued by these governments. Neither embraced a clearly defined doctrine, as was the case with Bishop and the PRG, but both leaders were influenced by the ideological orientation which was adopted by their regimes.

The genesis of the post-colonial state in Grenada, having been based upon a different set of class alignments than was true elsewhere in the West Indies, has produced different patterns with respect to its autonomy in relation to the various social classes. As a result of its different class character, the state in Grenada experienced a degree of autonomy from both the middle and upper classes that was not found elsewhere in the region. The unwillingness of the upper classes to accept or accommodate Gairy led him to use his control over state resources to punish them. His efforts at land reform and his support for unionization, though largely aimed at weakening his enemies, also had the effect of benefiting the lower classes and deepening his support among them. Though Gairy was by no means a socialist, his populist ideology, combined with his desire to punish the class forces who aligned themselves against him, prodded Gairy to pursue a strategy that at times brought tangible benefits to the lower class. While such policies did not increase Gairy's accountability to his lower class constituents, it did establish a pattern of their inclusion in Grenadain politics that was not evident elsewhere in the region. This pattern of working class inclusion has had a profound influence upon the actions and policies of the regimes that succeeded his.

Yet, it would be a mistake to conclude that because the Gairy regime enjoyed a degree of autonomy not found elsewhere in the region that its commitment to democracy was any greater. Gairy, like many of the other leaders in the region, had autocratic and, some would say, megalomanic tendencies. From 1967 on his regime was characterized by its brutal treatment of its opponents and blatant disregard for established legal practices. Moreover, like his counterparts in the region, Gairy did not attempt to challenge the foreign interests that controlled Grenada's economy; rather, he sought to personally enrich himself through his cooperation with them. In this respect, the Gairy regime conformed to the established patterns of neo-colonialism that have severely limited the possibilities for development on the island and in the Caribbean.[14]

Still, describing the ideological orientation of the Gairy regime is difficult, for Gairy was truly an eclectic when viewed on matters of principle and belief. When asked how he would characterize the ideological orientation of his party and government, he claimed that Christianity was the guiding doctrine (Interview 9/12/87). However, further analysis reveals a strong opposition to communism, though he was once labelled a communist by his opponents, with a strong commitment to Grenadian populism. Gairy remained a populist throughout his career, and though his contact with the masses decreased over the course of time, the policies and programs he enacted were still largely influenced by his unique form of populism. Even as he became more accepted among elites on the island and began to associate with individuals who were allegedly involved with organized crime during the 1970s, Gairy's policies retained much of their earlier populist orientation. The World Expo in 1970 and the Easter Water Parade in 1976 were two large extravaganzas sponsored by the government which attracted thousands of Grenadians, as well as many visitors from neighboring islands. Such events served as demonstrations of national pride and provided Gairy with ceremonies at which he could project his vision for the country to large crowds. Gairy also established the "Meet the People Tours," which many Gairyites claim were later copied by the PRG when it implemented its community volunteer programs. The "Meet the People Tours" were held to solicit volunteer labor in minor construction projects on roads, schools, bridges, and health clinics. Food and rum were often provided at no cost to the volunteers in exchange for their free labor on the projects. According to former participants, the tours were generally very successful in attracting large numbers of volunteers.[15] Programs such as these, as well as others, were devised by Gairy out of his populist orientation toward the common folk.

Blaize, on the other hand, had been influenced largely by his belief in the free market and a desire to preserve the social hierarchy established by the French and British. Within this social structure, the landed elites held the economic power on the island, while the brown-skinned middle class controlled government and the civil service. This arrangement suited Blaize and the GNP well. As leader of the GNP, Blaize championed the interests of the private sector, which in turn provided substantial political and financial support to him and his party. Moreover, while Grenada was a British colony, Blaize also worked very closely with the colonial authorities in devising policies for local government that met their approval. During his last term in office, he was influenced by U.S. economic advisors and relied quite heavily upon their advice in devising economic policies. As a result of this influence, the policies of the NNP government heavily favored the interests of the business sector and the wealthy, while the needs of the lower class were treated as less of a priority.

The conservative ideology of the Blaize regime was also responsible for undoing many of the social reforms that had been enacted by both the PRG and the Gairy regimes. As was mentioned previously, there were several cases in which lands that had been provided to poor people for squatting or permanent residence were returned to their original owners or merely taken by the government to be sold for private use. Beachfront property, which had previously been accessible to all Grenadians, was sold by the NNP government, with provisions enabling the new landowners to restrict public access. Social reforms such as the adult literacy effort, the free milk program, the house repair program and the school book subsidy program have all been either eliminated or greatly reduced. All of these actions were attempted under the influence of an ideology which placed the interests of capital ahead of the interests of the lower classes and were often carried out with the justification that the regime was righting past wrongs and bringing long overdue justice to those who had been victims of the previous regimes.

Hence, while it can be said that the ideologies embraced by the Gairy, Bishop and Blaize regimes were almost irrelevant to Grenadian citizens in their evaluations of the three regimes, ideology has had considerable influence over the regimes themselves. Ideology has shaped the policies which the regimes have adopted and has influenced the thinking of the leadership when goals for the future were made. Most importantly, ideology has been a key factor in influencing decisions when a regime has been confronted with choices over how to distribute and allocate limited resources. It is the ideology of the regime which has enabled it to rationalize and justify the choices that were made. Ultimately, ideology also serves as the basis through which regimes evaluate their own successes and failures.

The ideological orientation of Eric Gairy and Maurice Bishop may also be important to understanding why Grenada has deviated so sharply from the Commonwealth Caribbean with respect to its political trajectory. Gairy's emergence as a labor leader in 1951 not only delivered the country from its docility, which had allowed it to miss out on the nationalist upheavals that occurred more than a decade earlier elsewhere in the region, but also enabled him to assume a position of national leadership. While labor leaders were present in the leadership of several other islands, no other West Indian territory produced a leader of Gairy's class or color. Gairy's populism, combined with the challenge he represented to the social hierarchy in Grenada, in turn made it possible for yet another Grenadian deviation to occur nearly thirty years later, the rise of a radical socialist to a position of national leadership. With its open appeal to the interests of the lower class, Gairyism laid the basis for the socialism espoused by Bishop and the PRG. Whereas in other West Indian nations the anti-imperialist, Marxist-Leninist ideology of the NJM might have rendered them to the margins of mainstream politics, in Grenada the radical legacy of Gairy and the GULP created fertile ground on which the party could flourish.

The Role of Patronage in Consolidating Popular Support

Based upon the findings of the survey and the historical analysis of Grenadian politics, it is clear that for many of the respondents, improving the quality of life, for themselves as individuals and the country as a whole, has been the most central concern. 32% of the respondents who were asked what they would look for when selecting a leader in the next election stated that they would favor a candidate who had the ability to improve economic conditions. Similarly, in their criticisms of the three leaders, respondents most often cited poor performance on matters related to the economy or their own experience of economic hardships during the period that a particular leader was in power as the basis for their negative opinion.

An analysis of Grenadian political attitudes during periods of economic decline on the island reveals that concern over social welfare and the state of the economy has been the primary factor influencing popular opinion toward government. For example, the Gairy regime was most vulnerable to challenges from the New Jewel Movement during the 1970's when the prices of imports had risen sharply due to high rates of inflation in the economies of Grenada's primary trading partners (Canada, the United Kingdom and the United States). Similarly, the leaders of the NJM became most concerned about their support among the population as it became increasingly difficult for the government to pay the salaries of the expanded civil service due to shortfalls in foreign aid. Likewise for Blaize's NNP government, much of the dissatisfaction toward the regime was linked to rising unemployment and rising prices for consumer goods and housing.

All three of the regimes in this study established patronage systems to cope with the vagaries of an economy that is characteristically vulnerable to changes in foreign markets. Although Gairy's was by far the most extensive and perhaps the most effective, each regime developed a system of patronage which operated with informal rules and methods of compensation through organized channels. Since independence, the organizational apparatus has typically consisted of the ruling party, various trade organizations and the civil service, with loyal lieutenants serving as the functionaries between government and constituents. Each regime utilized both direct (employment, money, housing, etc.) and indirect (community services, infrastructure improvements, etc.) forms of patronage to satisfy the needs of clients.

Patronage Under the Gairy Regime

The patronage system developed by Gairy came into being shortly after his electoral victory in 1951. Throughout its tenure, the system was revised based upon changes in the constitution that increased the power of the elected leadership over public sector employees. As direct supervision by the colonial authorities over local government was gradually withdrawn, Gairy's use of patronage, in particular the employment of supporters in government controlled jobs, increased.

Upon returning to power in 1961, Gairy set out to develop a system of patronage which would enable him to satisfy the expectations of his followers whose quality of life he had promised to improve upon taking office. His efforts to do this during the first fifteen months he was in office led to the investigation of his government by the colonial authorities over charges referred to in the local press as "Squandermania." Prior to his ouster by Chief Administrator Lloyd, Gairy attempted to allow some of his allies to obtain monopolies as the sole providers of certain goods and services to government (Jacobs: 81). Jacobs describes the strategy as an attempt to "undermine the 'old elite,' headed by the plantocracy which had historically supported the GNP, and substitute a new elite created by their close association to the Gairy regime and, thus, beholden to Gairy himself" (Jacobs: 82). The strategy also involved an attempt to undermine the Tenders Board, which had authority to approve public works contracts so that Gairy could use government projects as a means to employ his supporters (Brizan: 237). In both cases, he used patronage to co-opt and neutralize groups and individuals who were potentially hostile toward him.

Gairy's attempt to establish a system of patronage generated considerable hostility from his opponents in the colonial administration, the civil service, the GNP and, later, the NJM, as well. For these groups, Gairy's attempts at consolidating power through the establishment of a patronage network was seen as a sign of the authoritarian tendencies inherent in Gairy's style of leadership. Following his defeat in 1957, Gairy believed that the new powers which accompanied the constitution of 1959 would greatly enhance his ability to exercise control over government and, thereby, enable him to secure power on the island indefinitely. Gairy understood that the key to his political success lay in his ability to deliver tangible benefits to his supporters. Fiery rhetoric and agitation could get him elected, but only "bread and butter" could keep him in power over time.

During the 1950s, Gairy's efforts to consolidate power by strategically placing his supporters in the civil service brought him into direct conflict with the colonial administrator, who still possessed ultimate control over government affairs. A.W. Singham describes the conflict which ensued and Gairy's dilemma in the following way:

> The moment the colonial politician assumes office, he must try to reconcile the demands of two opposing sets of people and problems. First he must come to terms with the complex financial procedures and the personnel of the bureaucracy, and at the same time, he must find ways and means to keep his supporters happy by providing services and goods. The latter forces him to spend a good part of his day meeting clients and proving how valuable his personal intervention is for them. Since the coffers of the state in a colony like Grenada are hardly overflowing, he becomes perpetually involved in finding sources of funds to satisfy his supporters. The politician is therefore faced with the problem of trying to increase the funds of the state, not only to satisfy the demands of his followers, but also to try to improve economic conditions. His mass support, after all, is based primarily on his promises to improve the lot of the voters (Singham: 171).

When Gairy finally returned to power in 1967, he found himself with greater authority than ever before, and in a better position to establish the system of patronage that he saw as vital to his long term political interests. The new constitution of 1967 provided total authority for managing domestic affairs to an elected Senate and House of Representatives, headed by a Premier who was to be selected by the party that had won the majority of seats in the national elections. With his newly gained power over government, Gairy was soon able to gain control over the civil service. Anti-Gairy elements were transferred from their jobs and subjected to various forms of harassment. All new hirings were filled by Gairy loyalists, often selected personally by him. Jobs in the public sector came to be a major pillar of Gairy's patronage system, and by 1972, enabled him to cultivate a political base for the first time among urban civil servants (Brizan: 247). In addition to the public sector, Gairy utilized the GMMWU to recruit workers in the private sector, which greatly increased the number of workers who were directly and indirectly dependent upon him for their livelihoods.

Aside from using land and jobs as a form of patronage, Gairy utilized a variety of other forms of personal power to maintain his control over government. Several Grenadians that I interviewed claimed to have received small gifts and money directly from Gairy upon making a request to his office during times of need.[16] Gairy was known to visit the homes of the elderly during the holiday season to distribute presents. He also made numerous appearances at weddings, funerals and other ceremonies that provided occasions for him to display his generosity toward the hosts and their guests. In areas where support for Gairy was high, such as Calliste and Grand Anse, indirect forms of patronage through the construction of health clinics, schools, post offices and recreation centers were utilized as well. Such actions by Gairy helped to sustain the support and loyalty of those who benefited from his patronage.

Patronage was, therefore, a very effective component of the survival strategy of the Gairy regime. Like the boss politicians of New York's Tammany Hall, Gairy was able to cultivate and maintain a solid base among the population by delivering tangible benefits to his constituents. Conversely, life for his opponents could be made extremely difficult. For those he considered hostile, disloyal or undependable, he was able to devise a number of ways to make life difficult. This carrot and stick approach was supplemented by other aspects of the regime's survival strategy, which effectively enabled Gairy to hold on to power continuously from 1967 to 1979.

Moreover, Gairy's use of patronage enabled him to counter the control of the economy exerted by the large landowners and larger retailers who had traditionally held a monopoly on power and political influence on the island. Using the resources of the state as his leverage, Gairy could make life difficult for his opponents through the imposition of tariffs and a variety of taxes. By organizing their workers, Gairy could also threaten his opponents with strikes and labor unrest. His effective use of his union and the state apparatus enabled him to become more than merely a figurehead, administering a weak government; Gairy was the boss of a large political operation that could control resources and their distribution, and in many cases, extract cooperation from those who sought to undermine him.

Patronage Under the Blaize
and Bishop Regimes

Like Gairy, the governments headed by Maurice Bishop and Herbert Blaize also utilized patronage as a strategy for maintaining popular support. However, unlike Gairy, their patronage networks relied more heavily upon indirect rather than direct forms of patronage. Whereas the Gairy regime could be described as a form of "personal rulership" (Bendix and Roth 1971) in which beneficiaries of the regime's largess were personally responsible for some form of reciprocity, the Bishop and Blaize regimes were more impersonal and their exercise of power more diffuse. Both regimes followed Gairy's example in employing their supporters in the civil service and utilizing government contracts to the advantage of their allies. However, those who received jobs from the Bishop and Blaize regimes were less likely to feel personally indebted or obliged to show tangible support for their patrons. This was due to the fact that the form of patronage used by the Bishop and Blaize regimes was implemented primarily to co-opt and control potential opponents of the regime rather than to insure their loyalty.

Neither the PRG nor the NNP governments were as entrenched as the Gairy regime of the early 1970's. For the PRG especially, there was constant concern over credibility among the masses and perceptions of legitimacy, both domestic and international, largely because of the manner by which the NJM gained state power. The PRG used patronage by dramatically increasing employment in the public sector, lowering unemployment and demonstrating the effectiveness of its policies. Jobs combined with increased social services were also intended to serve as tangible evidence that the benefits of the revolution would accrue to those whose needs had long been ignored. However, whereas individuals who gained employment under Gairy understood that retention of their jobs was contingent upon political support for him, public sector employees under the PRG felt no similar sense of accountability to the PRG. Such individuals were more likely to see the provision of jobs and services as part of the fulfillment of the promises of the revolution, rather than as a form of patronage.

The following quote from a thirty-two year old farmer from Birchgrove, a village located in St. Andrews parish in the center of the island, is indicative of how patronage under the PRG was perceived:

> Sure, a lot of people got jobs, and scholarships and all kinds of training, but these things are small compared to what the people in the party was getting. Look, these men promised that the revolution was going to make everything better for the poorer people in Grenada. I can't say that some did not benefit. I for one did, because I went to Bulgaria and became a mechanic. But that don't mean that them didn't take care of themselves first. All of them fellas in the party got nice cars and houses out of it. Them is the main ones that was benefiting from the revolution.

In addition to a general effort to maintain and increase overall support for the revolution through increasing the "social wage,"[17] the PRG also used government services to promote support among constituencies which were critical or even hostile toward them. By extending previously inaccessible services to a community through the construction of a health clinic or the rehabilitation of roads and bridges, relations between residents and the PRG could be expected to improve. For example, during their first two years in power, the PRG devoted considerable attention and resources to the island of Carriacou. Carriacou had historically been neglected by Gairy, due to its history of support for its native son, Herbert Blaize and the GNP. The PRG built new roads on the island and greatly expanded water and electricity services to residents. As a result, political support on the island for the PRG was high, as measured by rates of participation in the national literacy campaign, the militia, and the various other mass organizations.[18] Such forms of patronage often helped to reduce the degree of antagonism toward the regime emanating from those who felt deprived or unserved by the government.

However, the PRG experienced great difficulty in providing this form of indirect patronage on an ongoing basis and the costs could not be sustained. As economic hardships hit the country in 1983, it became increasingly difficult for the PRG to pay the salaries of the expanded public sector labor force. It also became increasingly difficult to continue to extend services and to complete development projects, as sources of foreign aid began to dry up. With the shrinking of available resources, recipients of government patronage became less restrained in their criticisms of the PRG and were less likely to participate in the mobilization efforts of the regime.

The use of patronage by Blaize's NNP followed a pattern similar to that of the PRG. Though swept into office by a wide margin at the polls, the NNP government found itself in a tenuous situation because it was confronted by high expectations that it would quickly succeed in the task of improving living conditions and reviving the economy. Even with the backing of the United States, reducing the level of unemployment which had soared to nearly fifty percent during the year after the invasion was not a simple task, particularly since the regime planned to rely heavily upon foreign investment in the private sector to bring about economic recovery. The fact that many of the unemployed were suspected former supporters of the PRG, as well as former soldiers from the People's Revolutionary Army, added to the pressure on the regime.

Like the PRG, the NNP's use of patronage did not necessarily ensure the loyalty of the recipients. Rather, the NNP used patronage primarily to discourage opposition to the regime. As it had in the past, the government took steps to ensure that its allies among the local elite benefited from the policies enacted while they were in control over the government. However, for the most part, to the extent that the regime's patronage extended beyond the elite and traditional GNP supporters, it was limited to those who were enlisted in the reconstituted military or employed in the civil service. Unlike the Gairy and Bishop regimes, large segments of the population were untouched by either direct or indirect patronage. Patronage was, therefore, not an effective component of the NNP's strategy to cultivate and maintain political support nor did it help the regime to expand its base of support beyond its traditional allies.

Though patron-client systems were developed by all three regimes, only the Gairy regime developed the kind of patronage networks that proved effective as a means of sustaining political support and stability. Elsewhere in the Caribbean, such systems have been instrumental in cultivating the loyalty of key constituencies and prolonging the longevity of several governments (Edie 1991; Thomas 1987; Stone and Henry 1983). Gairy's use of patronage proved effective because it was so extensive and matched his style of leadership. The beneficiaries of patronage were made to understand that they were personally indebted to Gairy. Conversely, Bishop and Blaize used patronage in an attempt to satisfy popular expectations that their governments could improve economic conditions. The grandiosity of their promises combined with the impersonal manner in which rewards were granted brought them substantially less political benefit.

Finally, it must be pointed out that excessive dependence on patronage contributed to the ultimate demise of all three regimes. In a developing society like Grenada, the ability of the government to extract and accumulate resources is not only limited, it is also subject to fluctuation. The control over the economy exerted by foreign interests who are able to determine the rates of exchange for Grenada's primary exports, the viability of the tourist industry, the flow of aid, and the cost of consumer goods makes it difficult for local government to engage in financial planning over an extended period. Retractions in the local economy are inevitable and unpredictable. Such fluctuations can undermine the credibility of those in power because the government has no way of fulfilling its commitments during periods of recession. Patronage systems have limited elasticity, and when the coffers of the state are empty, the state has few options available for satisfying the needs of its clients. Economic hardships, frustrated expectations and retrenchment in the public sector, while not the sole factor contributing to their demise, featured prominently in the downfall of all three governments. In this respect, reliance on patronage can set a trap for politicians in a small, poor nation like Grenada: it can serve as both the base of political power and the cause of decline and collapse.

The Use of Coercion as a Strategy for Regime Survival

At various times, most regimes rely on some form of coercion, either out of sheer expediency or because the leaders perceive there to be no other viable options for contending with opponents. The Gairy, Bishop and Blaize regimes were not exceptions. All three found it necessary to deploy the state's coercive apparatus against their opponents when other options appeared less viable.

Within the scope of coercive measures available to the state, there are a broad range of actions that can be taken to curtail the activities of political opponents and those whom the regime regards as subversive. All three regimes in Grenada had access to coercive resources that included: the enactment of legislation to limit the ability of opposition political parties to function legally, the use of the police and courts to arrest and detain opponents of the regime, the use of unofficial agents of repression in carrying out acts of intimidation and violence against dissidents, and the use of foreign support in the form of actual or threatened military intervention. While each of the three regimes employed coercion as part of its strategy for survival, the extent and nature of state sponsored coercion varied considerably between them.

While it is true that most regimes find it necessary to engage in some form of repression to ensure survival, excessive reliance on such measures is necessarily restricted by the fear that a regime may become stigmatized by its use of violence against political opponents, a characterization which invariably affects its external image. Particularly within the English speaking Caribbean, with its history of respect for civil liberties and democratic government, excessive use of repression by a state can lead to ostracism and isolation, as eventually happened to the PNC (Peoples' National Congress) government headed by Forbes Burnham in Guyana. For this reason, state sponsored coercion in Grenada has generally been employed strategically and, if possible, under a rationale that is presumably defensible to outsiders.

For example, when the PRG imprisoned the leaders of a rebellion that was allegedly being fomented within the ranks of PRA soldiers residing in Tivoli (a small village in St. Andrews parish), they defended their action by asserting that the soldiers intended to seize a privately owned estate and use the land for marijuana cultivation. Similarly, when the leadership of the NJM were beaten in November of 1973 by Gairy's police force and so-called police aids, the Gairy government attempted to rationalize the arrests and beatings by claiming that the NJM was plotting a coup against his government.

Particularly in a nation such as Grenada, where parliamentary democracy and the rule of law have been a part of political and civil traditions since the colonial period, the use of overt violence by the state or excessive infringements on personal freedoms has generally been avoided. One of the vestiges of Grenada's colonial past has been the availability of external avenues for appeal of legal matters through higher courts located outside of the island. These legal channels have provided victims of injustice with an important legal arena through which to air, publicize and seek recourse for violations of various kinds. This has been especially important for those who have been victims of politically motivated censorship, harassment and intimidation. The Commission of Inquiry headed by a Jamaican jurist, Herbert Duffus, that was called to Grenada to investigate allegations of injustice on the island following the beatings of the NJM leadership in November 1973, served precisely this purpose. More recently, Bernard Coard and the other NJM Central Committee members who received death sentences for their alleged involvement in the assassination of Maurice Bishop and others were able to appeal to the Privy Council in Great Britain for an appeal of the verdicts. The possibility of recourse through an external source of adjudication had considerable influence on the conduct of the three regimes and served as a restraint to the extent to which coercion was used. Despite this restrain, however, coercion was a part of the repertoire of tactics utilized by all three regimes for retaining power.

The Use of Coercion by the Gairy Regime

In many respects, it is ironic that the Gairy regime became infamous for its repressive character and that Gairy became widely regarded as a small but ruthless dictator. For all the charges of repression levelled against the Gairy regime and the accusations that Gairy had erected a dictatorship, at the time he was overthrown, there were no political prisoners being held on the island. Throughout the thirteen years of uninterrupted rule by Gairy, opposition parties remained legal and, though subject to harassment, were allowed to participate in elections. An independent judiciary continued to function, which, while manipulated by Gairy at various points, also became an arena through which NJM leaders Maurice Bishop and Kenrick Radix won important legal battles against the Gairy regime. Independent newspapers such as the anti-Gairy *Torchlight* remained operative throughout the Gairy years and political opponents of the regime were able to hold public demonstrations at which they openly called for his removal. Gairy's opponents were often subject to unofficial harassment and physical intimidation by the Mongoose Gang and the police force, but officially organizations in opposition were allowed to operate and they took advantage of these opportunities to the detriment of Eric Gairy. Why the image of the Gairy regime became permanently associated with violence and repression in ways that the others did not is a matter which warrants further exploration.

From the start of his political career in Grenada, Gairy was accused by his opponents of using force and physical intimidation to achieve political objectives. The threat of strikes, arson and violence on the estates, as symbolized by the dreaded code word "sky red" which was used to indicate the possibility that such actions would be directed at a particular estate, were employed by Gairy as a means of leverage against the colonial administration and the plantocracy (DaBreo: 61). Similarly, following the Black Power protests and the attempted military coup in Trinidad in 1972, Gairy announced to the nation, via the airwaves, the formation of auxiliary police units which would be used against those who attempted to engage in similar activities in Grenada. The Duffus Commission later referred to these units as "an unlawfully constituted body of men with a proclivity to violence" (Duffus Commission Report: 123). Gairy himself announced that he was recruiting the "toughest and roughest" into the ranks of these special forces. Shortly thereafter, opponents of the regime, including members of the NJM, GNP, journalists, and others considered unfriendly by the regime, became the object of physical intimidation, violent attacks and in some cases, politically motivated killings by the group which became popularly referred to as the Mongoose Gang.

Gairy did not always act outside of the law to persecute his enemies. He also enacted a number of laws to provide legal justification for his actions. For example, the Emergency Powers Act of 1970 provided the police with a free hand in their efforts to monitor and control "subversive elements" (Brizan, 1987: 13). Likewise, the Newspaper Amendment Act of 1976 was devised to make it difficult for the NJM to produce or distribute the weekly Jewel newspaper by requiring publishers to deposit $20,000.00 with the government. Finally, the Public Order Act was enacted by the Legislative Council in 1976, placing a ban on the use of microphones and loudspeakers at public meetings. Such measures provided Gairy with a legal basis by which to censor his opponents.

The use of coercion by Gairy is regarded by many as the factor most responsible for the forceful overthrow of his government (Jacobs: 84; Heine: 220). Gairy's use of the police and Mongoose Gang in the intimidation and victimization of his enemies, as well as his efforts to make life difficult for his opponents through the seizure of their property, contributed to the radicalization of the opposition. Particularly after the failure of the general strike in 1974, the leadership of the NJM became convinced that Gairy would not allow himself to be removed from power nonviolently. The foul play and fraud which characterized the election of 1976 added to the perception that Gairy would not allow himself to be unseated through a fair election either (*Torchlight* 2/12/76).

Despite its apparent usefulness is a technique for thwarting the efforts of those opposed to him, excessive use coercion by Gairy eventually contributed to the regime's demise by undermining its legitimacy at home and abroad. In part, this is because Gairy never figured out how to convincingly justify the use of force against his opponents such that the credibility of his government would not be compromised. Gairy's unabashed use of repression against his opponents helped to galvanize elite and middle class opposition to his government through organizations like the Committee of 22. Moreover, the increasing use of coercion coincided with a decline in Gairy's contact with the masses. There was, therefore, less reliance upon his personal ties with the masses at the very time that his regime took on a more repressive character. As a result, the regime had no way of countering the antipathy that developed toward it during the late 1970's which was exploited by its opponents.

The Use of Coercion by the Bishop and Blaize Regimes

The use of coercion by the PRG presented its leaders with a major contradiction. Bishop, Radix and the other leaders of the NJM had based much of their opposition to Gairy on the charge that the regime violated the rights of the citizenry. Ironically, after the NJM assumed power through the takeover of 1979, the newly formed regime proceeded to commit many of the same violations of political freedoms for which it had previously attacked the Gairy regime. During the weeks that followed the takeover, dozens of people were detained without trial, most of whom had been members of the Gairy government, the police force or the Mongoose Gang. Initially, these were justified on the basis that such persons posed a threat to the newly formed government and they would only remain incarcerated until the political situation stabilized and new courts could be established. However, as time passed, the number of detainees grew, and while some of the earlier detainees were eventually tried and released, increasingly, the number of people detained without trial grew significantly under the rationale that they posed risks to national security.

Included among the ranks of the detained were Lloyd Noel, the former Attorney General of the PRG and a former law partner of Bishop. Noel had become disenchanted with the regime largely as a result of the excesses associated with the detention practice. Noel and others were arrested and detained in 1982 after publishing the *Grenada Voice* newspaper which PRG officials charged was funded by the C.I.A. Several former NJM members were also detained by the PRG, including: Kennedy Budhlall, the NJM member accused of killing Innocent Belmar, Gairy's police chief, and who led the attack on the Grenville police station the morning of March 13, 1979, the day of the NJM takeover, Teddy Victor, the founder and past editor of the *Jewel* Newspaper; and several young Rastafarians who had been supporters of the NJM throughout the 1970's but later became targets for detention as a result of their differences with the PRG. Many Rastafarians were detained at the Hope Vale estate, which though officially described as a farm cooperative was actually a forced labor camp used for the purpose of producing food to feed PRA soldiers.[19] Since there was no independent press that was allowed to function after the closure of the *Torchlight*, news about repressive actions taken by the PRG was not widely known and, as a consequence, gossip and rumor served as the primary source of information. Because initially many of these charges could not be substantiated, supporters of the regime generally dismissed this information as propaganda.

As tensions within the ruling circles of the NJM intensified, members of the leadership, particularly those aligned with Bishop, also became victims of detention, as the split within the party led to polarization, incriminations and, finally, confrontation over what were considered irreconcilable differences. Kenrick Radix and George Louison, two of the original founders of the NJM, were among those detained by the Revolutionary Military Council. When I interviewed Radix in 1987 about the PRG's practice of detaining people, he remained supportive of the practice. "It was necessary for us to detain those who we felt were counter revolutionaries because we knew that imperialism sought to destabilize the government through the use of agents. Though I eventually became a victim of the policy, I still defend it." What makes Radix' response particularly surprising is the fact that after the invasion, he returned to his law practice and once again represented victims of police brutality and political harassment, acts which he claimed were committed by a government that "terrorizes the people."

Aside from the detentions, the PRG also utilized threats and intimidation against a variety of other opponents. When the Catholic church attempted to publish a newsletter which was critical of the government, the paper was immediately shut down. Minutes from central committee meetings also revealed that the party leadership perceived the churches on the island to be hostile to the revolution and plans were developed to curtail their activities against the government. Businessmen who opposed the PRG's policies or who attempted to undermine them were fined and threatened with imprisonment. Even labor leaders, who had previously been seen as key members of the NJM's constituency and who engaged in agitation that challenged the government, were subjected to harassment and punishment.

Yet, despite the frequency with which it applied coercive measures against its political opponents, the interviews conducted with Grenadians four years after the invasion do not suggest that the PRG was viewed as either overly repressive or brutal. In fact, several individuals who stated that they had been detained by the regime or who had family members who were mistreated still cited the PRG headed by Bishop as the government that had done the most to help the country. Even among the 13% who cited the PRG as the government which had done the least to help the country, only 40% based their answer on violations of political freedoms which occurred while the PRG was in power.

The fact that respondents to the survey did not emphasize objections to political harassment and repression as a major factor in their evaluation of the PRG does not necessarily mean that such actions on the part of the government were seen as unimportant or not perceived as insignificant by the population. Rather, it suggests that Grenadians take a more encompassing view of their governments when evaluating them. For example, one conservative businessman from Grenville whom I interviewed stated that he hated the PRG and described them as "shit." Yet, when he compared them with the Gairy and Blaize regimes, he said "at least them fellas in the PRG were competent." In their evaluations of the three governments, respondents to the survey were primarily concerned with how they fared as individuals with respect to living conditions. Aside from that, all other factors, including political repression, were generally deemed secondary. In fact, respondents to the survey were more likely to criticize the Gairy regime for its repressiveness than they were to make the same criticism of the PRG, even though an historical assessment of the use of coercion by the two regimes seems to reveal greater evidence of political repression being carried out by the PRG.

The reason for this apparent contradiction lies in the perceptions of the Grenadian people and what they believe constitutes legitimate versus illegitimate uses of force by the state. While the actions taken by the Mongoose Gang to control and intimidate opponents of the Gairy regime may have been less severe than those carried out by the People's Revolutionary Army or the People's Militia, the latter possessed legitimacy while the former did not. Thousands of Grenadians joined the militia in their local areas to prepare for defense of the nation because they believed that the island would be attacked by the United States.[20] The unveiled hostility emanating from the United States toward Grenada created a climate on the island which called for vigilance on the part of the citizens who were, therefore, more tolerant of restrictions on personal freedoms as a result of the perceived external threat.

One explanation for the apparent incongruity between the opinions of those interviewed on the degree of coercion employed by the PRG and the reality of political repression during the revolution is the popularity enjoyed by the PRG. Supporters of the PRG were more likely to accept the regime's rationalization for utilizing coercion than were its opponents. The PRG often claimed that certain individuals were working in cooperation with U.S. imperialism, and that these individuals needed to be brought under "heavy manners." Undoubtedly, many Grenadians accepted this rationale and more or less tolerated the use of force by the government as being politically necessary. Toward the end of its term however, it seems clear that this tolerance was waning, and that increasingly, formerly supportive elements were raising objections over perceived injustices committed by the government in the name of national security.

Perhaps, even more than the Bishop and Gairy regimes, governments which have been headed by Herbert Blaize seem to have had better records for respecting political freedoms and have been less guilty of utilizing force against political opponents. Coercion has of course been utilized by the earlier Blaize-led governments, as well as by the more recent NNP government, however when compared to the Gairy and Bishop regimes, the degree and number of actual incidents has been far less.

Under earlier Blaize-led governments (1957-1961 and 1962-1967) there were relatively few attacks that were reported which were directed by the regime against political opponents. There was an attempt in 1965 to ban strikes by agricultural workers, but this could not be enforced since the British retained ultimate responsibility for enforcement of all laws at the time and they held a more benign view toward labor activity on the island (Jacobs: 64). Opposition parties and newspapers functioned freely, with little interference from the government, and there were no political prisoners.

Although during the period immediately following the U.S. invasion, repression against those associated with the PRG/NJM and its mass organizations was quite severe, much of this activity was carried out by the U.S. military. One year later, when the NNP assumed power under Blaize, there were relatively few incidents of government sponsored repression. Political parties, including the remnants of the NJM, now known as the Maurice Bishop Patriotic Movement (MBPM), and Gairy's GULP, all functioned freely, holding rallies, distributing their newspapers, and generally were allowed to operate in the open as they expressed their criticisms of the new government. There were several cases of alleged police brutality and several members of the MBPM were subject to various forms of harassment. However, unlike the detainees under the PRG, those who claimed to have been victimized by the regime were all able to seek legal redress through the courts. Initially, the government made it difficult for doctors and others who received training in socialist nations, such as Cuba, to practice their professions on the island, but even these restrictions were eventually relaxed and most were allowed to enter the labor force.

Perhaps the only strong case which could be made against the regime with regard to its respect for political freedoms and civil rights was in regard to the treatment of Bernard Coard and the others who were accused of slaying Bishop and the other PRG leaders. There is well documented evidence that these individuals have at various times been mistreated and subjected to physical and mental abuse (Ferguson 1989: 94-96). It has also been argued that they never received a fair trial for the offense with which they have been charged (Amnesty International, 1984). However, in their efforts to win an appeal, Coard and the others have laid most of the blame for the miscarriage of justice on the United States and not the NNP.

Coard's charges of U.S. interference exposes a consistent pattern which was followed whenever Blaize held power, that of relying upon external powers for assistance and, ultimately, their coercive ability to achieve political objectives. As the party which was favored by the British colonial authorities, Blaize's GNP often relied upon the British to intervene in the political affairs of Grenada to provide him with the assistance he needed to prevail over Gairy. In each case, the intimidation of a foreign power worked to the political advantage of Blaize. This is perhaps the reason why the governments which were led by Blaize did not have to rely upon direct forms of coercion. With the backing of foreign powers such as the United States or Great Britain, the regimes that Blaize led possessed a degree of security which allowed considerable complacency toward domestic challenges to its authority. The assurance that a foreign power would intervene militarily if necessary provided Blaize with a measure of invulnerability, which the Gairy and Bishop regimes did not enjoy. It also served as a form of external coercion for the regime, which intimidated opponents of the regime and effectively restricted their activities on the island.

Foreign Support: The Key to
Regime Survival in the Periphery

There is no question that foreign support is essential to a small, poor developing nation such as Grenada. Its heavy dependence upon foreign markets for its major exports, its need to import most of its consumer goods, and its dependence on foreign capital for development necessitate that it maintain supportive relations with larger and wealthier nations. During the colonial period, there was no need to be concerned with the question of foreign support. As a British colonial possession, Grenada's economic and political affairs were controlled by the British colonial authorities. However, with the coming of independence in 1974, the door was opened to utilize foreign policy for the purpose of achieving political and economic objectives.

Gairy perceived independence as an opportunity to increase the amount of foreign aid Grenada received, which in the years preceding independence, had been reduced considerably by the British. The Bishop and Blaize regimes also attempted to utilize foreign policy to obtain aid, both economic and military. Because of the importance of economic stability to regime survival, the ability to obtain foreign aid has often been viewed by Grenada's political leaders as the key to political success. Foreign aid can make it possible for a regime to sustain and even expand its patronage network. It can also provide a regime with a degree of security through the assurance of military backing if the regime is threatened with subversion from within or aggression from a hostile neighbor.

Yet, despite its value, adequate levels of foreign support are difficult to maintain over time, largely because of Grenada's size and relative unimportance in the geo-political context. Lacking in precious minerals or natural resources, Grenada has no strategic significance. This changed temporarily when the PRG established ties with Cuba, the Soviet Union and its allies. That alliance made Grenada politically significant in geopolitical terms for the first time. As the only English speaking Caribbean nation outside of the U.S. sphere of influence, Grenada attained sudden prominence, attracting both increased levels of foreign aid and hostility from the United States, which perceived its new diplomatic ventures as a threat to its interests. While the move toward the Soviet bloc clearly involved many risks to the island's security, it also enabled it to be seen as a more attractive recipient of foreign aid, particularly to countries that were not friendly toward the U.S. Though the PRG never succeeded in convincing the Soviet Union to provide large amounts of aid, the level of assistance it received from Cuba was substantial. The PRG also developed a knack for packaging its aid proposals in ways that proved attractive to a broad cross section of donor nations, thereby making it possible for the regime to avoid being perceived strictly as a Soviet client (Pryor: 34-48).

The NNP government also received large amounts of aid, most of which came from the United States in the aftermath of the invasion. However, just as sources of foreign aid for the PRG began to dry up during the fourth year of its rule, the same happened to the Blaize government in each year after the invasion. Once Grenada lost its perceived geo-political value to the United States, it gradually became just another poor Caribbean nation and the volume of aid it received diminished substantially.

Despite its unpredictability, foreign support remains an important component in the survival strategy of any regime in Grenada, both because of the need for foreign aid and because of Grenada's dependence upon foreign trade. The Gairy, Bishop and Blaize regimes each devised foreign policy strategies to provide them with financial, political and military support. However, each strategy was influenced to a large extent by the ideological orientation of the regime.

The Isolation of Eric Gairy

Gairy's foreign alliances played an important role in his strategy for regime survival. Particularly because of his start as a militant labor leader, it was important for him to establish support from labor leaders on other Caribbean islands. He emerged as the leader of the Grenadian labor movement a few years after the labor unrest on the other British West Indian colonies had produced a new generation of leaders, some of whom would eventually lead their islands to independence. During the height of the strike in 1951, Gairy boasted before his followers during a speech at Market Square that "Bustamante (leader of the Jamaican labor movement) behind my back; Butler (Grenadian born labor leader based in Trinidad) there also, and several other leaders with me . . . I knew that someday I must have become a famous leader . . ." (Singham: 168). His claim of support from West Indian labor leaders was intended as a message to the colonial authorities that he could not be dealt with in isolation, and that in their efforts to deal with him they had to be cognizant of the ramifications which could be felt elsewhere in the region. The queries made by labor leaders from Trinidad and Jamaica during the height of the uprising made it clear that Gairy and the uprising he led had to be dealt with delicately (Singham: 87).

The coming of independence in 1974 brought with it the power to develop diplomatic relations with other sovereign states. For a small and impoverished state, such an opportunity brought with it the prospect of acquiring new sources of aid which previously had not been available. Membership in the Organization of American States and the United Nations opened the doors for development assistance in the form of grants, loans and technical exchanges. In a bid to attract foreign aid, Gairy used his newly gained access to the international political arena to call for an international campaign against "evil individuals and small subversive groups whose aims and objectives are mainly and simply to disrupt the peace and harmony of society in their attempts to overthrow governments . . ." (Jacobs: 119).

As word spread in the region of his growing reliance on repression against his political opponents, Caribbean leaders began to distance themselves from Gairy. Grenada continued its membership in regional associations within the Commonwealth Caribbean but, increasingly, Gairy found it necessary to cultivate ties with nations outside of the region, which he believed would be more likely to provide the military and financial assistance he needed. Diplomatic relations were established with the Pinochet regime in Chile and the military government of South Korea during the mid-1970's. From both nations, he obtained arms as well as technical assistance in counter insurgency tactics, and in exchange, his regime provided political support when either nation came under attack in international fora for human rights violations against their citizens (Jacobs: 119).

As his concern about the threat posed by the NJM to the stability of his government grew, Gairy also sought assistance from the United States, Canada and Great Britain. To this day, Gairy maintains that the unwillingness of those nations to "heed my warnings about the communist threat in Grenada," led to the 1979 NJM take over.[21]

Although at the time the U.S. was displaying a new interest in the region largely as a result of the development of diplomatic relations between Cuba and the Manley government in Jamaica, it was hesitant to embrace Gairy. His reputation as a tyrant, combined with his well known eccentric behavior, caused the United States to remain cautious in its approach to his regime. Moreover, Gairy had provided refuge to an American charged by U.S. courts with embezzlement, who was allegedly linked to organized crime (*Torchlight* 6/15/78). There were also reports that Grenadian banks were used to launder funds brought into the country by criminal elements from the United States (*Torchlight* 9/12/78). While the U.S. had no desire to see the radical NJM replace Gairy, they found it difficult to develop close ties with him, particularly under the Carter administration's foreign policy with its proclaimed commitment to human rights (Barry et al., 1984).

By the time of the NJM takeover, the Gairy regime was largely isolated. In early 1977, Gairy approached the British High Commissioner to request modern weapons to equip his forces. The Commissioner responded derisively, "to shoot what with," as a clear indication to Gairy that he could not even count on the former mother country for help as opposition to him mounted (Lewis, 1984: 24). The relatively short amount of time it took for the People's Revolutionary Government to gain official recognition and acceptance in the region and by the international community as a legitimate government was a further reflection of the lack of support possessed by the Gairy regime toward the end of its tenure.

While the Gairy regime clearly understood the importance of foreign support to its survival, Gairy and his colleagues failed to foresee how their domestic policies and the reputation it had developed would influence their ability to develop alliances externally. After independence, Gairy placed little importance upon his ties with other Caribbean nations, Grenada's traditional locus of foreign support, and instead chose to cultivate ties with nations such as Chile and South Korea, nations which were themselves isolated politically, while simultaneously attempting to garner support from the U.S. on the basis of his anti-communist and pro-western stance. He understood the need to develop supportive relationships with the major western powers, but he failed to realize that his authoritarian practices at home would reduce the possibility of receiving support from those countries. Gairy's foreign policy thus failed to serve as an effective part of the survival strategy of his regime, and as a result contributed to its eventual downfall.

The PRG's Strategy for
Obtaining Foreign Aid

From the onset, Bishop and the NJM were keenly aware of the importance of developing foreign support. Particularly because of the radical route to power taken by them, establishing credibility internationally was viewed as an essential first step by the NJM leadership in their efforts to consolidate power. The fear that Gairy would rally foreign support to stage a counter revolution against the newly formed government or that the United States would take the initiative on its own to remove them from power led party leaders to devise a fairly sophisticated strategy for obtaining foreign support early on.

To neutralize potential antagonists within the international arena and to gain acceptance from those they perceived to be potential supporters, the PRG devised a multi-faceted strategy in its foreign policy. This strategy essentially consisted of cultivating and projecting different images to different nations, depending on ideological orientation of the donors (Heine: 123).

In his analysis of the PRG's quest for foreign aid, Pryor has identified three elements of the strategy which the regime employed. The first component was aimed at attracting aid from the socialist nations. Pryor argues that part of this strategy involved establishing the regime's "radical credentials," which he asserts was largely accomplished through a deliberate effort on the part of Bishop to allow relations between Grenada and the U.S. to deteriorate (Pryor: 49). Robert Pastor, the former senior staff member for Latin America on the U.S. National Security Council, contends that there was a decision made to have the early talks between Bishop and U.S. Ambassador Rizzo go badly (Heine: 192). While it may never be known for sure if the early deterioration in relations between the U.S. and the PRG were planned or accidental, it is clear from other actions taken by the regime that steps were taken to attract support from socialist nations, which the PRG must have understood would alienate the United States.

For example, Grenada was one of few nations in the United Nation General Assembly which did not support the resolution condemning the Soviet invasion of Afganistan. In a similar move, Bishop used his address before the Non-Aligned Nations to call for Third World unity in the fight against U.S. imperialism, and support for liberation movements in Central America and Southern Africa. While such actions were undoubtedly a genuine reflection of the political sentiments of Bishop and the NJM, it is also clear that such statements were made with knowledge that they would have a negative impact on the possibility of cultivating positive relations with the United States. A review of central committee discussions following Coard's visit to the Soviet Union also reveals that the party leadership believed its pro-Soviet stance on international issues would result in larger amounts of aid from that country and other socialist nations (Grenada Documents: Document 94).

This diplomatic offensive represented a significant gamble for the regime. As a colonial possession and during its short period of independence, Grenada, like most of the other island nations of the Caribbean, had been firmly tied to the Western sphere of influence and had been essentially pro-U.S. on most international matters. In altering its alignments with foreign powers, the PRG ran the risk of jeopardizing relations with its traditional trading partners, as well as existing financial arrangements in the area of trade, currency and loans from regional organizations such as Caricom, the Organization of Eastern Caribbean States, and the Caribbean Development Bank. As it undertook this diplomatic offensive, the PRG was well aware of the risks involved. To reduce these risks, it developed the two other components of its foreign policy strategy.

The second component of the strategy was aimed at soliciting aid from Western, non-socialist countries. This diplomatic offensive required that the PRG leaders present themselves as the leaders of an underdeveloped nation, whose economy was being run by fiscally prudent managers rather than ideologues. Externally, Grenada's revolution was described as a peaceful overthrow of a brutal dictator where a new form of participatory democracy was being created. Assurances were made that some form of elections would eventually take place and that the rule of law would continue to prevail on the island. Such marketing tactics proved to be extremely advantageous to the regime's fund raising efforts, and led to a diverse array of nations providing aid to Grenada, including the EEC (European Economic Community) and France, which previously had shown little interest in the Anglophone Caribbean. It also helped to boost the regime's prestige internationally, which for a time served as a somewhat effective means of countering the hostilities emanating from the United States.

The key to the success of the second component was a recognition on the part of the party leadership that the domestic situation and the image of the revolution that was projected abroad would have tremendous bearing upon the ability of the regime to attract foreign support. This is a lesson which Gairy failed to grasp, and which subsequently undermined his diplomatic efforts in foreign policy. The PRG invited visitors from a broad array of countries to show off the progress achieved under the revolution and to dispel the images propagated by the U.S. of an island taken over by "communist thugs." The tours by foreign visitors combined with effective marketing by the regime's representatives, particularly Bishop, who was well received in most of the nations he visited, provided the regime with large amounts of foreign aid and political support. In describing the PRG's approach to foreign policy, Anthony Payne writes that ". . . in some contexts, the PRG was prepared to deal pragmatically with whatever regimes would deal with it. The nature of the relationships varied, . . . but they were all regarded as valuable in some way" (Heine:145).

The third component of the strategy was aimed at obtaining grants and aid from international development organizations. The international airport became the primary objective for the regime's solicitations of development aid. To obtain support for the airport project, the PRG first had to overcome concerns generated by the United States that the airport would be used for military purposes by the Soviet Union. Visits by foreigners to the construction site, combined with explanations of how the new airport would boost the tourist industry, helped to allay the fears of many international agencies, including the EEC and the European Development Fund, both of which ended up being among the group of donors that supported the project (Pryor: 46).

After three years in power, the PRG had proven itself to be extremely capable in the area of international relations. On a per capita basis, it ranked among the top five aid receivers in the world from 1980 through 1983 (Pryor: 44). It successfully pulled off its strategy of marketing the country differently to different donors, and it used its membership in the Socialist International, an organization whose political aims it did not support (Grenada Papers, 132), to obtain political and financial assistance.

Yet, for all its adeptness in foreign affairs, the PRG's strategy for obtaining foreign support eventually fell apart. Its success in attracting foreign aid led to excessive dependence on the steady flow of large amounts of aid. Once Grenada's initial popularity began to level off, and countries which had promised aid began to renege for various reasons, this dependence began to produce severe economic problems. Many of the domestic reforms which had been implemented by the PRG were made possible only by the infusion of cash from abroad and were difficult to sustain without it. Moreover, the gamble involved with alienating the U.S. could only pay off if other nations would block or counter U.S. efforts to intervene or to destabilize the island. The assassination of Bishop and the other PRG leaders completely undermined the possibility of such assistance, and paved the way for the long expected military assault by the U.S. Although it seems likely that problems in obtaining aid would have persisted even if Bishop had not been killed, it is not clear that the U.S. would have been able to invade had he survived.

It is questionable whether the PRG would have been able to withstand the antagonism that had developed with the United States indefinitely, even if the split in leadership had not occurred. There is substantial evidence which suggest that the U.S. was engaged in planning to invade Grenada long before the assassination of Bishop, and was only awaiting the most appropriate conditions under which to strike (See footnote 88). This fact, combined with the actual acts of subversion that took place, provided an important justification for the use of coercion by the PRG against its domestic opponents.

With the death of Leonid Brezhnev, the Soviet Union substantially reduced its commitments abroad. Its allies who were engaged in combat in countries such as Ethiopia, Angola and Mozambique were encouraged to seek accommodation with their enemies. Later, the fall of the Soviet Union and the ongoing economic and political crisis in Russia forced traditional aid recipients (i.e. Cuba and Vietnam) either to devise strategies for pursuing socialism on their own or, if possible, to pursue a new foreign policy course. Undoubtedly, had the PRG survived, the recent turn in world events would have resulted in even less support for small nations like Grenada. Moreover, without the assurance of Soviet support in response to U.S.

aggression, the PRG would have remained extremely vulnerable to the possibility of U.S. military intervention.

The NNP's Dependence Upon the United States

After returning to power in 1984, Blaize and the NNP relied upon a foreign policy strategy which consisted largely of dependence upon the United States. This dependence included reliance on financial, military and political support, which the U.S. provided because it considered the NNP the only party at the time with the ability to insure stability and prevent communist insurrection. Knowledge of U.S. support provided the regime with considerable confidence. For a time, its leaders believed that if the economy faltered or if the government was threatened, the U.S. would come to its rescue. Such sentiments were expressed to me by several high ranking advisors to the government and were reflected in the optimism of the NNP delegates at the third annual convention in 1987 which I observed. Several delegates cited the continuing support of the U.S. for their party as a factor likely to assure them of victory in future elections. The presence of a representative from the U.S.- backed Caribbean Democratic Union was seen as further evidence of U.S. interest and support.

The confidence of the delegates was based on the fact that the U.S. had carried out its promises of support in the past. The United States provided the NNP government with budgetary supplements, on at least two separate occasions, to meet payroll and other recurrent expenditures, a practice which was unheard of in most other countries that received U.S. aid.[22] It had also provided large amounts of development aid through private organizations, such as Project Hope and the National Endowment for Democracy, as well as subsidies to American businessmen seeking to do business in Grenada. Such practices reinforced the belief that the NNP government could rely upon U.S. support in times of need, and created the impression that the NNP was the only Grenadian party blessed with such backing.

However, the extent and level of U.S. aid to Grenada took a dramatic decline in 1987 and 1988. In all probability, the decline in U.S. aid will lead to the adoption of new attitudes toward the U.S. by those who will lead the government in the future. The political crisis which occurred within the NNP and which brought about the ouster of Herbert Blaize from leadership of the party by its members at the August 1989 party congress, even as he retained the position of prime minister, was undoubtedly prompted in part by recognition that his total dependence on the U.S. as a strategy for retaining power was no longer viable. For some time it was clear that the United States was looking for an opportunity to decrease its presence on the island and cut back on the level of aid. Instead of anticipating this reduction and adjusting in a timely manner, the NNP clung to the hope that the flow of U.S. aid would continue.

Once again a Blaize-led government repeated the same type of mistake that it had made in the past. Whenever Blaize held power, he relied heavily upon foreign aid to support the economy and maintain control over government. Under colonialism, the GNP's dependence upon the British was one of the reasons why it was so distrusted by the peasantry. In the aftermath of the uprising of 1951, there was considerable anti-colonial sentiment among the peasantry, due to the British role in putting down the rebellion, as well as its traditional support for estate owners. As the party aligned to both the British and the estate owners, the GNP was viewed with suspicion and some degree of hostility by large segments of the lower classes.

Likewise today, the perception of NNP subservience to the United States was often cited by respondents to my survey as one of the reasons for their dislike of the regime. Though a small nation and an economically dependent one, Grenada has a population that expresses a high degree of nationalism which translates into a distrust toward heavy influence by foreigners in Grenadian affairs and a strong belief in national sovereignty. This is substantiated by Brathwaite's survey, which found that while 59% of the respondents felt the Cubans contributed positively to the country, 63% expressed concern about their influence on the government. Similarly, he found that while 88% supported the U.S. invasion of the island, 56% were opposed to a permanent American military base on the island (Brathwaite: 19).

Aside from alienating certain elements within the population through its dependence on the United States, the NNP government also boxed itself into a corner. Of all the tactics available to the regime to prolong its survival, the NNP relied most heavily upon foreign support, so much so that other strategies were not fully developed. When support from the United States began to taper off, the regime had little to stand upon and undoubtedly collapsed because no other external sources of support could be found. Even with U.S. military support intact, by 1988 the regime was in serious trouble as a result of in-fighting and deteriorating economic conditions. Its poor showing in the 1990 elections was predictable, even though the replacement of Blaize by former Construction Minister Keith Mitchel seemed to offer hope of new leadership and new directions.

Notes

1 For analyses of challenges to British rule in South Africa and India, see *White Supremacy* by George Fredrickson (London: Oxford University Press, 1981) and *The Social Origins of Dictatorship and Democracy* by Barrington Moore (Boston: Beacon Press, 1966).

2 The election of Prime Minister Silvio Berlusconi and his coalition Fuerza Italia in Italy might be seen as a radical departure from the more moderate character of democratic governments in western Europe, due to the presence of neo-fascist elements within the ruling coalition. However, on most political and economic matters, the direction of the new regime appears to differ only slightly from that of its Christian Democratic predecessors. (See *New York Times*, July 23, 1994 for discussion of political orientation of the Berlusconi government).

In Eastern Europe, socialist oriented governments have been returned to power in Poland and Hungary, despite prior victories by pro-western reformers following the fall of communist regimes in 1989. (See "The Rebirth of Socialism" by Christopher Hitchen in *The Nation*, June 8, 1994). Socialist also appear headed for an electoral victory in Brazil, following decades of military rule and political instability. (See the "Ground Swell of Support for Workers Candidate in Brazil" by Mark Brown in the July 17, 1994 issue of the *New York Times*.)

3 The departure of Raphael Fletcher from the GULP was consistent with past patterns within that organization, which has tended to be run like a "one man show" by Gairy.

4 Since the election of 1951, the voting constituencies of St. George's Town and Carriacou have consistently voted for candidates other than the GULP. The only exception to this pattern was the election of 1972, in which H.R. Scipio, the GNP candidate, lost by 21 votes to J.M. Morris of the GULP. See Brizan, G. *Grenada Island of Conflict* (London: Zed Books, 1984) p. 364.

5 It has been argued that charismatic leaders are particularly likely to emerge during the post-colonial period. See Ake, Paul *A Theory of Political Integration* (Homewood, Illinois: The Dorsey Press, 1967) p. 61 and Young, C. *Ideology and Development in Africa* (New Haven: Yale University Press, 1967) p. 123-147.

6 In describing the radical trade union leadership that emerged in the Crown Colonies of the Windward Islands, Gordon K. Lewis writes: ". . .

Gairyite politics were traditional small island style, the particular brash forcefulness, half confident, half petulant, so characteristic of the political condition that lies halfway between the unadorned colonial status and complete independence . . . Gairy in his own flamboyant person represented the Negro of working class origin and limited education who has reached eminence through union leadership and mass voting . . . There is a strain of ribald irreverence in West Indian life; Gairy brought it into the open with his guying of prominent local personalities, the 'big boys' . . . in *The Growth of the Modern West Indies* (New York: Modern Reader, 1968) p. 156.

7   For a discussion of Obeah and its influence on Caribbean cultures, see *The Rastafarians* by Leonard Barrett (Boston: Beacon Press, 1977) p. 103-113.

8   Gairy earned several honorary titles during his many terms in office. He was knighted by the Queen of England and received an honorary doctorate from a university in South Korea. He was generally referred to as the Right Honorable Doctor Sur Eric Mathew Gairy. He was also fond of wearing medals and other emblems he had received.

9   For a detailed eye witness account of the events leading up to Bishop's house arrest, release and assasination, see "'Blow by Blow' A Personal Account of the Ravaging of the Revo" by Akinyele Sadiq in *Black Scholar* Spring 1984, vol xx, no. 4.

10   There is evidence that Coard's supporters on the Central Committee were aware of the support possessed by Bishop and regarded it as a threat to their move for joint leadership. The architects of the plan figured that the public could be convinced to accept the plan because Bishop would still serve as the figure head in most public settings. Liam James, the member who made the proposal, said that this would allow the party to continue to take advantage of Bishop's strengths. See *The Grenada Documents* "The Extraordinary Meeting of the Central Committee" September 14-16.

11   In an attempt to justify Bishop's murder, Hudson Austin, the head of the armed forces and a close friend of Bishop, made an address of Radio Free Grenada attacking Bishop: "Maurice Bishop and his other petty bourgeois and upper bourgeois friends had deserted the working class and working people of Grenada . . . today Wednesday, 19th of October, history was made again. All patriots and revolutionaries will never forget this day when counter-revolution, the friends of imperialism, were crushed." For a detailed discussion of the immediate aftermath of Bishop's assassination see O'Shaugnessy, H. *Grenada* (New York: Dood, Mead Co., 1984) p. 136-144.

12   For a discussion of how the social programs created by the PRG related to the goals of the revolution and the ideology of the government, see *African and Caribbean Politics* by Manning Marable (London: Verso Books, 1987) p. 225-235.

13   For a discussion of the role of ideology in the foreign policy of the PRG see Payne, Anthony "The Foreign Policy of the PRG" in *A Revolution Aborted* by Heine, J.

14   For a discussion of how neo-colonial development patterns have influenced the political economy of Caribbean nations, see *The Poor and the Powerless* by Clive Thomas (New York: Monthly Review Press, 1988) p. 351-363.

15   Several of the Gairy supporters I interviewed mentioned the Meet The People Tours as an example of the things that Gairy had done to help the country. The Tours were organized by Gairy supporters in rural villages to provide voluntary labor for community projects (i.e. school construction, road repair, etc.). Food, drink and occasionally music would be provided to the volunteers, along with materials needed for carrying out the task. Beyond their instrumental purpose, the tours provided tangible evidence of Gairy's interest in rural residents.

16   Several Gairy supporters said that they were able to petition Gairy directly for assistance during times of need. One woman told me that after she went to see Gairy for help that he paid for the cost of her husband's funeral. This type of patronage seemed to have a lasting effect upon the recipients who were some of Gairy's most ardent supporters, even though the actual amount of money distributed may have been quite small.

17   On several occasions, Maurice Bishop and Bernard Coard, the deputy prime minister, characterized one of the goals of the revolution as an effort to elevate the social wage. The point was that while they could not guarantee actual wage increases, by increasing social benefits (i.e elimination of school fees, free books and uniforms, free health care, etc.) and services, household expenditures would be reduced and living conditions would improve. For examples of how these positions were articulated, see *Is Freedom We Makin* (p. 18-25) and the Report on the National Budget (St. Georges Grenada: Government Printery, 1982).

18   For a description of how participation in the literacy campaign and other mass initiatives were related to political support, see "Mass Literacy As a Political Strategy: The Role of Adult Education in Revolutionary Grenada" by Pedro Noguera in *International Journal of University Adult Education*, vol.XXXI, No.2, July 1992.

19   The Hopevale labor camp was described in detail to me by two former detainees. Conditions at the camp are also described in the November 21, 1985 issue of the *Grenada Voice*.

20   There is evidence that the invasion had been planned long before October 25. According to the Pacific News and Information Service, a Special Army Ranger Unit of the 75th Infantry Division conducted military exercises between September 23 and October 2 at Port Ephrata, Washington. The exercises involved Rangers parachuting onto an airport runway and securing the area around the runway before more troops arrived. A similar procedure was used on the morning of the invasion. According to an article printed in the February 27, 1983 issue of the *Washington Post*, former C.I.A. Director Casey had proposed covert operations against Grenada and Surinam as early as 1981, but the idea had been blocked by the Senate Intelligence Committee. For more details on U.S. covert operations against Grenada, see *Covert Action Information Bulletin*, No. 2, Winter 1984.

21   In my interview with Gairy, he claimed to have to have warned the U.S. in advance of communist attempts to subvert his government. He claimed that his warnings were ignored because the U.S. did not take the threat seriously at the time.

22   In my interview with Phil French (1917/87) at the U.S. embassy, I was informed that the 6 million dollar budgetary supplement that Grenada received in 1987 was an anomaly and that it would not be repeated in the future.

Chapter 10

Assessing the Significance of a Study on Regime Survival and Regime Support in Grenada

Interpreting Findings from the Data

Having presented two sources of data on popular responses to political change in Grenada, historical and contemporary survey research, we turn now to a summary of the findings. Though each of the regimes we have focused upon in this study differed significantly with respect to its constituent base, its style and manner of governance and its ideological orientation, political lessons related to regime survival and regime support do emerge from a comparative analysis. Using the five themes that have served as the analytical framework for this research, we will now attempt to extract these lessons and illuminate the central findings.

Charismatic Leadership

Though Grenada's political history clearly reveals that the presence of a charismatic leader can be invaluable to a party during its bid for power and to a government seeking to maintain popular support, the experiences of the Gairy and Bishop regimes also reveal several fundamental weaknesses that arise from over reliance on the appeal of the charismatic leader. As Weber pointed out years ago, charismatic regimes tend to be inherently plagued by at least two major issues: the tendency toward personal rulership and the problem of succession (Weber, 1968: 48-66). The Gairy regime was primarily affected by the former, while the PRG suffered from the effects of the latter. The overwhelming popularity of the charismatic leader tends to lead to an inappropriate centralization of authority and the dominance by the leader of all decision making. Weber suggests that charisma can be routinized through institutionalization to counter this tendency, however this necessarily requires a willingness on the part of the leader to cede power and authority to an organized party or bureacracy (Weber: 54, 55). Failure to do so results in inefficiency, arbitrary decision making, and ultimately instability, since it is typically not possible for one leader to manage and control all of the important political operations and functions of government.

Undoubtedly, Eric Gairy and his cohorts would have benefited from reading Weber. Throughout his tenure in office, Gairy engaged in a highly personal form of rulership, preferring to keep most powers of government under his personal control and influence, rather than delegating or sharing authority with others. For many years Gairy realized several political benefits from such an approach. Not only were his supporters loyal to him personally, but for a time, he was seen as indispensable to the elites and colonial authorities on any matter of conflict involving estate workers, for he alone had their trust and support. However, Gairy's unwillingness to institutionalize his authority ultimately contributed to his isolation at home and abroad. His refusal to work cooperatively with any interest group that was not willing to submit itself to his political agenda prevented him from developing strategic alliances that may have prolonged the longevity of his regime. Moreover, his expectation of blind obedience from his subordinates deprived his government of capable advisors and ministers, who might have been more effective in developing, administering and implementing government policy.

In contrast, Bishop and the PRG went to great lengths to decentralize authority and institutionalize charismatic appeal. Unlike Gairy, Bishop did share power with others in his party and government and did not develop a similar kind of personal style of rulership. However, despite fearing what they termed as "one manism," the central committee of the NJM realized that Bishop was by far its most persuasive spokesperson and that he was, therefore, the most effective at cultivating support for the revolution at home and abroad. Hence, because of his personal power and efficacy, Bishop came to personify the regime. The danger this posed to the government was eventually realized when Bishop's opponents on the central committee attempted to remove him from power. Popular reaction to their decision to place Bishop under house arrest in October of 1983 was so strong that it made it impossible for the regime to reclaim any legitimacy, particularly after Bishop was executed. Though Bishop was willing to share power within the party and government, the regime itself was unable to survive without him.

Finally, the experience of Blaize and the NNP suggests that the absence of a charismatic leader may have actually limited the ability of the regime to withstand the difficulties which arose when political and economic problems became more acute in 1986 and 1987. Lacking a leader who could effectively explain to the population why there had been defections in the ruling party and why unemployment and taxes were rising, the regime became open to even more intense infighting and turmoil. This is not to suggest that a charismatic leader is necessary or essential to regime survival, but given Grenada's vulnerability to economic crises which almost always have political consequences, it certainly does help if there is a leader who can use the power of personality and persuasion to communicate to the populace.

Grenada's current Prime Minister, Keith Mitchel,[1] is not regarded as charismatic, but he is widely regarded as a clever politician whose style and tactics are similar to those of Eric Gairy. Mitchel is also viewed widely as an untrustworthy leader, having been charged in the past with various forms of corruption.[2] Only time will tell if his government will be hurt by his lack of charisma. Given that past experience has shown charismatic leadership to be like a double-edged sword, bringing with it both advantages and disadvantages, there is undoubtedly no way of predicting what the future will hold for the new government.

Ideology
Despite arguments that have been made by several other writers about the importance of ideology to Grenadian politics (O'Shaughnessy, 1984; Seabury and McDougal, 1984; Lewis, 1984; Vigilante and Sandiford, 1984), the research that has been presented here suggest that this is not the case. This is

not because Grenadians are either apolitical or too uneducated to discern the ideological orientation of prospective political leaders. However, my research experience in Grenada, which includes conducting one hundred and fifty interviews, leads me to conclude that most Grenadians take on a pragmatic perspective when assessing the merits of politicians. Rather than judging a regime or a leader through a particular ideological lens, Grenadians are more likely to ask more basic questions related to their personal economic circumstances, the overall state of the economy, and the reliability, effectiveness and trustworthiness of the regime.

Ideology is important to understanding Grenadian politics mostly because of the way in which it influences the character of the regime in power. The ideological orientation of the Gairy, Bishop and Blaize regimes had considerable influence over the types of economic and social policies that were pursued and the constituencies, both foreign and domestic, that were courted. In fact, it is largely on the basis of their ideological orientation that the three regimes are differentiated. However, insofar as the process of cultivating and maintaining political support is concerned, ideology is a relatively insignificant factor.

Certainly, for some sectors of the Grenadian populace, ideological issues have had greater pertinence. For the island's elites, Gairy's populism represented not only a challenge to their control and authority, it also came to constitute a serious threat to their ability to wield power. Prior to the emergence of Gairy, the Grenadian lower class was unorganized and had no voice in political matters. After his rise to power, the interests of the lower class, as articulated by Gairy, could no longer be dismissed. Even those who might regard Gairy as ultimately a traitor to his populist roots can not deny the impact that his organizing had upon social and political relations in Grenada. Many of Gairy's enemies recognized this impact and hated him because of it.

Similarly, much of the opposition to the PRG was related to its ideological character. The Catholic church hierarchy became the source of important opposition to the regime out of their fear that the government's policies would lead to atheism and a reduction in church influence. Large business owners and farmers opposed the regime because of its commitment to progressive taxation, its support for progressive labor laws, and its willingness to impose price controls on consumer goods. Finally, and perhaps most importantly, the external opposition to the regime, especially that which emanated from the United States, was largely related to the perceived threat posed by the PRG's ideological orientation. Fearing the rise of another Cuba within the U.S. sphere of influence, hostility from both the Carter and Reagan administrations was tied almost entirely to the ideological threat that Grenada was perceived as posing.

For Blaize and the NNP, ideological opposition to the goals and direction of the government was largely a non-factor. In the aftermath of the U.S. invasion, partisans of the NJM were either in prison, at war with each other, or so badly disorganized that they were unable to mount a credible electoral challenge in the elections of 1984, and still aren't able to do so to this day. Others who have opposed the policies of the Blaize-led government have been more likely to do so out of practical disagreement than because of ideological differences.

Of the three regimes, only the PRG had a small but significant group of ideologically committed supporters. While this was not enough to rely upon, it did prove extremely helpful to the regimes efforts to mobilize the population for various efforts. However, for many ordinary Grenadians, ideological appeals for support amount to little more than the typical rhetoric of politicians. Most are tired of this rhetoric, for they know all too well that once a party or individual is in office, retaining power becomes far more important than realizing ideological commitments. Past experience has shown this to be the case with both the Gairy and Bishop regimes. There is little reason to think that the future will be different.

Patronage

Of all the factors that have been considered thus far as being relevant to understanding political support and regime survival in Grenada, the use of patronage by the three regimes under study seems to have had the most significant impact. The use of patronage by the three regimes has addressed in a practical and meaningful way concerns that are relevant to nearly all segments of the population: material needs, living conditions and economic opportunity. As was mentioned previously, Grenadians are largely a pragmatic group of people, and as the survey demonstrated quite clearly, their evaluations of the three regimes are based to a large extent on the ability of those in power to satisfy material/economic needs. This is not to say that this is the only concern or that Grenadian votes can simply be bought by the highest bidder, but it does suggest that satisfaction of the disparate needs of the population, or segments of it, is the key element to maintaining political support and ensuring regime survival in Grenada.

There is no secret or magic to this realization. In fact, since the enactment of adult suffrage in 1951, "rum and roti" have been the bread and butter of Grenadian politics (Will, 1989). Grenadian politicians of all types have understood for sometime that largess is at least part of the key to winning support during any election. That part is easy, for although the cost of running a campaign can be expensive when parties are expected to provide plenty of food and drink at political events, given the rewards at stake, the expense is usually seen as being worth it. The difficulty comes in taking care of constituents once power has been attained. Although the forms of patronage are plentiful, civil service jobs, government contracts, community services, etc., there is a limited supply of resources. Moreover, the availability of resources is typically unpredictable, in that the coffers of the state are susceptible to the ebbs and flows of the economy.

For this reason, over reliance on patronage can be as dangerous as over reliance on a charismatic leader. The drop off in support experienced by the PRG during its last year in power was, to a large extent, influenced by the government's inability to sustain the patronage system it had erected. In this respect, Ted Gurr's (1970) axiom that frustrated expectations can be worse than expectations that go unfulfilled provides an important political lesson. Politicians who cultivate economic dependency through patronage may eventually experience more trouble when they cease to be able to satisfy needs than those who make promises but fail to deliver. This is even more true with indirect forms of patronage than with direct forms. When those who receive jobs or services perceive these as public entitlements rather than as political pay-offs, they may be even more likely to resent the regime that fails in its ability to deliver than the clients of a patron who is unable to deliver at a particular point in time. As Carl Stone has shown through his research on the role of patronage in Jamaican politics, a personal relationship can more easily withstand stoppages and reductions in the flow of goods or services than an impersonal relationship (Stone, 1994: 34-41).

It is for this reason that the patronage system developed by Eric Gairy was far more effective as a strategy for retaining political power than the forms of patronage utilized by either the Blaize or Bishop led regimes. Throughout the society, individuals were made to feel personally indebted to Gairy and, as part of their reciprocity in the patron-client relationship, they could be expected to deliver politically when called upon. Gairy went out of his way to let individuals and communities know when Uncle Gairy had provided something. To this day, Gairy supporters are able to remember small amounts of money, favors, or community projects that were given to them by him. Gairy recognized early on that the wider he could expand his patronage network, the more secure his position in politics would become. He creatively went about doing this, using his union and public sector employment as the primary source of his largess. He also consciously and deliberately punished his opponents, using the carrot and stick approach to masterfully retain powers for several years.

Neither the Blaize nor the Bishop led governments utilized patronage in this type of highly personalized manner. Those who benefited from employment or services provided by the regime were not necessarily more likely to become active supporters of the government. Such measures may have prevented certain individuals and constituents from becoming openly antagonistic toward the regime, as was the case with several former PRA soldiers who were recruited to the reconstituted Grenada Defense Force, but they were unlikely to feel personally or politically indebted to the party or individual leader in power.

Hence, patronage did not produce the same type of benefit or support for the Blaize and Bishop regimes that it did for Gairy. Long after his union ceased to serve as an effective advocate of the poor, Gairy could continue to rely on personal connections to deliver support and votes. However, even for the crafty Eric Gairy, problems sustaining patronage eventually contributed to the demise of his government. The economic recession of the 1970's weakened the Gairy regime's ability to satisfy the material needs of supporters. With the NJM growing in influence and actively organizing lower class Grenadians into opposition against Gairy, the regime became increasingly vulnerable. The fact that so few Grenadians even attempted to defend the regime following the largely non-violent takeover by the NJM on March 13, 1979 was indicative of the thin layer of support the regime enjoyed. At least the PRG could count on several dozen ideologically committed cadre to fight U.S. troops at the time of the invasion. Neither Gairy nor Blaize could muster a similar show of support when their regimes were threatened with collapse.

For all its practical appeal, therefore, patronage has not proven to be a reliable means of insuring political support. Government jobs, land, contracts, gifts and services do not necessarily win the hearts or minds of supporters. It may win votes at election time, but it may not, and in Grenada's history it has not guaranteed political support to the patron or the regime.

Coercion
Unlike the other measures which are used primarily to generate political support, state sponsored coercion is used to thwart the opposition, and while such a strategy may seem to accomplish essentially the same objective, that of retaining political power, the consequences of its use are quite different. All three regimes adhered to Machiavelli's warning to the Prince that it is better to be feared than to be loved (Machiavelli, 1952), though not all were affected in the same way by the use of coercion. The Gairy regime's image was far more tarnished by its use of coercion than was the PRG, even though from an objective standpoint the PRG may have been more repressive. This is because the ability of a regime to effectively use coercion against its opponents is intimately tied to the degree of legitimacy that it enjoys.

The PRG understood this point well and, as a result, was able to carefully use coercion to achieve political objectives without engendering an despotic image abroad. In fact, the four and one-half years of the revolution were positively referred to as the peaceful revolution, with far greater emphasis given to the government's efforts to improve social conditions than was directed at its abuses of power.

Gairy failed to understand this point, and repeatedly allowed his vindictive desire to punish his opponents to undermine his credibility at home and abroad. Gairy was unable to characterize his opponents in ways that would make them less supportable. Because he also allowed freedom of the press and independence for the judiciary, the repressive measures utilized by his regimes could be widely publicized. As a result, each exercise of coercion by the Gairy regime further undermined its credibility and legitimacy, which in turn helped to create the conditions for the unseating of his government.

In both cases, Grenada's history shows that any government must be extremely careful in the ways it uses coercion against its opponents. Grenada's political history and culture have been too strongly influenced by the liberalism of British colonialism for the population to tolerate the excesses of a repressive government for long. Even for the PRG, pressure had been mounting within the Caribbean and the international community for the scheduling of elections and the release of political prisoners. Left leaning newspapers such as the *Caribbean Contact* that supported the goals of the revolution joined the chorus for government restraint. There is no doubt that had the internal differences within the party not reached the boiling point when they did, that greater opposition to the regime's coercive tactics would have grown both within and outside of Grenada.

Seymour Martin Lipset (1963) has described the art of politics as the ability to accurately read social conditions and adapt one's message accordingly, so that the politician says what the people want to hear (1963 p. 13). In Grenada, a reading of social conditions and political culture would provide the following warning to any politician: coercion must be used sparingly and carefully. The brutal excesses of slavery, combined with the long history of exploitation of the majority by an all powerful elite has left a bitter memory about the abuse of power. Having broken with the harsher forms of brutality associated with that legacy, Grenadians seem generally unwilling to tolerate any reversion to the past, regardless of how it is rationalized. Opponents can be punished, but future political leaders in Grenada would do well to heed the admonishment of Machiavelli: ". . . the prince should not make himself so feared that he is hated, for hatred can lead to revolt"(p. 90).

Foreign Support
Like patronage, effective use of foreign support can also enable a regime to address the basic material needs of the population and, thereby, help in generating and sustaining popular support. Foreign aid and investment are vital to a poor developing nation like Grenada, and all three regimes have had to rely on some form of foreign support not only to fulfill their political objectives but to stay in power.

Yet, foreign support is inherently unpredictable. Donor nations are often fickle and their willingness to give is almost always contingent on the state of their economy. Private investment is just as unpredictable, and more often than not, is only attractable if quick and substantial returns are guaranteed.

For these reasons, while foreign support was a boon to all three of the regimes when they had it, over reliance upon it proved to be dangerous. This was clearly the case for the PRG, and perhaps even more so for Blaize's NNP, which set its hopes on the belief that U.S. support was indefinite. Having been delivered to victory in the 1984 elections with the backing of the U.S., Blaize and the NNP believed that their hold on power could withstand internal challenges, scandals, and even economic crisis, because ultimately the U.S. would intervene to safeguard their hold on power, as the colonial government had done in the past. My interviews with NNP supporters revealed a surprising confidence in U.S. support. Some, such as Keith Mitchel, the current leader of the NNP, believed that the U.S. would never risk allowing the country to fall back into the hands of the socialists, and for that reason he felt confident that political and economic support would remain intact in the years ahead. However, since 1989, Grenada has ceased to be even a minor priority for U.S. foreign policy. Since 1984, U.S. aid to Grenada has declined steadily, and the promise of foreign investment from American businessmen has never been realized. Today, Grenada receives no more support than any other small island in the Eastern Caribbean, neither from the U.S. or any other foreign power.

Hence, for all its desirability, exclusive relaince on foreign support has not and undoubtedly can not be a viable part of the survival strategy for any Grenadian government. Grenada is too insignificant in strategic terms to warrant sizeable amounts of foreign aid, and it has no comparative advantage over any of the many other beautiful islands in the Caribbean to garner a greater share of foreign investment for its tourist industry. Careful use of foreign policy has been and will continue to be important for any Grenadian government. Gairy's failure to recognize this contributed to his fall from power. However, foreign support will undoubtedly never rise to such a level that a government can pin its hopes for longevity on it. Instead, it must be seen as part of a strategy for regime survival, which when combined with other elements, can provide crucial support to a regime in power.

When considered together, the five variables considered here offer several possibilities for understanding political support and regime survival in Grenada. However, when considered in isolation, none of these variables can stand alone as an essential ingredient to political success. That is, while the presence of a charismatic leader, the effective use of ideological appeals, patronage and coercion, and receipt of significant amounts of foreign support can be instrumental to maintaining political support and power in Grenada, none of these elements is sufficient to guarantee either. Under certain conditions, even the combination may be insufficient in that the state of the economy, which may at times be an overriding factor, can undermine even the craftiest political leader.

However, what analysis of the variables does provide is a means of interpreting and making sense of forty years of political history that belies simplistic or straightforward explanation. Why has Grenada developed a pattern of populist politics that distinguishes the country in such significant ways from its counterparts in the Anglophone Caribbean? Because the Grenadian middle class failed to organize and provide leadership to the lower class majority, thereby creating the opportunity for Eric Gairy to do so later. Why is Grenada the only member of the Commonwealth Caribbean to have experienced an armed, socialist takeover of government? Because the populist Gairy lost touch with his popular base, and the middle class GNP was largely discredited, a political void was created that the more radical NJM could fill. Gairy, therefore, in a literal and figurative sense, made it possible for Bishop to come to power. Why didn't the repressive measures taken by the PRG tarnish the image of Maurice Bishop, and why did Gairy develop a reputation as a dictator even though his regime was relatively less repressive? Furthermore, why didn't Blaize's NNP government benefit politically from its respect for civil liberties and the rule of law? This is an important question, for while Grenadians certainly have strong feelings about government violations of constitutional rights, the majority do not examine these issues in isolation from the overall performance of government. Hence, the success of the PRG's social programs outweighed the negatives associated with its repressive tactics in the eyes of many Grenadians. Conversely, the NNP received little credit for its respect of civil liberties due to the generally poor performance of the government, while Gairy came to be regarded as a small time despot because of his inability to effectively rationalize the repressive actions he took against his opponents.

Perhaps the most important question that can be answered from this study and which has the greatest relevance to other cases concerns the social basis of popular support for government. On what basis have Grenadians chosen to support a regime and by what criteria have they judged the performance of their political leaders? The answer to this question is important not only because it sheds light on the perplexing nature of political change in Grenada, but because it may also shed light on other cases where the behavior of voters seems incomprehensible to analysts and observers that are not familiar with local sensibilities. Based upon our historical analysis of Grenadian politics and drawing on the data collected from interviews and the survey, we can conclude the following: Above all else, Grenadians support political leaders who champion their interests, not just instrumentally through government policies, but symbolically through personal appeals and deeds. The average Grenadian judges their leaders not just by what they do, but by what they say, how they say it, and who they say it to. The political culture that has developed in Grenada is fundamentally populist. The lower class majority is unwilling to accept being marginalized to the sidelines of civil society as it was in the past, and large numbers of Grenadians are no longer willing to even accept the paternalism of an Eric Gairy.

When I spoke to Grenadians about what they liked best about the revolution, over and over I was told that they appreciated the sense of collective participation in political, economic and social activities that was encouraged by the PRG. According to one thirty year old woman in Gouyave:

> During the Revo, for the first time you had Grenadians working together to do things for themselves. We were meeting together to talk about the needs of our villages and the country. It brought us closer together. There was a sense of excitement and caring that never existed before. People helped one another to do simple things like farming and building. There was more concern about the youth. That is what I liked the best. During the revolution everyone counted, not just the rich. Even the poorest person could be involved in the revolution.

I witnessed first hand the participation, the volunteerism and the excitement that this woman described. In rural villages where there had been no prior history of grassroots politics or collective action, I attended meetings where residents discussed how they would go about addressing community needs and what kinds of support and resources they would expect from the government to do so. The activities and involvement promoted by the PRG during its four and a half years in power left an indelible impression on many Grenadians. And though many seemed more cynical and less trusting toward politicians in the aftermath of the revolution's demise, there was also a widespread sense that what occurred during those years was truly extraordinary.

In the future, popular support for government in Grenada will undoubtedly be judged to a large extent by the standard set by the PRG. Already since its collapse, it is evident that new governments will be judged quickly and more critically than those of the past if they fail to meet popular expectations. These are difficult times for politicians in Grenada. It is widely recognized that with the exception of Eric Gairy's remaining die hard supporters, none of the many new parties have a lock on the sympathy of the voters. For this reason, there has been constant jockeying within parties and coalitions, and within the parliament, as individual leaders maneuver to distinguish themselves from other politicians, and opposition parties constantly search for ways to exploit the failings of the ruling party and turn it into their own political advantage. The future appears uncertain, for thus far none of the parties or leaders that have come forward have demonstrated that they have the ability to rekindle the sense of hope and participation that was evident during the revolution.

Conclusion

Assessing the significance of a study on political change in Grenada is made difficult in part by Grenada's size which understandably forces one to question the generalizability of findings from a such a small society. To a certain extent, difficulty in generating meaningful lessons from the Grenadian experience also arises because of the unique political drama which has unfolded there over the last forty years. Few nations have experienced such drastic shifts in political leadership as have occurred in Grenada. As a result, there is a tendency to treat Grenada as a special case, a deviation not only from its counterparts within the Commonwealth Caribbean but among nations generally.

Yet, despite the real limitations imposed by Grenada's size and the singularity of its political experience, the process of political change in Grenada contains elements which are common to other developing societies and to other cases more generally. A close examination of the island's political history reveals patterns of political change in which the structures of political and economic power, at both micro and macro levels of analysis, influence the course of political events by limiting the range of options for action available to political leaders. Identification of these patterns makes it possible to use the history of political change in Grenada as a case from which to generate concepts and theoretical propositions that may have relevance to other cases. In-depth analysis of cases like this one will undoubtedly play a central role in the formulation of new theories or theories of the "middle range" on the nature of political change in the developing world.[3]

Despite the tendency to think otherwise, Grenada's history is more than just an intriguing political drama played out on an obscure tropical island. The intrigue created by both the plot and the characters is certainly part of what makes this an interesting case study, but beneath the travails and tragedies of the story lie some lessons that are important to understanding the connections between politics, culture and social change. Illumination of these lessons may undoubtedly prove relevant and useful to a larger audience.

To mitigate against the exceptional nature of the case, five themes have been used to provide an analytical framework for this work: charisma, ideology, patronage, coercion and foreign support. These themes are indeed relevant to the study of politics in many countries, industrial and non-industrial, as well as smaller units of government, including states, cities and even villages. Use of these themes along with our focus on regime survival and the basis of regime support will hopefully make it possible to use this study on political change in Grenada for comparative analyses that extend across a range of cases.

This is not the first time that Grenada has been selected for a study with broad implications for the study of political sociology of developing societies. A.W. Singham's *Hero and the Crowd*, a study of charismatic leadership in a colonial polity, has made major theoretical, analytical and methodological contributions to studies of political behavior and charismatic leadership in less developed nations. In part, because Grenada is a small country, the nature of political and social relationships are more intense and direct, and the influence of foreign economic and political constraints are relatively uncluttered by other factors (i.e., regional economic differences, ethnic, religious and linguistic variations among the population, etc.) It is my contention, therefore, that the theoretical propositions derived from a study of this kind can be used to further our understanding of other cases or sets of cases.

The factors which make regime survival possible under certain conditions and which lead to its downfall under another set of conditions would appear to elude theoretical explanation, given the variation which has existed between and among regimes in Grenada. Yet, when examined from the standpoint of the survival strategies employed by the three regimes within the context of the political economy of this particular nation and the global context of the international economy, patterns of survival and decline emerge. It is the identification of these patterns based upon the use of generalizable concepts such as those that I have employed in this case study which can eventually form the basis of a theory of political change in developing societies. The relevance of each concept may vary from case to case, depending on its suitability to the political economy and culture of the nation or nations in question, but the identification of patterns of political behavior, as well as effective and ineffective strategies for regime survival, can serve as a reference for future studies of this kind.

In her exhaustive study of social revolutions, Theda Skocpol (1979) attempted to identify the factors that were responsible for revolutions in certain countries, and the absence of revolutions in others. Through an examination of structural factors, both internal and external, to the societies she focused upon, Skocpol attempted to draw out the specific conditions that led to particular outcomes. Despite her ambitious effort, one is still left wondering about the degree and significance that should be attached to human agency via the role played by particular individuals and organizations in making history. Would the Russian revolution have been possible without Lenin or the Chinese revolution without the leadership of Mao Tse-Tung? The fact that their equivalents did not emerge in either Germany or Japan, the two nations she uses for contrast, strongly suggests the importance of the intangible human factor. Similarly, for those who seek to understand and interpret the changes that have occurred in Grenada, we must ask ourselves how important were the roles played by particular individuals and organizations to the events that transpired there, and to what extent should their roles be emphasized as we seek to explain Grenada's deviations from its counterparts in the Caribbean.

To the extent that this study on political change in Grenada contributes to the development of theory may depend largely upon the willingness of readers to overlook the island's size as a factor prohibiting generalizability. Size is certainly a factor that has had considerable bearing on the political process in Grenada. So many of the political players in Grenada are related either by blood, marriage or circumstance, that at times Grenadian politics takes on the characteristics of a soap opera. Maurice Bishop's cousin, Pram Bishop, was a leader of the Mongoose Gang, while the current leader of the NNP, Keith Mitchell, ran for office in the election of 1972 in coalition with the NJM. Raphael Fletcher contemplated running for office with Eric Gairy, even though his brother was married to a relative of Bishop. Antagonisms that may be created by political differences are often eased by ties that bind partisans together in other ways. As a result, while Grenadians may appear on the one hand more inclined to engage in fierce political conflict than their West Indian neighbors, they are at the same time perhaps more forgiving and less likely to allow political differences to separate them indefinitely. Unless one chooses to leave the island or to eliminate his/her opponent, one can not avoid encountering long term political opponents either in town, at the beach, at the market, or in some other public space. For this reason, most political partisans have eventually learned to accept each others existence; live and let live has been an abiding principle in Grenada.

I saw this principle being practiced on numerous occasions while I was in Grenada. On one occasion I was interviewing a young man on Grande Anse Beach who had been detained by the PRG and sentenced to the Hopevale labor camp in 1981. He spent two years at the labor camp, during which time his dreadlocks were shaved and he was forced to produce food for PRA soldiers without compensation. As we walked along the beach, we crossed paths with another young man who, it turned out, had been a prison guard at Hopevale. Without speaking, the two men nodded at each other when passing, in effect acknowledging their past acquaintance. When I asked the young man how he felt about his former jailer, I was surprised to find that he harbored no resentment or anger. He explained: "What's done is done. Its in the past now. Neither one of us has a job now. He's scrunting to survive the same as me. I can't blame him for what happened. I can't take it personal." It may be that the island is simply too small and the country's history too wrought with conflict for forgiveness not to be the abiding practice; otherwise, it seems there would be far more violence and hostility than the population could possibly bear.

It must also be said, that despite its history of political conflict, Grenada has largely been an island at peace with itself. Even after the assassination of Bishop and the U.S. invasion, the island has returned to the state of relative calm and tranquility which has been prevalent throughout much of its past. These events have certainly had a significant impact on the island's politics, and have brought about important transformations in social relations among the island's population, but the traditional peaceful coexistence and slow pace of life has for the most part been preserved.

In this respect, Grenada is not unlike most other small island-states of the world, where the parochialism which is derived in part from being surrounded by sea often results in a stubborn persistence of tradition and a reluctance to accept change. If one visits the estates in the interior of the island, one can witness laborers performing the same tasks, often with the same tools, that were performed by African slaves hundreds of years ago. There are still people who are born and raised on the estates, who are bound psychologically and financially to the owner and the land and who, despite the literacy campaigns, can not read or write. Their lives appear to have been largely untouched by the tumultuous events of the last several years. Watching women sort nutmeg in the town of Victoria, using only their bare hands to separate the nut from the shells in the same manner that it has been done for the last two hundred years or more, one can see clearly that continuity and tradition characterize many aspects of life on this small island. Even in the center of the capital, St. George's, at Market Square where women sell their produce or on the wharf where they sell fresh fish and haggle over prices with their customers, one can appreciate that these activities are daily routines which have been repeated for generations and which will continue in much the same way for years to come.

Yet, inasmuch as tradition persists in Grenada, the island has not managed to insulate itself from the influences of the outside world or to escape the problems associated with modernization. At the time of my visit, Grenada had one of the highest rates of AIDS in the Western Hemisphere, thirteen known carriers with another twenty six tested positive for the HIV virus (Project Hope Report on Grenada, 1987). On an island of 100,000 people, this is an extremely large number, and given Grenada's interconnectedness, the risks to the larger population are quite high. Since the invasion, Grenada now has a a flourishing underground drug trade, with crack and other forms of cocaine appearing on the island for the first time in significant amounts. In 1987, a Kentucky Fried Chicken restaurant was opened on the island, and for the first time, American fast food is available to the Grenadian public. There are more reports of violent crime than ever before and a rise in juvenile delinquency (Police Commissioners Report on Crime Statistics, 1987). Finally, there is growing concern that Grenadians are hostile to tourists, so much so that radio programs have been developed to instruct Grenadians on how to treat their foreign guests.

These are just some of the more obvious indications that Grenada has not been able to avoid the trends and problems occurring elsewhere in the world. Given this lack of immunity, it is indeed possible to draw some lessons from the Grenadian experience which may be applicable or at least relevant to studies of similar nations. The starting point for comparisons and contrasts might begin with other English speaking nations in the Caribbean that share a similar culture and heritage with Grenada. From there, the scope of comparisons can extend to other islands in the Caribbean, and then to other small island states elsewhere in the world. Still greater leaps are possible to case and recognizes that the differences with respect to culture and structure are not to be overlooked.

The important point is that comparison becomes the necessary next step to any case study, because it is the starting point for developing an understanding of categories of nations and sets the stage for the development of theory. While this has been a case study of a single nation, it has also been a comparative study of regime survival. The three regimes analyzed in this study have been compared and contrasted both historically as well as within the contemporary framework provided by the survey. The selection of regime survival as the focus of the analysis was done because it is a theme that is relevant not only to Grenada but to most other countries. For developing countries in particular, a study of regime survival is potentially even more useful, given the frequency of political instability and the regularity of regime collapse and political disorder. It is neither a conservative nor radical construct, given that those who seek to preserve the status quo and those seek political change share a common interest in insuring regime survival. Furthermore, given the centrality of the role of the state to the process of economic development, a study of regime survival takes on even greater relevance to the study of the sociology of development in peripheral societies.

Yet, a focus on regime survival does not necessarily help to further our understanding of the process of political change in developing nations. To explain the factors responsible for regime survival, or conversely, to explain how and why regimes collapse, represents a significant retreat from earlier efforts to predict the direction of future political developments in the Third World. I chose the question of regime survival as a starting point for this study because I felt that existing theories of political development could not adequately explain the events which had occurred in Grenada. Neither the transition to socialism predicted by Marxist theorists nor the evolution of free market democracies prescribed by Modernization theorists has come to pass in the Third World. The countries which are part of this vast region of the globe follow no unilinear path to economic prosperity and democratic governance. The direction of change in these societies appears far more precarious, uncertain and volatile.

At the outset of this research, I purposefully adopted an inductive approach to study regime survival in Grenada. I placed particular emphasis upon the social structure of Grenadian society, the political economy, the relations between Grenada and its traditional trading partners, patterns of political behavior exhibited by leaders, parties and various social classes within the polity. My goal was to limit the effect of my personal bias through the utilization of an analytical framework which evaluated each of the three regimes by a common criteria. When judgements were made, I attempted to base these on the opinions of Grenadians themselves, in response to the survey, rather than projecting my own prejudices. As I spoke to the people and interviewed local leaders, I began to realize the complexity of opinions toward not only the PRG, but toward the Gairy and Blaize regimes, as well. Through the survey I gained an appreciation for the political values of the people and came to realize that they could not easily be placed in either "right" or "left" political categories. The longer I remained in Grenada, the more I knew that this study would have to reject ideology and partisan positions. I came to realize that I would have to strive for an approach that would lend itself to greater objectivity.

I believe that I have done that; not that I have eliminated my bias, but that I have accurately reflected the views of the Grenadian people I met and interviewed. As I carried out my research in Grenada I was often asked if I would ever return to the island with a copy of the book once the research was completed. I was told that many others have written about Grenada since the invasion, but few have ever returned or even sent down copies of their publications. I promised the people I interviewed that I would return. I promised that I would accurately represent what they told me in the interviews, and I pledged to be fair in my analysis. While I am certain that there will be several Grenadians who will disagree with what I have said in these pages, disagreement will undoubtedly come from across the political spectrum. There will also be those who will appreciate my attempt to be fair, and whose only question may be what difference will it make to their lives. While I can not answer that question, I can say this: there are powerful lessons to be learned from Grenada's political history, and to the extent that this work contributes toward sharing those lessons, then perhaps it will help in furthering understanding of how to avoid some of the more tragic aspects of Grenada's recent history.

Notes

1 Mitchel's NNP won eight seats in national elections that were held on June 19, 1995. George Brizan and the NDC won five seats, and Gairy's GULP won two seats, although Gairy himself was defeated in his race to represent south St. George's. As leader of the winning party, Mitchel will become the next prime minister.

2 While I was in Grenada, the corruption charges targeted at Keith Mitchel included allegations of drug trafficking, embezzlement of government revenues, and nepotism within the Construction Ministry which he formerly headed. See *The Informer*, October-November 1987 for details regarding these allegations.

3 Robert Merton used the term theories of the middle range to describe theories "that lie between the minor but necessary working hypotheses that evolve in abundance during day-to-day research and the all-inclusive systematic efforts to develop a unified theory that will explain all the observed uniformities of social behavior, social organization and social change." (p.39) Middle range theories are used to guide empirical inquiry and can serve as a foundation for the development of "grand" theories. For further discussion, see *On Theoretical Sociology* (New York: The Free Press, 1967) p. 39-72.

Bibliography

Ake, Claude (1967). *A Theory of Political Integration.* Homewood, Ill.: Dorsey Press.

Alavi, Hamza and Shanin, T. (1982). *Sociology of Developing Societies.* New York: Monthly Review.

Almond, Gabriel and Verber, Sydney (1963). *The Civic Culture.* Princeton, N.J.: Princeton University Press.

Almond, G. and Powell, G. B. (1978) *Comparative Politics.* Boston: Little Brown Company.

Ambursley, F. and Cohen, R. (1984) *Crisis in the Caribbean.* London: Heinemann Educational Books.

Ambursley and Dunkerley (1984) *Grenada: Whose Freedom?* London: Latin American Bureau.

Andrain, Charles (1988) *Political Change in the Third World.* London: Unwin Hyman Ltd.

Apter, David (1965). *The Politics of Modernization.* Chicago: University of Chicago Press.

Arendt, Hanna (1951) *Origins of Totalitarianism.* New York: Harcourt, Brace and Company.

Bagchi, Amiya (1982) *The Political Economy of Underdevelopment.* Cambridge: Cambridge University Press.

Bates, Robert (1988) *Toward A Political Economy of Development.* Berkeley: University of California Press.

Baran, Paul (1952). "On the Political Economy of Backwardness" in *Imperialism and Underdevelopment*, Robert Rhodes Editor. New York: Monthly Review.

Barry, Wood and Preusch (1984) *The Other Side of Paradise.* New York: Grove Press.

Beckford, George (1972) *Persistent Poverty.* New York, London: Oxford University Press.

Bell, Wendel (1964) *Jamaican Leaders: Political Attitudes in a New State.* Berkeley and Los Angeles: University of California Press.

——— (1967) *The Democratic Revolution in the West Indies.* Cambridge: Schenkman Publishing Co.

Bendix, Reinhard and Roth, Guenther (1971) *Scholarship and Paryisanship: Essays on Max Weber.* Berkeley: University of California Press.

——— (1964) *Nation Building and Citizenship.* New York: Wiley Books.

Binder, L. et. al. (1971) *The Crises and Sequences in Political Development.* Princeton, N.J.: Princeton University Press.

Brizan, George (1984) *Grenada: Island of Conflict.* London: Zed Books.

Brizan, George (1987) *Autocracy, Repression and the Emergency Powers Act of 1987.* St. George's, Grenada: Tribune Publication

Castells, Manuel (1983) *The City and the Grassroots.* Berkeley: University of California Press.

Chailand, Gerard ((1977) *Revolution in the Third World: Myths and Prospects.* New York: Viking Press.

Chirot, Daniel (1977) *Social Change in the Twentieth Century.* New York: Harcourt, Brace and Javanovich.

Clark, Steven (1987) "The Second Assassination of Maurice Bishop" in *New International.* New York: Pathfinder Press.

Danns, George (1982) *Domination and Power in Guyana.* New Brunswick, New Jersey: Tansaction Books.

DaBreo, Sinclair (1984) *The Grenada Revolution.* Castreies, St. Lucia: Management Advertising and Publicity Services Publication.

Dahl, Robert (1963) *Modern Political Analysis*. Englewood Cliffs: Prentice-Hall.

Demas, William (1965) *The Economics of Development in Small Countries With Special Reference to the Caribbean*. Montreal: McGill University Press.

Edie, Carlene (1994) "Clientelism, Dependency, and Democratic Stability" in *Democracy in the Caribbean, Myths and Realities* edited by Carlene J. Edie. Westport, CN: Praeger.

Edie, Carlene (1991) *Democracy by Default: Dependency and Clientelism in Jamaica*. Boulder, CO: Lynne Reinner Publishers.

Eisenstadt, S.N. (1980) "The Social Framework and Conditions of Revolution" in *Research in Social Movements, Conflict and Change*, edited by Kreisberg, L. Greenwich, Conn.: J.A.I. Press.

Enloe, Cynthia (1973) *Ethnic Conflict and Political Development*. Boston, Mass: Little, Brown and Company.

Evans, Peter (1979) *Dependent Development*. Princeton, N.J.: Princeton University Press.

Evans and Stephens (1987) "Development and the World Economy" in *Handbook of Sociology*, Edited by Neil Smelser and Ronald S. Burt. Beverly Hills, CA: Sage Press.

Evans, P., Rueschemeyer, D. and Skocpol, T. (1985) *Bringing the State Back In*. Cambridge: Cambridge University Press.

Fagen, Richard (1969) *The Transformation of Political Culture in Cuba*. Stanford: Stanford University Press.

Fanon, Frantz (1967) *Black Skin White Masks*. New York: Grove Press.

——— (1963) *The Wretched of the Earth*. New York: Grove Press.

Ferguson, James (1989) *Grenada: Revolution in Reverse*. London: Latin American Bureau.

Field, Lowell (1967) *Comparative Political Development*. Ithaca: Cornell University Press.

Frank, Andre Gunder (1969) *Latin America: Underdevlopment or Revolution.* New York and London: Modern Reader.

Geertz, Clifford (1963) *Old Societies and New States: The Quest for Modernity in Asia and Africa.* New York: Free Press.

Giddens, Anthony (1987) *The Nation-State and Violence.* Berkeley: University of California Press.

———— (1982) *Classes, Power, and Conflict.* Berkeley: University of California Press.

Gerth and Mills (1974) *From Max Weber.* London: Oxford University Press.

Glazer, Barney and Strauss, Anselem (1967) *The Discovery of Grounded Theory.* New York: Adeline Publishing Co.

Gramsci, Antonio (1971) *Prison Notebooks.* New York: International Publishers.

Gurr, Ted (1970) *Why Men Rebel.* Princeton, N.J.: Princeton University Press.

Gurr, Ted and King, Desmond (1987) *The State and the City.* Chicago: University of Chicago Press.

Henry, Paget (1985) *Peripheral Capitalism and Underdevelopment in Antigua.* New Brunswick, New Jersey: Transaction Books.

Henry, Paget and Stone, Carl (1983) *The Newer Caribbean: Decolonization, Democracy and Development.* Philadelphia: Institute for the Study of Human Issues.

Heine, Jorge (1987) *The Lessons of Grenada.* San Juan, Puerto Rico: University of Puerto Rico Press.

———— (1990) *A Revolution Aborted.* Pittsburgh: University of Pittsburgh Press.

———— (1992) "Ethnicity and Class in Post-Colonial Caribbean Politics" in *El Caribe Hacia el Ano 2000*, edited by Serhin, A. San Juan, Puerto Rico: ILDIS.

———— (1991) "Arthur Lewis and the Development of Middle Class Ideology" in *Sir Arthur Lewis An Economic and Politi-*

cal Portrait by Ralph Premdas and Eric St. Cyr. St. Augustine, Trinidad: Institute of Social and Economic Research.

Hintzen, Percy C. (1989) *The Costs of Regime Survival: Racial Mobilization, Elite Domination and Control of the State in Guyana and Trnidad.* London: Cambridge University Press.

Huntington, Samuel (1968) *Political Order in Changing Societies.* New Haven: Yale University Press.

Inkles, Alex and Smith, David (1974) *Becoming Modern: Individual Change in Six Developing Countries.* Cambridge, Mass: Harvard University Press.

Jacobs, W. Richard and Jacobs, Ian (1980) *Grenada The Route to Revolution.* Havana, Cuba: Casa de las Americas.

Johnson, Chalmers (1964) *Revolution and the Social System.* Stanford, Cal: The Hoover Institute, Stanford University.

Kahl, Joseph (1976) *Modernization, Exploitation and Dependency in Latin America.* New Brunswick: Transaction Books.

Kuhn, Thomas (1962) *The Structure of Scientific Revolutions.* Chicago: University of Chicago Press.

Lewis, Gordon K. (1968) *The Growth of the Modern West Indies.* New York: Monthly Review.

———— (1987) *Grenada: The Jewel Despoiled.* Baltimore: John Hopkins University Press.

Lieden, Carl and Schmitt, Karl (1968) *The Politics of Violence: Revolution in the Modern World.* Englewood Cliffs, N.J.: Prentice Hall.

Lerner, Daniel (1958) *The Passing of Traditional Society: Modernizing the Middle East.* New York: Free Press.

Leys, Colin (1975) *UNderdevelopment in Kenya.* London: Heineman Press.

Lipset, Seymour M. (1959) *The Political Man.* New York: Anchor Books.

Machiavelli, Niccolo (1952) *The Prince.* New York: Mentor Press.

Magdoff, Harry (1969) *The Age of Imperialism: The Economics of U.S. Foreign policy.* New York: Monthly Review Press.

Mannheim, Karl (1936) *Ideology and Utopia.* New York and London: Harcourt, Brace and Javanovich.

Marable, Manning (1987) *African and Caribbean Politics: From Kwame Nkrumah to Maurice Bishop.* Norfolk: Thetford Press.

Marcus, Bruce and Taber, Michael (1984) *Maurice Bishop Speaks.* New York: Pathfinder Press.

McClellan, David (1961) *The Achieving Society.* Princeton, N.J.: Van Nostrand.

Merton, Robert K. (1967) *On Theoretical Sociology.* New York: The Free Press.

Miliband, Ralph (1969) *The State in Capitalist Society.* New York: Basic Books Publishers.

Mintz, Sidney (1974) *Caribbean Transformation.* New York: Columbia University Press.

Moore, B. (1966) *The Social Origins of Dictatorship and Democracy: Lord and Peasant in the Making of the Modern World.* Boston: Beacon Press.

Noguera, Pedro (1983) *The Role of Adult Education in Economic Development: A Comparative Analysis of the Cuban and Tanzanian Experience.* Unpublished Masters Thesis. Brown University, Providence, Rhode Island.

Oberschall, Anthony (1969) "Rising Expectations and Political Turmoil". *Journal of Development Studies* 6:1

O'Shaughnessy, Hugh (1984) *Grenada: Revolution, Invasion and Aftermath.* London:

Oxaal, Ivor (1968) *Black Intellectuals Come to Power.* Cambridge, Mass.: Schenkman.

Payne, A., Sutton, P. and Thorndike, T. (1984) *Grenada: Revolution and Invasion.* New York: St. Martin's Press.

Parsons, Talcott (1960) *Structure and Process in Modern Societies.* Glencoe, Ill.: The Free Press.

———— (1977) *The Evolution of Societies.* Englewood Cliffs, New Jersey: Prentice Hall.

Pearce, Jenny (1982) *Under the Eagle.* London: Latin American Bureau.

Petras, James (1970) *Politics and Social Structure on Latin America.* New York: Monthly Review Press.

Poulantzas, N. (1975) *Classes in Contemporary Capitalism.* London: New Left Books.

Pryor, Fredreric (1986) *Revolutionary Grenada: A Study in Political Economy.* New York: Praeger Publishers.

Pye, Lucien and Sydney Verber (1965) *Political Culture and Political Development.* Princeton, N.J.: Princeton University Press.

Reuschemeyer, Dietrich, Stephens, E.H. and Stephens, J.D. (1992) *Capitalist Development and Democracy.* New York: Polity Press.

Rostow, Eugene (1960) *The Stages of Economic Growth: A Noncommunist Manifesto.* Cambridge, Mass.: Cambridge University Press.

Schurmann, Franz (1966) *Ideology and Organization in Communist China.* Berkeley: University of California Press.

Scott, J.C. (1972) "Patron-Client Politics and Political Change." in N.T. Uphoff and W. F. Ilchman (edc.) *The Political Economy of Development.*

Seabury, Paul and McDougall, Walter (1984) *The Grenada Papers.* San Francisco: Institute of Contemporary Studies.

Seers, Dudley (1969) "The Meaning of Development" *International Development Review.* Vol. 11. no. 4. Reprinted in *The Political Economy of Development.* Edited by Norman Uphoff and Warren F. Ilchman. Berkeley: University of California Press.

Shils, Edward (1971) "The Intellectuals in the Political Development of New States." *Political Development and Social Change*. Edited by Finkle and Gable. New York: John Wiley and Sons.

Singham, A.W. (1968) *The Hero and the Crowd in a Colonial Polity*. New Haven, Connecticut: Yale University Press.

Skocpol, Theda (1979) *States and Social Revolutions*. Cambridge: Cambridge University Press.

Smith, M.G. (1965) *The Plural Society in the British West Indies*. Berkeley: University of California Press.

Stephens, Evelyne Huber and Stephens, John D. *Democratic Socialism in Jamaica*. Princeton, New Jersey: Princeton University Press.

Stone, Carl (1977) *Democracy and Clientelism in Jamaica*. London: Zed Press.

—— (1985) *Class, State and Democracy in Jamaica*. Kingston, Jamaica: Blackett Publishers.

Sunshine, Catherine (1982) *Grenada the Peaceful Revolution*. Washington. D.C.: EPICA Taskforce.

—— (1984) *Death of A Revolution*. Washington, D.C.: EPICA Taskforce.

Thomas, Clive (1974) *Dependence and Transformation: The Economics of the Transition to Socialism*. New York: Monthly Review Press.

van der Mehden, Fred (1969) *Politics of the Developing Nations*. Englewood Cliffs, N.J.: Prentice Hall.

Valenta, J. and Ellison, H. (1986) *Grenada and Soviet/Cuban Policy: Internal Crisis and the U.S./OECS Intervention*. Boulder, Co.: Westview Press.

Vigilante, R. and Sandiford, G. (1984) *Grenada The Untold Story*. New York: Madison Books.

Wallerstein, Immanuel (1979) *The Capitalist World Economy*. Cambridge, U.K.: Cambridge University Press.

—— (1980) *The Modern World System II.* London: Academic Press.

Watta, David (1987) *The West Indies: Patterns of Development, Culture and Environmental Change Since 1492.* Cambridge: Cambridge University Press.

Waters, Anita (1989) *Race, Class and Political Symbols.* New Brunswick, N.J.: Transaction Publishers.

Wiarda, Howard (1982) *Politics and Social Change in Latin America.* Boston: University of Massachusetts Press.

Wilbur, Charles (1973) *The Political Economy of Development and Underdevelopment.* New York: Random House.

Will, Marvin (1989) "From Authoritarianism to Democracy: Observing the 1990 Election in Grenada" *Journal of Commonwealth and Comparative Politics*, Vol. XXVII, No. 3, November 1989

Wriggins, P. (1977) *The Rulers Imperative.* New York: Praeger.

Young, Crawford (1982) *Ideology and Development.* New Haven: Yale University Press.

Zeitlin, Maurice (1967) *Revolutionary Politics and the Cuban Working Class.* Princeton, N.J.: Princeton University Press.

Reports, Documents, Newspapers, Pamphlets and Magazines

Brathwaite, Farley (1985) "The 1984 Grenada Elections" Article printed by the University of the West Indies, Cavehill, Barbados.

Budget Speech (1986) Herbert Blaize, Prime Minister, Printed by the Government Printer.

Budget Speech (1987) Herbert Blaize, Prime Minister, Printed by the Government Printer.

Coard, Bernard (1973) "The Meaning of Political Independence in the Commonwealth Caribbean" Paper delivered at the University of the West Indies, St. Augustine, Trinidad.

Free West Indian Newspaper, St. George's Grenada (Out of Print)

Grenada Cooperative Nutmeg Association, Financial Statement, 1986

Grenada Cooperative Nutmeg Association, Financial Statement, 1987

Grenada Voice Newspaper, Published in St.George's Grenada. Reviewed issues from 1984-1988.

Grenada Documents: An Overview and Selection (1984) Released by the Department of State and Department of Defense, Washington, D.C.

"In the Spirit of Butler" Pamphlet Published by the Peoples' Revolutionary Government (1981)

Informer Newspaper, Published in St. George's, Grenada. Reviewed issues from 1984-1988.

"Is Freedom We Making" The New Democracy in Grenada. (1980) Published by the Government Printing Service.

Manifesto of the Grenada United Labor Party (1973)

Manifesto of the New National Party (1984)

Manifesto of the Maurice Bishop Patriotic Movement (1984)

New Jewel Movement Manifesto, Manifesto for Power to the People.

Population Census of Grenada (1980) Published by Caricom

Report on the Commission of Inquiry into the Control of Public Expenditure in Grenada (1961)

Report of the Duffus Commission of Inquiry into the Breakdown of Law and Order and Police Brutality in Grenada (1975)

Report on the Grenada Gneral Elections (1984) St. Georges Grenada: Parliamentary Office oon Elections.

Report on the National Economy (1982) Presented by Bernard Coard, Deputy Prime Minister. Published by the Government Printing Office.

Ryan Selwyn (1984) *Grenada Political and Social Outlook.* Pamphlet Published by St. Augustine Research Associates, Trinidad.

Sadiq, Akinyele (1985) "Blow by Blow: A Personal Account of the Ravaging of the Revp" in the *Black Scholar.* March 1985.

"Social Stratification in Grenada" Paper delivered by Beverly Steele at University of West Indies Conference on Grenada Independence, 1973.

Torchlight Newspaper, St. George's Grenada (Out of Print) Reviewed available issues from 1950-1979.

West Indian Newspaper, St. Georges Grenada (Out of Print) Reviewed available issues from 1950-1972

West Indian Royal Commission Report on the Economic Conditions of the Grenada Peasantry (1939)

Appendix

Questionaire

1. Where do you live?

2. What is your occupation?

3. How far did you go in school? (primary, secondary, post secondary)

4. Since independence in 1974, do you think that. Grenada has made much progress? If so, in what ways? If not, why not?

5. Of the following leaders, (Gairy, Bishop and Blaize) which one do you believe has done the most to help the country? Why?

6. Which leader (Gairy, Bishop, Blaize) has done the least to help the country? Why?

7. Which one do you believe was Grenada's best leader? What made him the best?

8. Were your living conditions good or bad during the time that Gairy, Bishop and Blaize were in power? In what ways?

9. When you vote for someone in an election, what is the most important quality you look for to determine who would make the best leader?

10. Of the three leaders (Gairy, Bishop and Blaize) which one do you believe was most supported by the people? Why?

Chart #16
Grenada Population by Education

No Education	2.7%
Primary	82.2%
Secondary/Comprehensive	12.5%
Other Secondary	3.2%

Chart #17
Grenada Population by Occupational Group

Professional	6%
Clerical	5%
Agriculture	33.4%
Production	38%
(low skill labor including fishing, factory, etc.)	
Business	6%
Skilled Craft	7.9%
Unemployed	4%

Source: Grenada Population Census, 1980-1981, Vol. 1; CARICOM

Index

TECH LIBRARY LOAN

MAY 2 0 1992

JUN 2 9

MAR 27

JUL 3 0 2003

OCT 2 5 2000

APR 2003